PARADISE DESTROYED

France Overseas: Studies in Empire and Decolonization
SERIES EDITORS: A. J. B. Johnston, James D. Le Sueur, and Tyler Stovall

PARADISE
DESTROYED

CATASTROPHE *and* CITIZENSHIP
in the FRENCH CARIBBEAN

Christopher M. Church

University of Nebraska Press | Lincoln and London

Portions of chapter 4 were originally published in
French as "'Strikingly French': Martinique, agitation
ouvrière et politique métropolitaine au tournant
de siècle," in *Le mouvement social: Revue d'histoire
sociale*, trans. Myriam Faten Sfar and Aemmanuelle
Saussier, 109–24 (Paris: La Découverte, 2014).

Library of Congress
Control Number: 2017952686

Designed and set in Arno Pro by L. Auten.

CONTENTS

ILLUSTRATIONS

MAPS

TABLES

ACKNOWLEDGMENTS

This work began long ago at the University of California, Berkeley, where I was fortunate to be advised by Tyler Stovall, Thomas Laqueur, J. P. Daughton, and Percy Hintzen—to whom I am indebted for their advice, feedback, and support over the course of my intellectual career. I thank Tyler Stovall for his unending guidance in bringing this work to fruition; J. P. Daughton for his advice on colonial ideology and humanitarianism; Thomas Laqueur for always pushing me to keep sight of the forest and not get lost in the trees; and Percy Hintzen for his engaging recommendations with respect to my work's theoretical implications for the Caribbean Basin.

I also thank all my fellow scholars for their help, support, and critiques over the years. Without my supportive friends and colleagues—Gene Zubovich, Katherine Eady, Jennifer Allen, Terry Renaud, Vanessa Lincoln-Lambert, Scott McGinnis, and many others—I never would have made it through graduate school, let alone bring my book into the world. I am grateful for my former colleagues at UC Berkeley's Social Sciences Data Lab (D-Lab), in particular Savet Hong for assisting me with my demographic analysis. Without the D-Lab's founding director, Cathryn Carson, I would not have had access to the invaluable digital tools and data science methodologies that have influenced and enabled much of my work. Neither would I have had the opportunity to learn from so many other disciplines—sociology, demography, education, political science—all of which shape the pages to follow.

Additionally, I acknowledge those who helped edit my prose and shape my narrative, especially my close friend Eric Kalisher, who has provided essential feedback on nearly all my work for the better part of two decades, as well as Kate Epstein, who gave me invaluable advice on narrative flow and structure. Above all, however, I thank the University of Nebraska Press for making the publication process seamless and transparent. Working with UNP has been a wonderful experience, in large part due to Bridget Barry's professionalism and editorial advice.

Last, but not least, this book would not exist if it were not for my family. The unconditional support of my loving and wonderful partner, Courtney, who accompanied me on this long and demanding journey, has helped me throughout the writing process and kept me grounded over the years. The shenanigans and levity of my rambunctious daughters, Elise and Chloe, have helped keep my spirits up while I created data sets, gathered archival documents, hunted through libraries, and wrote this book.

And finally, I'd like to thank my parents for instilling in me a love of knowledge and an unending respect for education.

Introduction

Colonialism, Catastrophe, and National Integration

At five-thirty in the morning on 3 May 1902, the young schoolteacher Roger Portel awoke to an eerie scene outside his window in Saint-Pierre, Martinique. Everything was closed: shops, governmental buildings, and schools. The sky blackened under what looked like a gray snow, as roads, homes, and even people were covered in a thin layer of a substance like ground cement. Remarking to a friend that it was now "winter without the cold," Portel shuffled outside to take stock of what was happening. Mount Pelée had lurched awake, and Saint-Pierre teemed like a kicked anthill. Joining a crowd of Saint-Pierre's disoriented denizens, Portel quickly realized he could not see more than thirty feet in front of him, and he choked as his nose burned. While he pinched it to ward off the smell of sulfur, he wondered, "Are we all going to die of asphyxiation? . . . What's coming tomorrow? A column of lava? A shower of stones? A wind of suffocating gas? Mass drownings? No one knows." Portel had awakened to a living nightmare, a hellish postapocalyptic scene plucked straight from the pages of the Bible. And he suspected that his death was imminent. "Should I die," he wrote to his brother, "don't be too sad." Unfortunately, Portel's worst fears came true. Five days later, he and everyone else in the crowd in Saint-Pierre was dead—suffocated by sulfur, petrified by ash, frozen in a winter without cold. Ascension Day had come. Mount Pelée had erupted.[1]

Forty kilometers away, in the city of Fort-de-France, the island's acting bishop, Gabriel Parel, said a mass commemorating Jesus's entrance into heaven. Later, when he stepped onto his balcony shortly after eight o'clock in the morning, night descended as ash blocked the morning sun and a hail of stones assaulted Martinique's capital. While helping his congregation seek refuge, Bishop Parel wondered what was happening at Saint-Pierre. When he learned that Pelée's fury had obliterated the so-called Paris of the

Antilles, turning it into what witnesses would describe as "one vast brazier" and claiming thirty thousand lives in a quarter of an hour, a cry of horror went up "like the funeral knell of Martinique" that "would take the pen of Dante and the accents of Jeremiah" to accurately describe.[2] Thousands of miles away, a Parisian journalist, who described himself as an "old republican . . . [with] an absolute faith in the progress of the human race," asked, "Our race, is it as grand as we had imagined it? Hasn't this disaster belied all [our] grand ideas?"[3] Pelée's eruption had shaken the convictions of the French Republic, and all eyes turned toward relief and recovery lest French civilization in the Caribbean come to an end.

The Caribbean environment had sparked French fears about the obliteration of their colonial project since France's occupation of Martinique and Guadeloupe in 1635. Two centuries of the forced migration of Africans shackled into slavery had thrown fuel onto those sparks, and by the end of the nineteenth century, nature's wrath collided with social conflicts within France and its old empire. In the span of thirty years, the French islands of Martinique and Guadeloupe endured catastrophes from all the elements— earth, wind, fire, and water—as well as a collapsing sugar industry, civil unrest, and political intrigue. In 1890 Martinique experienced a fire that burned down its capital city, and a year later a cyclone destroyed the island's primary source of income: sugar. Since 1884 the islands' economies had been in a tailspin, and by 1899 labor unrest ignited an urban fire that destroyed the largest city in Guadeloupe and launched a general strike in Martinique the following February. And in 1902, the eruption of Mount Pelée became the deadliest volcanic eruption in modern memory, solidifying the association of the Caribbean environment with death and destruction.

Nationalist fervor was at its height in this period, as the French empire grew to its greatest extent and politicians of France's Third Republic vied to build a democratic consensus and distance themselves from France's recent autocratic past. With the humiliating defeat during the Franco-Prussian War in 1870 came the first democratic government in France in a generation—the Third Republic. Republicans projected a fantasy of assimilation onto the Caribbean islands of Martinique and Guadeloupe, two of France's oldest colonies, where the Constitution of 1875 had bestowed full citizenship and governmental representation on the predominantly nonwhite population.

Contemporaries described the Caribbean as "one of France's oldest and most dear colonies," where former slaves and indentured servants had been successfully integrated politically and culturally into the French nation-state, and republicans cast the Antilles as evidence of the "civilizing mission made good." As the nineteenth century ended, however, environmental disasters threatened this republican fantasy by bringing to the fore existing racial and social tensions that held France's ideological convictions of assimilation and citizenship to the fire. Disasters catalyzed the already rapid decline of the Antillean sugar economy, and injections of capital into the islands in the form of disaster relief rapidly made the former valuable financial assets a drain on the French economy. As Antilleans put forth an alternative image of Frenchness defined by its tropical surroundings and demanded state aid, disastrous moments precipitated a discussion of economic welfare and colonial assimilation and challenged republican cohesion.

When disaster struck in the French West Indies—whether the whirlwinds of a hurricane or the stirrings of an open rebellion—France faced a tempest at home as politicians, journalists, economists, and ordinary citizens debated the role of the French state not only in the Antilles but in their own lives as well. During the age of new empire, therefore, the "old colonies" of Martinique and Guadeloupe redefined what it meant to be a French citizen by prompting a discussion over economic rights and social welfare, and by laying claim to a definition of tropical Frenchness that preserved French civilization against a hostile environment. Disasters exacerbated existing societal tensions and marked a rupture in the status quo, however, and while centuries of cultural association demanded public assistance and political incorporation after these disasters, economic considerations led the French state to reexamine the long-term viability of its Caribbean colonies.

Disasters: Environmental Catastrophe and Civil Unrest in the French Caribbean

Disasters are never natural but are induced by either nature or humanity. Irrespective of what causes it, a disaster is always predicated on an event's interaction with human civilization.[4] Only the trappings of human society can make natural events into disasters—for example, construction in flood plains or on tectonic plate boundaries, lax or nonexistent building codes, high population densities, insufficient or crumbling public facilities and infrastructure. That is, it is our own built environment—roads, housing, sewers, aqueducts—that comes into conflict with what are natural cycles, and the natural ebb and flow of droughts, tempests, and seismic movements seem entirely unnatural when framed by the contours of human society: our notions of time, space, and location.[5] As with nature-induced disasters, human-induced disasters—such as the 1899 fire in Guadeloupe and the 1900 strike in Martinique—disrupt what we see as normal time, space, and location by destroying the built environment, unseating or challenging cultural mores and political givens, and disturbing the pace of everyday life. Moments of environmental catastrophe and civil disturbance are, in their effects, two sides of the same coin, as all such emergency situations ultimately bring forth and make public systemic political prejudices and social tensions, ultimately leading to a crisis that precipitates a change in or reaffirmation of the status quo. This revaluation is particularly salient during events that strike contemporaries as significant ruptures (hurricanes, fires, strikes) rather than those that develop slowly over time (climate change, drought, economic hardship). Such large, singular events present the state with an immediacy to confront, even as officials attempt to contextualize such apparently extraordinary occurrences within a longer time frame. Therefore, the present work focuses on those disasters that the state understood as quick to unfold, even as it contextualizes them against longer historical and environmental trajectories.

At stake in the disasters and civil discord that struck the French Caribbean at the close of the nineteenth century were the population's citizenship rights and the French state's relationship to those citizens. The Third Republic's invocation of the Jacobin ideals of the French Revolution—liberty, equality, and fraternity—to grant citizenship rights to the French Caribbean (and all the inhabitants of its "old colonies," including French Guiana and Réunion) coincided with its beginning to make subjects of countless West Africans and Indochinese. Citizens are those who enjoy full legal rights and obligations within a state; possess membership in a political community in which they have the right to participate; and are entitled to the protection of the sovereign state to which they owe allegiance.[6] Noncitizens, or subjects, lack some or all of these characteristics: they enjoy limited legal rights, cannot participate in the political community, or are not entitled to the protection of the sovereign state. Whereas in West Africa and Indochina officials applied a harsh indigenous legal code with expectations and penalties out of step with those applied in the French Caribbean, the people of the French Antilles were citizens and not subjects, in spite of France's sordid history marred by slavery and forced migration, and they demanded a quality of life equal to their metropolitan counterparts via their political participation in the French legislature.

That Antilleans were indeed citizens and not subjects, however, did not ensure equal treatment under the law. While citizenship confers a certain degree of protection by the state, the exact rights that citizenship bestows are always in debate. At various points, France permitted Antilleans of color to voice their demands upon the state as citizens, and at other times it levied accusations of criminality or colonial disorder to muffle their voices and back an economically privileged white elite threatened by the political participation of Antilleans of color. Developments within the metropole, or the parent nation of the colonies, influenced and mirrored this slippage, as the poor, destitute, and disenfranchised there demanded equality in the face of industrial hazards and unfair labor practices. The end of the nineteenth century was the height of French demands for a social republic that properly attended to the needs and demands of its citizenry, and Antilleans were at the forefront of the conversation over what citizenship rights entailed.

Insufficient responses from the metropolitan government often fostered tension between creole elites in Martinique, local governmental bureaucrats in Guadeloupe, and mainland officials. As the following chapters describe, many prominent colonial administrators thought first and foremost of the sugar economy after both environmental catastrophes and moments of civil disorder. Though they might cast the French Caribbean as colonies of settlement on the path to assimilation, where French values and mores had taken root in a tropical soil, they tacitly treated the islands as colonies of extraction where economic profit was paramount and civil rights were curtailed. Regardless of the size of the disruption, ministerial reports following hurricanes or the eruption of Mount Pelée focused primarily on the disaster's immediate effect on the sugar economy, secondarily on its impact on the alternative economies (fruit, cocoa, coffee, tafia—a rum made from cane juice), and only thirdly on its consequences for the citizens living there. Even the ardent assimilationist official Eugene Étienne claimed in 1897 that "the sole criterion to apply to every colonial enterprise is its degree of utility, the sum of the advantages and profits flowing from it to the *métropole*."[7] Colonial governments saw catastrophic events as an opportunity for restructuring society. And for many, this restructuring focused on a revitalization of, or in some cases a repudiation of, the colonial economy. At the same time, however, a language of civic inclusion that heralded the Frenchness of the people of the French Antilles challenged this focus on the economy. As a result of this tension between an economic calculus of disaster and a republican language of citizenship, moments of catastrophe serve as a lens through which to observe the contemporary values of French society and polity alike. And in the case of the French West Indies, which had been integrated in many ways into the metropolitan structures of government, the demands and expectations for disaster relief had substantial repercussions in the mainland.

"Old Colonies" in an Age of New Empire

Despite their legacy of plantation slavery and forced migration, the colonies of Martinique and Guadeloupe had become "assimilated colonies" par excellence in the eyes of French contemporaries. That is, while the republican myth of assimilation purported that all colonies could one day become part of a Greater France and that all colonial subjects, after receiving French education and culture, would become active French citizens, this myth was in many ways made real in the French Caribbean. From 1848 onward, non-white inhabitants of the old colonies—including Martinique, Guadeloupe, Reunion, and Guyane—possessed full French citizenship, in theory if not in practice, thereafter rallying to the cause of the republican values of liberty, equality, and fraternity. After a period of "curtailed" citizenship during the Second Empire, wherein vagabondage laws limited islanders' movement and only 2.6 percent of Guadeloupe, for example, was enfranchised in 1868, the French Antilles achieved universal manhood suffrage and became fully integrated into the French legislature under the Third Republic, receiving two deputies and a senator to represent their interests in Paris.[8] The islands' general councils, much like their departmental counterparts in the metropole, served as the local legislative bodies. The Law of 8 January 1877 replaced the colonial penal code with metropolitan law in the Antilles and Réunion, and later that year was fully extended to French Guiana and partly applied to French Indochina. No longer were the old colonies under the jurisdiction of a separate penal code; rather, the same juridical framework that governed their metropolitan compatriots governed these "colonial citizens."[9] In many ways, the descendants of the forcibly migrated Africans who populated the island were construed as tropical French citizens who had settled the colony in the name of France. In fact, since the *Declaration of the Rights of Man and the Citizen* in 1789, free people of color in the French Caribbean had appealed to Enlightenment ideals in order to undermine the authority of local white planters and overturn a regime that precluded their political participation based on their skin color since the 1760s.[10] While free men of color typically advocated a hierarchical society based on wealth rather than race, their unfree counterparts fought for emancipation and self-sufficiency in the eighteenth century, and later for class consciousness and societal equity in the nineteenth and twentieth centuries.[11]

Despite their appeals, the state met tropical Frenchmen with prejudice and inequity. As historian Jacques Dumont illustrates concerning its Antillean citizenry, the meritocratic Third Republic compromised between equality in principle and inequality in practice, which repeatedly culminated in strike activity persisting up to the present day.[12] Though the Third Republic proclaimed equality for all in the French colonies, the ideal of equality always fell short of the reality. For instance, the Law of 8 January 1877 had some important exceptions to its extension of the metropolitan penal code to the old colonies. Most notably, the restrictions and laws that forbade public vagabondage and set up mandatory "work sentences" in public workshops, enforceable by the local police, remained in place.[13] The Antilles also remained under the thumb of a colonial administration—an appointed governor, and the Ministry of the Marine until 1894 and the Ministry of the Colonies thereafter.

Nonetheless the French Antilles were politically represented in the same fashion as departments in France despite their colonial status, helping to shape the very policies that the French executive branch carried out. Since the Law of 28 July 1881, Martinique and Guadeloupe each had two representatives in the French legislature, up from the initial single deputy after the ratification of the constitution in 1875.[14] Unlike other colonies such as Indochina and Senegal, which limited suffrage and had minimal representation in the legislature, the Caribbean colonies received representation in the Chamber of Deputies on par with that of departments within metropolitan France.[15]

Historically the French West Indies participated vociferously in the French Republic. Taking up arms during the French Revolution of 1789 and rejoicing during that of 1848—and even proclaiming a republic in southern Martinique in 1870—the predominantly nonwhite population of France's old empire defined itself as inherently French and undeniably republican.[16] In fact, the legality of the Third Republic hinged on the political participation of the French Antilles. The Guadeloupean deputy, Germain Casse, permitted the ratification of the Constitution of 1875 on 30 January 1875. The Wallon amendment to the constitution, which established the president of the republic as the chief executive and thereby finalized the political order of the Third Republic, passed by only a single vote: that of Germain Casse. As *Le Figaro* put it after Casse's death in 1900, "At the time of the Third Republic's founding, . . . the establishment of the government in France depended on the support of a colonial deputy."[17] Those who represented Martinique's interests in Paris were by and large members of the island's mixed-race middle class, or in the case of Guadeloupe, dedicated members of a mounting black socialism during the 1890s. Coupled with the flagging Caribbean sugar economy, which sapped the political power of the islands' *grands blancs* and pushed people of color into administrative, legislative, educational, and bureaucratic posts, the onset of the Third Republic thrust the French Antilles' population of color into social and political prominence, though the islands' endogamous white elite continued to dominate its economic sphere.[18]

Therefore, the islands of Martinique and Guadeloupe were almost-but-not-quite departments of France. While they had been folded into the metropolitan legal code, were free from the harsh indigenous code applied elsewhere in the French empire, and had representation on par with other departments—if at the lower end of the spectrum—they still faced very real hurdles to integration, most notably the economic realities of sugar cultivation and the political realities of their still colonial status. Given their legislative representation as well as their economic subjugation, the French West Indies were indeed colonies of citizens.

Colonialism, Catastrophe, and National Integration

Scholars of the French West Indies have extensively examined the importance of assimilation in Antillean politics and culture, elucidating the significance of the short-lived emancipation of 1794; the transient citizenship gained in 1848 and suspended in 1851; and finally the full citizenship restored in 1871 and codified in the Third Republic's Constitution of 1875. From Richard Burton's *La famille coloniale: La Martinique et la mère patrie* (1994) and his edited volume *French and West Indian* (1995), to Mickaella Perina's *Citoyenneté et sujétion aux Antilles francophones* (1997), to Jean-Pierre Sainton's *Les nègres en politique* (2000), and, more recently, to Serge Mam Lam Fouck's *L'histoire de l'assimilation* (2006), scholars have probed the entry of Antilleans into the political sphere during the Third Republic and explored their demands for civic and economic rights.[19] This work seeks not to retrace their steps but to explore for the Third Republic, as Laurent Dubois does for the First Republic in *A Colony of Citizens* and *Avengers of the New World*, how disruptive events in the French West Indies—in this case, disasters both natural and manmade—shaped and interacted with broader developments in the metropole itself.

Disasters constitute a crucial aspect of a state's relationship to its citizenry. Recent works such as Matthew Mulcahy's *Hurricanes and Society* and Sherry Johnson's *Climate and Catastrophe* evidenced how disastrous events propelled individuals toward the poles of revolution and reconciliation, reshaping how historians understand the effect of ecology on national and transnational political developments in the Atlantic world. Meanwhile, Jeffrey Jackson's *Paris under Water* has underscored how disasters and the state's technocratic response heightened nationalist sentiments among Frenchmen. In unpacking these nationalist sentiments, however, scholars must be attentive to race as well as class. As evidenced by the work of Jennifer Anne Boittin, Gary Wilder, Tyler Stovall, and others, narratives of France in the nineteenth and twentieth centuries must incorporate the notion of a "black France" distinct from, and yet part of, a national French history—one with a trans-Atlantic dimension that pushed the limits of French reasoning about its nonwhite subjects and citizens.[20] Republican dogma and nation building stretched their muscles in France's old colonies during the second half of the nineteenth century, but as Myriam Cottias has pointed out, despite their vital role in France's national story, the old colonies have occupied a blind spot in national French history and consequently in our understanding of French identity.[21]

By combining the literature's recent focuses on ecology and race, as well as its redefinition of French national history as colonial history, the present work demonstrates that the cultural reaction of France to natural disasters in Martinique and Guadeloupe proved vital in defining French civilization at the close of the nineteenth century, torn as it was between an economic calculus that heightened Antilleans' second-class status and a language of inclusion aimed at their assimilation. French officials understood Antilleans' relevance to the French nation first and foremost as a function of their economic utility. As Elizabeth Heath has shown, Guadeloupeans struggled amidst a flagging sugar industry and ultimately failed to secure agricultural subsidies and governmental support akin to that provided to their metropolitan compatriots who toiled phylloxera-ridden vineyards in southern France.[22] Heath's excellent work has demonstrated how an uneven economic playing field between Guadeloupean and metropolitan Frenchmen interacted with administrative racism to preclude a truly inclusive social republic in France, and she has accurately shown that deep-seated racial prejudices and colonial disparities undercut the Republic's claims to truly universal values and eased the rejection of Antillean rights to governmental assistance, increasingly in the decade leading up to Guadeloupe's great strike of 1910. In the Third Republic's Caribbean, this mistreatment was as undoubtedly true for downtrodden workers at it was for victims of catastrophe. And yet disasters and their cultural responses complicated France's economic and civic exclusionism. Tropical Frenchmen of color fought for civil rights and national inclusion during moments of climatic and civil catastrophe that put the strength of liberal values and national integration to the test, to be sure, and at times this popular activism produced an administrative distancing that underscored the islands' legacy of economic exploitation. At other times, however, disasters resulted in a public outpouring of support that seemed to wash away racial difference, particularly since the French prided themselves on having incorporated their West Indian populations as citizens. As the following pages will show, natural disasters—large, singular events like hurricanes, fires, and volcanic eruptions that captured the French imagination—and resulting civil unrest simultaneously prompted an exclusionary "calculus of disaster" that justified civic disparity through racially coded economic language, as was the case for Guadeloupe's sugar workers, and an inclusive "language of citizenship" that underscored compatriotism and national community.

In some ways, this process mirrored what took place across the Caribbean at the close of the nineteenth century. As Bonham Richardson has rightly shown for the British West Indies, conflict arose when a collapsing sugar industry combined with what seemed to racist colonial officials to be a veritable onslaught of environmental hazards marking Antilleans as fundamentally different from Europeans.[23] To them, such difference justified discrimination. While this phenomenon rings true in the French West Indies to some extent, in many ways the French case differed. Though French Antilleans were similarly plagued by an economic downturn and marked as distinct by their tropical environment, and even as contemporaries understood them through the lens of racist tropes, French West Indians' status as citizens discouraged the French government from discriminating against them on the basis of their skin tone alone, leading republican officials to justify their exclusionism in financial as well as geographic terms. In turn, this exclusionary rhetoric ran up against the countervailing force of French national integration that was in part predicated on the republican faith that the civilizing mission could actually work.

As Eugen Weber reminded us, the process of making Frenchmen out of a rural, disconnected peasantry at the close of the nineteenth century was uneven and fraught with tension.[24] He deemed it a form of internal colonization in which urban values permeated the countryside through school systems, transportation and communication networks, and military service. Similarly, historian Benedict Anderson has demonstrated that nations are not natural or foundational givens but "imagined communities" in the modern world produced through print capitalism, the political action of provincial elites, and the ever-increasing bureaucratic apparatuses of the state. The

French Caribbean was part of this dual process of "internal colonization" and "national imagination" in that its population participated as citizens in the national integration of France. Rather than forming an independence movement struggling to imagine a separatist community, most Antilleans sought to gain recognition as a French one. The republican middle class and the socialist laboring class, not the white creole elites, led the charge because of the complex position of white elites in relation to the legacy of slavery and the particularities of French republicanism. Where the demand by colonial elites in the United States had represented a form of nascent nationalism a century before, Antillean planters' centuries-long demands for increased autonomy represented a form of secessionism that ran counter to the political ambitions of the islands' predominantly nonwhite middle and working classes. That is, colonial nationalism meant not independence but integration into the French nation.

Internal colonization forms a crucial backdrop for the political tensions brought to light by disasters and civil unrest in the Caribbean as well as in the metropole, because cataclysmic events cast societal problems and dynamics in their starkest relief, and the debate over who belongs in the national community takes center stage. The major crises this book addresses ignited public debates over Antillean belongingness in the national community and a political dialogue between the Antilles and metropolitan France as French society questioned who belonged and who did not. In the process, commonplace French understandings of citizenship, colonialism, and community were unearthed and challenged. By tracing the peculiarities of the Caribbean environment—as well as the increasing role of the French nation-state in distant localities—in relation to the rise of French nationalism and demands for political inclusion and social welfare, this book provides a fuller picture of the development of late-nineteenth-century nationalism and its ramifications for the colonial world.

How and to what extent the French Caribbean is part of metropolitan France remains a prominent issue to this day. Antillean society reveals a tension between a sense of commonality with an African heritage—most clearly elucidated through the writers and artists of the *Negritude* school—and a drive by the Creolité movement for difference from, or rather a synthesis of, the cultural or geographic antecedents to Caribbean peoples. The Caribbean during the late nineteenth century was not only a space of fragmentation and insularity but also one of a shared connection to the physical tropical environment and a shared bank of local knowledge. Undoubtedly distinct from their metropolitan counterparts, Antilleans nevertheless saw themselves as both French and Caribbean as they participated in the politics and social developments of the French Third Republic. While it is important not to reduce Antilleans to a singular cultural antecedent—either that of France or Africa—Antilleans have long engaged with their French nationality. In times of both natural disaster and civil unrest, French conceptualizations of nationality and citizenship simultaneously included and excluded them.

As a "colony of citizens," the French Caribbean was simultaneously a colonial territory and an integral part of France. Under French control longer than Nice, Savoy, or Alsace-Lorraine, the colonies of "la France lointaine," as it was called, were inextricably entangled in metropolitan concerns and arguments about the meaning and significance of "liberty, equality, and fraternity" as demands rose for a social republic in France. Rather than treating the colonies as a space to which national ideologies were either applied or one in which local circumstances pushed back on national discourses, this book looks beyond the dichotomy between metropole and colony in order to explore not only how republicanism was refracted in the colonies but also how the colonies shaped the Third Republic by challenging and redefining French ideology and serving as the battleground where a language of civic inclusion challenged, and was challenged by, economic imperatives.

Demands from the metropolitan government as well as conditions within the colonies shaped the French state's imperial policy. The French had a strong desire to view the French Caribbean as the embodiment of the civilizing mission "made good"—that is, contemporaries explained, as a place where French values and culture had taken root in the tropics. The old colonies themselves had a voice in the legislature and thereby a say in government's colonial policies. The political realities in Martinique and Guadeloupe were such that the islands' mixed-race middle class and black laboring class championed assimilation, demanding disaster relief from the central government as if the Antilles were departments, and requesting economic parity with metropolitan citizens. Oftentimes these claims fell on deaf ears. However, the increasing prominence of socialists from the islands upheld the ideal of a "Social Republic" during times of natural catastrophe and civil discord. The French Caribbean's relationship to the metropole during times of unrest and disaster under the Third Republic thus reveals the inextricability of colonialism, catastrophes, and democratic nation building in the nineteenth and twentieth centuries.

Overview of Chapters

The late nineteenth-century French understood disasters as an assault on the nation, though people in its oldest colonies always saw compatriotism through the lens of colonialism. Nevertheless, French Antilleans were by law citizens of the French nation, and while disasters were alienating events, they opened the opportunity for black Frenchmen to fight for their rights of inclusion. This book explores how the metropolitan French projected their prejudices and misconceptions, as well as their political hopes and aspirations, onto a tropical environment far removed from France; and how that faraway space—with its hurricanes, fires, and earthquakes—in turn influenced the conceptualization of the French nation itself by bringing forward existing racial and social tensions that put under scrutiny France's ideological convictions of assimilation and equal citizenship.

Chapter 1 establishes that the "old colonies" are distinct from the "new colonies," exploring the relationship of race to space to show that the colonial population of the French Antilles—particularly the middle class of Martinique—figured into the French imaginary as "tropical Frenchmen" who served as a bastion of French identity in a hostile environment that perpetually threatened to destroy all civilization there. Despite the fact they had been extractive sugar colonies in reality, France treated the French Antilles as colonies of settlement and thus as an extension of France in the tropics. The colonial citizenry had, according to contemporary journalist Auguste Terrier, "attained a certain degree of civilization" in this "faraway France," and an intense struggle over French identity and nationality waged there between liberal French republicans and a reactionary right composed of monarchists and Bonapartists. Race, politics, and socioeconomics were intertwined in the Caribbean. Faced with an intransigent population of white planters who maintained the old aristocratic mores of prerevolutionary France but who were increasingly becoming obsolete at the hands of international market forces, liberal officials turned to Martinique's burgeoning mixed-race middle class as the bearers of the French Republic.

Chapter 2 explains how Frenchmen socially identified with and supported distant "compatriots" in the Caribbean who suffered during the 1890 fires that burned down the administrative capital of the island of Martinique and an agricultural town in Guadeloupe. The fires of 1890, and the French government's relief campaign, illustrated the French state's need to safeguard its Antillean citizenry in times of natural disaster. Though the climate of the Caribbean was diametrically opposed to that of France, the French state and national press depicted people living there as inherently French—"more French than the French," as many in France describe Antilleans today. The dire situation following the Great Fires of Fort-de-France and Port-Louis met an outpouring of public support from across France and throughout the empire, as Frenchmen heeded the call for the Caribbean's compatriots to open their wallets to their brothers in peril.

Chapter 3 examines the role economics played in distinguishing "colonial" populations from "metropolitan" ones, looking at how the French business elite, whose financial operations in the islands had been repeatedly hampered by natural disasters and undercut by a worldwide sugar crisis, attempted to distance itself from the French Caribbean in the aftermath of the 1891 hurricane. As disaster fatigue set in, officials began to reevaluate the economic importance and vitality of the French Caribbean, downplaying the importance of its shared culture and instead emphasizing its economic history as the site of extractive colonies. To the chagrin of assimilationist politicians fighting for West Indian political rights, the Caribbean's Frenchness seemed to hinge on its economic utility.

Chapter 4 explores the consequences of the downturn in the Antillean sugar economy caused by international competition and local environmental catastrophes. It examines the mounting agitation and incendiarism in Guadeloupe that eventually burned down the island's largest city, Pointe-à-Pitre. On the heels of this fire, a general strike erupted on Martinique that foregrounded labor unrest in metropolitan France, as French socialists rallied to the cause of their compatriots in the Caribbean. The military had opened fire on strikers at Le François in Martinique, and that same year, the military used force in Chalon-sur-Saône in eastern France to suppress an industrial strike in the metropole. These events made it difficult to consider the problems of the French Caribbean exotic or strictly colonial: the issues brought to light by the shooting at Le François, when cast with the unrest evident at places like Chalon, reinforced French cultural identification with their compatriots in Martinique.

Chapter 5 turns toward the deadliest natural event in the Western Hemisphere in recorded history: the 1902 eruption of Mount Pélee and the destruction of Saint-Pierre, "the Paris of the Antilles." If disaster had previously characterized how the French understood the Caribbean and the tropics more generally, the eruption of Mount Pelée solidified that association. As one of the world's deadliest catastrophes, this eruption became the prevailing leitmotif for Martinique in the French imaginary, solidifying the ideological division between the Frenchness of the Antilleans themselves and the tropical space in which they lived.

The epilogue looks at a new form of catastrophe: the violence inflicted by the First World War. The book moves, therefore, from the barbarity of the Caribbean climate to the barbarism of the European battlefield, which challenged the very idea of French civilization. Therefore, as this race of tropical Frenchmen left the West Indies for Europe, they defended French civilization not from the harshness of a tropical climate but from itself. The cycle of catastrophe closed around colony and metropole, and the dynamics and political struggles surrounding disasters at the turn of the century, coupled with Antilleans' role in the First World War, set the French Caribbean on a path toward eventual departmentalization in 1946. While departmentalization was in no way predetermined, the debates over inclusion and exclusion, as well as the habits of practice forged during times of catastrophe, helped set the stage for the struggles over "black France" that characterized French discourse in the twentieth century. French citizens in the Caribbean—whose race, geographic distance, and exposure to environmental risks often cast them as outsiders in France—continue to demand parity with their metropolitan counterparts, evidenced most recently by the 2009 general strike, and this book explores the roots of this dynamic.

1

French Race, Tropical Space

The French Caribbean during the Third Republic

In 1888 the soon-to-be president of the École Coloniale's administrative council, Paul Dislère, compiled his *Notes on the Organization of the Colonies*, in which he distinguished the assimilable from the nonassimilable colonies—that is, between those colonies that had enough in common with France proper that they could be assimilated into the French nation and those that could not. Though Dislère was an anti-imperialist earlier in his career, viewing overseas expansion as an economic drain and an utter waste of resources, by the time of his tenure at the École Coloniale—the college that trained all functionaries in the French colonial service to improve the quality of French colonial administrators from 1889 onward—he was an ardent assimilationist who dominated the school's directors and set the agenda for school policy.[1]

Leaving aside religious propagation for other bureaucrats to handle, this former director of the Ministry of the Marine and Colonies succinctly outlined five key motifs of French imperialism: (1) the expansion of the French race, (2) the extension of the powers of the state, (3) the satisfaction of commercial interests, (4) the creation of *points d'appui* or strategic locations from which military actions could be launched, and (5) the founding of places to which exiles from the metropole could be sent.[2] Placing an emphasis on the first three of these driving factors of French imperialism, Dislère drew the same divide historians of empire highlight today: the difference between colonies of settlement and those of exploitation, between colonies of citizens and colonies of subjects. He applied this division to the Antilles, which he described as "a very weak part of the ancient colonies of settlement, because the French race there is today a very weak minority, [though] they are no less true fragments of the French nation, with which everything is in common: language, education, and patriotism."[3] Dislère's statement glosses over the more unsavory parts of the colonial legacy in the Antilles, for the French Caribbean colonies were founded not as colonies of settlement but as exploitative sugar plantations where 1.1 million Africans were forcibly migrated to work as slave labor.[4] Historically, the Antilles were colonies of resource extraction: the backbone of the slave labor economy that harvested sugar and amassed the capital necessary to catapult Europe into modernity.[5]

However, in 1888, republicans had a selective memory, and they chose to view these old colonies as poor examples of colonies of settlement. Dislère was not alone in making the distinction between the French Antilles and the new colonies of exploitation in Africa and Indochina—the financially important colonies, according to Dislère and others.[6] The French Antilles were old hat to the French government, populace, and financial sector. Popular colonial periodicals like *Les Journals des Voyages* focused the reading public on the exoticism of the newer colonies, and the waning importance of the older colonies in the face of European beet sugar left economists and financiers underwhelmed.[7]

Arguing that the old colonies represented assimilable spaces that could one day become full French departments, while the new represented spaces of economic extraction that benefited the French economy, Dislère elucidated a distinction many understood at the time. At the height of new imperialism, the old colonies of Martinique and Guadeloupe represented a colonial space categorically different from France's newer colonies in Indochina and Africa. The legal system, which held separate judicial regimes for the old colonies and for the new, reflected this distinction. As citizens, inhabitants of the old colonies were exempt from the harsh indigenous code and by and large fell under the jurisdiction of the metropolitan legal system.

In describing the Antilles as a very weak example of colonial settlement, Dislère revealed his racialized understanding of Frenchness—only descendants of the white planter class were "true" Frenchmen in the region. However, Dislère underscored the holistic similarity of Antillean and French culture. Despite the lack of economic utility in the old colonies, their French culture, republican patriotism, language, and educational system called on France to treat them as part of the Republic. Dislère's thinking revealed the tension between civic and racial understandings of French nationalism that underpinned the Third Republic: from a racial point of view, the French

Antilles were not France's United States or Australia, where white expats formed autonomous colonies of settlement. Yet civically they were "true fragments of the French nation."

The fact of the matter is that what Dislère saw as a selective process of colonial assimilation in 1888 was well under way in the old colonies from the onset of the Third Republic. A decade after full citizenship and legislative representation were extended to the old colonies, the tension in French imperialism was evident. A racial conceptualization of French civic identity—one that theoretically should seek to exclude Antilleans from the French nation on the basis of their skin color, as in the newer African colonies—conflicted with the civic conceptualization of French civilization prevalent within both the metropole and the old colonies.

For many during the Third Republic, the distant Caribbean islands represented, in the words of the famous black Martiniquais intellectual Paulette Nardal, "a little France, a faraway France [where] [t]he social manners do not differ principally from French social manners. Life, over there, is only an adaptation of European life to the necessities of a tropical climate."[8] As part of this faraway France, Martinique reflected the sociopolitical struggle that characterized the unstable Third Republic from the brutal suppression of the Paris Commune onward, while its sister island of Guadeloupe draped itself in the legacy of the Communards. This extension of France in the tropics became the site of an intense struggle over French identity and nationality. Faced with an intransigent population of white planters who maintained the old aristocratic mores of prerevolutionary France, liberal officials turned to the islands' burgeoning mixed-race middle class. This political move in turn raised a challenge to the prevailing French conception of race during the height of "new imperialism," which witnessed the ascendancy of "scientific" racist thought, and it harks back to the oldest days of French colonialism in the New World when *métissage*, or miscegenation, was treated as expedient rather than threatening—at least before an ideology of "white purity" established a color line that politically and socially alienated free people of color after the 1760s.[9] Even then, however, French understandings of race contrasted sharply with their American counterparts': for instance, those with at least "one drop" of white heritage were permitted to marry "other whites" under Napoleon's ban on interracial marriage.[10]

The Third Republic leaned heavily on imperialism to maintain its legitimacy. Politicians like Jules Ferry and Paul Dislère intricately tied together racial typology and notions of French civilization, arguing that the unification of the French nation after the bloody beginnings of the Third Republic in 1870–71 required imperialism. With regard to this racialist typology, historians like Frederick Cooper and Ann Stoler have shown that French policy makers increasingly frowned on racial mixing, viewing miscegenation as threatening to state power and European racial superiority. In *A Mission to Civilize*, Alice Conklin has aptly shown that for republican officials in French West Africa, who simultaneously championed French pronatalism and imperialism, racial mixing would inevitably lead to the degeneration of the French race and the undermining of colonial authority. In the view of many French officials, the person of mixed race—the *métis*—"should not and could not become French," and functionaries must practice endogamy to preserve their Frenchness.[11] At the same time, however, others argued for an older model of "métissage" forged in the Americas that could "Gallicize" African races through intermixture with Europeans or buttress dwindling European populations in colonial spaces.[12] At the turn of the century, disdain for miscegenation, which would become so prevalent among the French after African involvement in the First World War, had not yet overcome the much longer tradition of *métissage* dating to the New World conquest and intermarriage between settlers and Native Americans. French authorities saw Antillean society as a relic of this old empire and a product of interracial mixing that served to strengthen rather than diminish French culture and civilization abroad.

As historians like Eric Jennings have shown, at play throughout the Third Republic was the juxtaposition of French race with hostile, tropical spaces: in short, the distinction between white and nonwhite, between European and colonial.[13] The religious, economic, political, and cultural integration of Martinique and Guadeloupe complicated these understandings. In a time when national unity and the civilizing mission were of the utmost concern, racial typologies were mapped onto the old colonies in surprising ways. In the Caribbean, French identity was not, and still is not, a black-and-white issue. In fact, many colonial functionaries saw racial mixing as necessary and laudable, and old world whiteness as antiquated and antithetical to the republican project. The old colonies in the Caribbean occupied a space separate from that of the new colonies, for unlike the new colonies they had come to represent French culture and ideals in a tropical world far removed from France; that is, though they were tropical and dangerous, they were "civilized" spaces in the French imaginary. To be precise, the French viewed the population living there as "civilized," whereas the environment perpetually threatened that civilization. This contrasted sharply with prevalent attitudes in the newer colonies, even in Algeria, which had become a province of France itself, that increasingly identified French civilization with political boundaries on a map rather than the populations living there and sought to maintain cultural markers that distinguished between the two.[14] Therefore, during a time of rampant imperialism that heightened the distinction between the French and the non-French worlds—in particular between the white and the nonwhite worlds—the separation between Frenchness and racial mixture in the French Caribbean collapsed under the weight of the republican myth of assimilation and unity, much as the division between metropole and colony began to give way from pressure by mulatto politicians who sought departmentalization.[15]

In the French Caribbean, political motives, social stratification, environmental concerns, and racialist attitudes intermingled to produce a sphere that turned the gaining vogue of European racial supremacy on its head. Racial purity—either white or black—was seen as antagonistic to republicanism in the Antillean tropics. For various reasons and to various ends, racial mixture was considered a bulwark against the danger of a tropical environment to French culture. Therefore, the Antilles held a peculiar place within the French Empire, as French ideology was applied across the empire in variegated ways and French racialist thought followed as well as directed French politics.

Sources from those who sought to explain the Antilles to contemporaries in the metropole—not only the writers, educators, and scientists who traveled to the island over the course of the Third Republic but also the popular guidebooks, textbooks, and encyclopedias that shaped the way in which republicans understood the old colonies—show the complex ways in which French racialist attitudes were mapped onto the French Caribbean. As home to Saint-Pierre—the so-called Paris of the Antilles—until its destruction by the eruption of Mount Pelée in 1902, Martinique exemplified for Frenchmen a space that was simultaneously French and tropical, domestic yet foreign. On the one hand, Saint-Pierre's European-style gardens and architecture, as well as its social life, represented the transplantation of Parisian life in a tropical climate. On the other hand, the flora and fauna, as well as the perpetual danger of tropical diseases and hurricanes, drove home the difference from the metropole. In this liminal space, the French looked to Martinique's mulatto population—an interstitial group who represented the convergence of two worlds—rather than the white planters as the embodiment of French civilization, that is, as the standard bearers of the French Republic in the tropics.

In a similar fashion, malcontented laborers and intellectuals in France looked to Guadeloupe's mounting social tensions as a reflection of civil strife in the metropole, and in parliamentary meetings Guadeloupean politicians encouraged such coidentification. After civil discord in Guadeloupe in 1899 and strike activity in Martinique in 1900, Guadeloupe's deputy, Gerville-Réache, a powerful advocate for colonial assimilation, argued that West Indian collective action represented not a colonial insurrection but measured strike activity, suggesting Antilleans were participating in a markedly French phenomenon.[16] Similarly, Guadeloupe's Senator Alexandre Isaac—a prominent man of color and passionate supporter of colonial equality—based his political platform on the maxim that "it is essential to eventually persuade France that colonies are not properties to exploit, nor are they conquered countries subject to the exigencies ransomed by war."[17] Isaac argued that the discord affecting Guadeloupe resulted from an economic sugar crisis that had torn the island's political parties asunder, and he warned that if unattended, economic discontentment would turn into a social crisis.[18]

Economic tensions led contemporaries to map social cleavages onto the island's topography—a geography that was sharply divided. Guadeloupe's tropical and mountainous southern island, Basse-Terre, contrasted sharply with its plantation-economy-driven northern island, Grand-Terre. As a middle-class encyclopedia explained in 1886, Basse-Terre has "elevated mountains, covered by forest, numerous waterfalls, volcanic soil, and no plains; [whereas] Grande-Terre [has] flat land, few water cascades, and calcareous soil."[19] Upon this flat land with few cascades sat numerous sugar plantations, amid what one scientist unflatteringly described as swampland full of "stagnant water" and "detritus contributing to the mephitism of the wet and muddy terrain."[20] Due to the swampy land and what were seen as characteristic miasmas of disease, officials created lazarettos outside Pointe-à-Pitre in the 1890s and early 1900s to deal with the increasing number of malaria and yellow fever cases.[21] To their anxiety regarding the environment, Guadeloupe's colonial administration added the worry that Antillean workers had become arsonists by 1899 and strikers by 1910 bent on destroying the island's economy. The physical contrast between Basse- and Grande-Terre, therefore, carried over into the political and social division of Guadeloupe's two halves: the island's capital and bureaucratic center in the south made up largely of functionaries and menaced by the fumes of La Soufrière, and the fertile, marshy sugar plantations and buzzing factories threatened simultaneously by malaria and by a roiling mass of increasingly class-conscious workers in the north.[22]

Within the broader historical context of economic, political, and cultural developments in Martinique, Guadeloupe, and the metropole, this chapter will focus on how contemporaries described the islands' population and environment and compared it with those of mainland France. To explain the mythos of the civilizing mission as well as foresee the eventual redesignation of the old colonies as French departments, the question to answer is this: with regard to climate, culture, and population, what does France look like in the tropics?

The French Caribbean and the Metropole: Political Aspiration and Economic Reality

The islands of Martinique and Guadeloupe came under French control in 1635. Slavery persisted on the islands until 1794, when, responding to the Haitian Revolution as well as other republican uprisings in the Lesser Antilles, the French National Convention abolished slavery for the first time. However, Martinique passed into British control that same year, and the abolition of slavery was never enacted. Meanwhile, Guadeloupe erupted into open insurrection to force the Republic to make good on its claims, briefly earning the liberty it so desperately desired and so obviously deserved. Yet the island's white planters soon forced Guadeloupe's black citizenry back into shackles. When Martinique returned to France under the First Empire with the Treaty of Amiens in 1802, Napoleon seized the opportunity to reinstitute slavery within the French empire—an act staunchly resisted by Louis Delgrès, a mulatto military officer who championed the values of revolutionary France, led a revolutionary militia, and fought Napoleon's reoccupation of Guadeloupe. With Delgrès's defeat, however, Guadeloupeans lost their short-lived liberty. Martinique fell back under British control in 1807, as did Guadeloupe in 1810, and the islands did not return to France until the Restoration. The slave plantation economy became even more important once Haiti had been lost, and slavery persisted until the 1848 revolution, when, upon the creation of the Second French Republic, it was abolished for a second and final time.

In the spirit of liberty, equality, and fraternity, the French Republic granted full citizenship to all emancipated slaves in the French colonies by decree on 27 April 1848, though abolition was meant to be delayed for two months to allow for the sugar cane harvest. The enslaved in Martinique did not wait for the news to cross the Atlantic before forcing the hand of the governor through an open rebellion that began on 22 May 1848, prompting Guadeloupe's governor to enact emancipation days later, on 27 May.[23] Martinique and Guadeloupe had earned representation in the National Assembly in Paris on the basis of universal suffrage. Martinique elected Pierre-Marie Pory-Papy, an enfranchised mulatto lawyer who backed the republican insurrection in Martinique in May 1848, and Cyrille Bissette, a free mulatto merchant who championed racial equality and French republican values, but who, under the Restoration government, had been arrested for political agitation, branded, and sold into slavery in 1824. His arrest had aroused French frustrations with "ancient regime" justice, and after being exonerated a few years later, he participated in the transnational crusade to outlaw slavery. Guadeloupe elected Charles Dain, an abolitionist from the extreme left; Louisy Matheiu, a former slave and typesetter; and François Perrinon, a mulatto military officer from Martinique who agitated for abolition alongside the legendary abolitionist Victor Schoelcher. As evidence of their republican and abolitionist character, the newly enfranchised on both islands elected Schoelcher, who ultimately chose to sit for Martinique.[24]

Despite the gains made with the rise of the Second Republic, which had already been marred by electoral misconduct, civil disorder, and a state of emergency declared in Guadeloupe in 1850, the rights concomitant with citizenship were suppressed on the creation of the Second Empire, when Napoleon III established an authoritarian regime on the islands that benefited the white plantocracy and maintained slavery in all but name.[25] Emancipated slaves were highly restricted in terms of political rights and mobility in the French West Indies. For economic as well as ideological reasons, vagabondage laws required former slaves to continue to work on the plantations. Nonwhite citizens had to carry passports documenting both their employment and their movement on the island, and if they could not prove employment, they were sent to involuntary workhouses. In addition, ex-slaves accrued debts that placed them in a new form of "wage slavery."[26] Such vagabondage laws, which were common across the Caribbean, undercut the freedom of choice demanded by emancipated slaves. While black resistance thwarted such laws at every turn and the number of plantation workers in Guadeloupe and Martinique either decreased or remained stagnant over the period, vagabondage laws nevertheless created a legal regime that suppressed black citizenship rights and disproportionately supported French planters. In Guadeloupe in 1858, for example, only two of 261 breach-of-contract disputes favored the employee over the worker; the rest levied penalties against the nominally free black workers.[27] Under the Second Empire, there was little recourse to change the legal situation, for while ostensibly citizens, black Antilleans comprised only 15 percent of the islands' voting population from 1852 to 1870.[28]

The legal status of French Antilleans improved with the creation of the Third Republic on 4 September 1870. Universal male suffrage and citizenship rights were reinstated in the colony, though they were not codified until the Constitution of 1875, and by 1881 Martinique and Guadeloupe had full representation in the French Republican government: each with two deputies in the National Chamber of Deputies and a senator in the National French Senate.[29] During the first decade of the Third Republic, the wealthy white planter class dominated politics in Martinique and Guadeloupe. From the early 1880s onward, however, mulattos came to the political fore in the French Caribbean.[30] By the end of the decade, so too had black socialists and advocates for a social republic risen through the political ranks, particularly in Guadeloupe.

As a result of the close relationship between the French Republic and the abolition of slavery, the French Antilles became markedly republican in political stature over the course of the nineteenth century, often staking their claims in the French political arena, like their metropolitan counterparts, with reference to the republican values of the French Revolution. As the governor in Guadeloupe proclaimed in 1886, without regard to real political differences between the left and right on the island, "everyone here is republican."[31] In fact, the sway of republican ideology was so intense on the island that many Antillean politicians, much to the chagrin of the white islanders who wanted to gain more autonomy, demanded assimilation into the metropole throughout the Third Republic.[32] In fact, the General Council of Martinique first expressed an interest in assimilation on 24 November 1874, when it proclaimed that Martinique was a French land with French values, language, culture, and dress. Shortly after the political gains of criminal juries and the freedom of the press in 1880 and 1881, respectively, the assimilationist sentiment was reiterated more forcefully in 1882 by mulatto republicans led by Osman Duquesnay in the General Council, who proclaimed, as representatives of a "patriotic population,"

> Considering that Martinique, which has been French for more than two centuries, which has enjoyed since 1870 the same political rights as the metropole, finds itself in the best possible conditions to be assimilated completely into the mother-country; . . . we renew the wish that was made on 24 November 1874 and ask that Martinique be constituted as a French department as soon as possible.[33]

Such a sentiment was echoed by some metropolitan republicans. Dislère had already elucidated for the École Coloniale that the Antilles denoted an assimilable space. Similarly, Albert-Marie-Aristide Bouinais—a well-traveled and award-winning naval officer and colonial geographer who strongly supported French colonial expansion—complained about the misalignment between the colonial and metropolitan administrations in Guadeloupe during the Third Republic, a shortcoming he thought "will be filled the day the colony's assimilation into a department is complete."[34] Nevertheless, although the French Antilles were integrated into the metropole in important ways and seen by many republican functionaries to be a colony of settlement—if only, according to Dislère, a "weak" one—the islands were first and foremost colonies of extraction.

*

Paradoxically the end of slavery had accelerated the growth of sugar production on the islands, as planters now faced labor shortages and pivoted toward industrialization to maintain production levels. It had taken nine to ten workers to produce a barrel of mediocre-quality sugar on a *habitation-sucrerie* (a traditional sugar plantation combined with a refinery), whereas five to six workers could produce a barrel of higher-quality sugar in one of the nineteenth century's new factories.[35] While industrialization progressed sluggishly in the first decades after emancipation, after 1860 planters allied themselves closely with the newly created colonial bank, the Crédit Foncier Coloniale, and lobbied the metropole for funds to mechanize and consolidate what were quickly becoming large-scale, industrial sugar factories distinct from sugar cane plantations.[36] Between 1868 and 1872, the Crédit Foncier Coloniale provided nearly 80 percent of all capital investment for central factories in Martinique, and by the end of the 1860s, what had once been smaller-scale *habitations-sucreries* predicated almost exclusively on biological power were centralizing into steam-powered *usines centrales*, increasingly dominated by a capitaled, white financier class drawn from the plantation owners of old and the wealthy of the metropole.[37]

All but a handful of the old sugar estates that had comprised the countryside since the onset of slavery had disappeared by the century's end, as agriculture became an enterprise increasingly separate from industrialized sugar refining.[38] For instance, of Guadeloupe's 620 *habitations-sucreries* in 1830, only ninety-seven remained by 1883.[39] While Martinique lagged behind Guadeloupe's industrialization and maintained about half its *habitations-sucreries* into the 1880s, the technical superiority of central factories, which could produce more refined sugar with less sugar cane, saw Martinique's *habitations-sucreries* virtually disappear between 1884 and 1900.[40] Meanwhile, centralized sugar factories in Guadeloupe doubled from twelve in 1844 to twenty-three by 1882, refining 77 percent of all exported sugar and using nearly 20 percent of the island's total land area.[41] Likewise, twenty-one centralized factories operated in Martinique at the end of the nineteenth century.[42] The new division of labor, in which now-consolidated agricultural estates solely grew sugar cane and sold it to industrial refineries, allowed Antillean sugar to continue to compete in an increasingly competitive world market.[43] Mechanization saw the production of Antillean sugar skyrocket, from roughly forty thousand to fifty thousand tons of sugar immediately after emancipation to upwards of one hundred thousand tons of sugar by the 1880s (figure 1).[44] Industrialization further entrenched the sugar monoculture, which by 1880 constituted 87 percent of all Guadeloupe's exports, used 60 percent of its land, and occupied 60 percent of its labor force.[45] Likewise, the sugar monoculture employed over half of Martinique's cultivated land—eighteen thousand hectares out of thirty-three thousand—and the bulk of its population.[46]

The dominance of metropolitan capital was more pronounced in Guadeloupe, where centralization brought about the virtual disappearance of the *habitants-sucriers*—the landed white aristocracy who had dominated the island's economy since the seventeenth century—than in Martinique, where the traditional white planter class was more unified, maintained its economic and political power, and continued to direct the island economy.[47] Nevertheless, by the 1880s the colossal economic shift wrought by emancipation and industrialization had marked demographic effects on both islands. Many former slaves now worked entirely outside the sugar industry, instead owning small plots and growing foodstuffs. This small planter class had doubled in size after emancipation, further exacerbating the labor shortages on the cane fields. Planters met the agricultural labor shortage with indentured servants from Asia, of whom they brought nearly seventy-five thousand to the French Caribbean between 1853 and 1889.[48] Virtually all indentured servants worked the cane fields, whereas the factories were predominantly staffed by the islands' creole black population.

The move toward factory work did not mean that the islands became urbanized, as the population remained mainly rural by approximately a two-to-one ratio. In Martinique, for instance, roughly forty-eight thousand people lived in urban areas, whereas 113,000 lived in the countryside, according to a report in 1877.[49] What had changed was the way in which workers

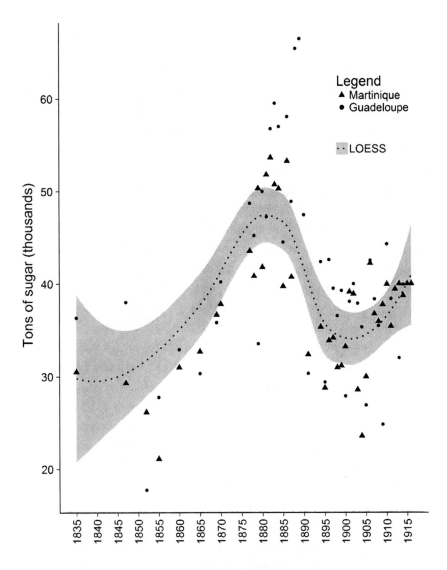

FIG. 1.   **Sugar production in the French Antilles, 1835–1916**
Local regression trend line (LOESS), on average, for Martinique and
Guadeloupe. Graph created in R statistical package with information from
Rolph, *Something about Sugar*, 242; Chemin-Dupontes, *Les Petites Antilles*,
241–42; *Projet de budget (Département de la Martinique)*, 1913–14; Block,
Statistique de la France, 623; France, *Bulletin: Documents officiels, statistique,
rapports*, 643; France, *Annuaire statistique de la France*, 15:73; Schmidt,
Abolitionnistes de l'esclavage, 32.

interacted with the island economy, as many former slaves made up a "rural proletariat." Though over half the islands' working population continued to labor in sugar cultivation and production, the changing nature of the sugar industry saw the decline of the *gens-casés*, former slaves who toiled and lived on the sugar plantations of old, and the growth of sugar factory workers, who formed the backbone of the islands' strike activity from 1900 onward. As Guadeloupe's governor remarked in 1895, "the population of Grande-Terre lives exclusively on factory salaries."[50]

Industrialization brought changes for the financiers as well. In their fever to mechanize and thus meet mounting international competition, economically minded colonialists considered the islands woefully under-exploited and underdeveloped, a sentiment that deepened as financiers received disappointing profits with the onset of a worldwide sugar crisis in 1884. As one contemporary put it, "In 1870, the budget of Martinique was 3,214,191 francs; in 1901, it was 7,763,768 francs. . . . Public works cost 950,000 francs each year. In 7 years, we've spent 6.5 million. Where are the works that represent this infusion of capital? Where are the roads? Where are the canals? Where are the railways? There aren't any."[51] Despite a long history of subsidies for the colonial sugar industry, which by 1900 had produced hundreds of miles of railways and factories containing what U.S. reports deemed "excellent machinery, most of it modern," French contemporaries considered both the islands' sugar production and economic infrastructure to be lacking by the close of the nineteenth century.[52] Some, such as sugar lobbyist M. L. de Feissal, argued that the current infrastructure existed in spite of underwhelming governmental investment.[53] Subsidies and capital investment could not keep apace the destruction wrought by disasters, nor the advance of beet sugar. In the words of Ferdinand Peck, the U.S. commissioner-general to the French World's Fair in 1900, "Notwithstanding the individual efforts made, climatic influence, such as earthquakes, cyclones[,] floods, etc., have caused much [financial] discouragement," as French investment in infrastructure had shifted toward beet sugar, which the Ministry of Agriculture described in 1882 as "one of the industrial glories of France."[54] In light of divestment in the French Antilles, a French lawyer and graduate of the École Coloniale, André Blancan, argued against assimilation and contradicted Dislère's division between old and new colonies, defining, as did several of his contemporaries, a colony's worth and economic value to be the true measure of patriotism. Instead of assimilation on the grounds of cultural similitude, he promoted autonomy as an economic solution that would attract capital investment in Guadeloupe.[55] Such a sentiment became increasingly commonplace among many wealthy financiers and colonialists who saw Guadeloupe's political and economic climate as "decadent" and illustrative of the "fallacies of assimilation."[56]

It is undeniable that the French Caribbean's economic production struggled during the end of the nineteenth century, and in fact the white community saw the islands as, in the words of contemporary R. S. Reisch, a "lost land, or *pays perdu*."[57] This decline was largely the result of the increasing beet sugar market, which cut into the demand for Antillean cane sugar; the hurricane of 1891, which devastated Martinique; and the unanticipated eruption in 1902 of a volcano thought to have been extinct, Mount Pelée, which utterly destroyed Martinique's political and financial capital, Saint-Pierre. The inclusion of Martinique and Guadeloupe in the customs tariff of mainland France in 1892 helped to improve sugar production on the islands, but it also brought them into direct economic competition with mainland beet sugar and prevented trade with the United States—eventually leading to civil disorder in 1899 and 1900. While the majority of Martinique's and Guadeloupe's land remained under sugar cultivation and the two islands continued to produce roughly two-thirds of all colonial sugar in the French empire, the French market began to shift toward the cheaper, domestic alternative.[58] By 1900, colonial sugar satisfied only about 12 percent of France's sweet tooth, with Martinique and Guadeloupe producing between 5 and 10 percent of all sugar consumed in the metropole.[59] Between 1887 and 1897, sugar cane production remained the same, while beet sugar production doubled, and by 1900 twice as much beet sugar as sugar cane was annually produced worldwide.[60]

Despite the declining importance of Antillean sugar in the world market, production remained fairly high except in the immediate aftermaths of natural disasters. Sugar yields stabilized in the first decade of the twentieth century, and production remained a fundamental aspect of the French Caribbean's economy and society. Though net profits declined as sugar became cheaper to produce, the cane sugar economy remained an influential factor in the creation of colonial policy, and Frenchmen saw it as the prime characteristic of the French Antilles until the reconfiguration of the islands' economies around banana production after a devastating hurricane once again hampered sugar production in 1928. Sugar production resulted in one of the fundamental dividing lines of Antillean society: rich white families owned most of the sugar plantations and factories while poor black laborers operated them, and as a result race was by and large mapped onto class divisions. The sugar crisis deepened this divide, as many capitalists took out their financial frustrations politically on the nonwhite laboring populations, whom they criticized as averse to hard work.[61]

On Guadeloupe, for instance, economic strife turned to political malfeasance in 1906 and a general strike in 1910, during which the gendarmerie opened fire on a striking crowd and, as metropolitan politicians remarked, "French blood flowed."[62] Despite the French legislature's insistence that French blood had been spilled, racial conflict lay at the root of the strike, which had been prompted by a recent uptick in production that led workers to demand a wage increase. As the socialist paper *L'Aurore* sarcastically asked days after the strike, "Fundamentally, what are the troubles in Guadeloupe? That blacks have bruised [*font des bleus*] the whites."[63] Oftentimes cross-Atlantic solidarity failed to gain traction in the press, despite many Antilleans feeling that it should. Guadeloupe's socialist deputy, Gérault-Richard, complained about the double standard: "If the bloody brawls of Halluin [in France] occurred in Guadeloupe or Martinique or Reunion, we'd never hear the end of it! The Press never misses a chance to proclaim that all is aflame and bloody in the colonies and to ask a puritanical deputy for the suppression of colonial representation."[64] Regrettably, international embarrassments caused by increased socialist agitation led many in the French government to consider suppressing universal suffrage on the islands, though this action never came to pass.[65]

Although the French Caribbean remained an extractive colony centered on sugar, the blurry line between metropole and colony, championed by Antillean representatives like Gérault-Richard, created an imperative to see the islands as colonies of settlement and presaged their uneven incorporation into French culture and politics. Sugar production became a contested issue, and dissatisfaction on the plantation became tightly bound to metropolitan labor unrest. Strikers in the Antilles invoked the 1892 Law of Labor Arbitration, which contained provisions extending its applicability to the old colonies. Labor unrest and arbitration, both successful and unsuccessful, were a widely spread French phenomenon. In the ten years between 1893 and 1903, there were 5,874 strikes and lockouts in France, approximately 10 percent of which were successfully resolved via the arbitration outlined in the law of 1892.[66]

Labor troubles in the Antilles, therefore, resonated with those dissatisfied with the Third Republic's politics. To commemorate the twenty-ninth anniversary of the brutal May 1871 repression of the Paris Commune, somewhere between twelve thousand and twenty-five thousand people took to the streets and marched through the Père-Lachaise cemetery, shouting "Long live the Commune" and waving red banners which read "To the victims of Galliffet! To the victims in Martinique!"[67] In remembering the Commune, as well as its brutal suppression by troops under the command of the Marquis de Galliffet, who in 1900 served as the minister of war, the protesters drew a straight line from "Bloody Week," the foundational moment of the Third Republic, to the violent repression of strikers in Martinique. In fact, Galliffet resigned his post two days after this funereal demonstration due to public pressure and ideological conflicts with his colleagues. Contemporaries saw the French Caribbean as politically occupying a space distinct from that of the new colonies—a space that in many ways coincided with metropolitan France.

During these demonstrations in 1900, the Universal Exposition opened in Paris as a demonstration of France's military might and colonial breadth. Nearly fifty-one million people visited the exposition, which sprawled across 112 hectares and housed eighty-three thousand exhibitors from over twenty-five countries.[68] Organizers made a marked attempt to exoticize the exhibits of Martinique and Guadeloupe to lure visitors, but with labor unrest in the Caribbean fresh in the minds of the French populace, they failed. Their failure underlined the coincidence of French Caribbean and metropolitan identity, as an exotic image of the Antilles stood at odds with its political and economic familiarity. One American observer described Martinique's pavilion as "quaint" and Guadeloupe's as "simple," tucked as they were behind the Indo-Chinese pavilions, whereas he described Madagascar's pavilion as an "immense structure . . . of three floors" that matched the stature of "[t]his large and important French colony."[69] Upon visiting the Guadeloupean exhibit, the United States' commissioner-general remarked that the "sugars exhibited offered no special interest."[70] Such lack of interest characterized the Antillean pavilions at the 1890 World's Fair a decade prior, when observers "passed them over in silence" because, in the words of Martinique's delegate at the exposition, sugar was too common a product to hold any allure for fairgoers.[71] Similarly in 1900, one contemporary French reporter explained that Parisians did not buy into the exoticization, because they saw the French Caribbean as a space far apart from more exciting colonial locales and a political culture that mirrored France in terms of end-of-the-century social conflicts, like strikes and workers' arbitration.[72]

Visitors to the exposition had little interest in the French Caribbean, because the recent strike activity, as well as the colonial home design of the Antilles' pavilions, undermined its claim to exoticism. Though brightly dressed creole women chatted with visitors, serving rum while gracefully balancing ornate fruit headdresses on their heads, the pavilions seemed banal, and they invoked the history of slavery.[73] A French past rather than an exciting imperial present lay within the construction of the pavilions, and according to an observer, placid workers in the Trocadero belied the turmoil Guadeloupe and Martinique had lately experienced.[74] Simply put, the Caribbean pavilions did not command the interest garnered by the newer colonies.'

The failure to attract interest cannot be attributed to a lack of effort in creating a tropical atmosphere. According to an observer, the Martinique pavilion, full of vibrant colors and resonant with high-pitched creole music, gave visitors the impression that they had entered a cage full of exotic birds. Rather, a familiarity with the islands led to the pavilions' failure to attract visitors who were looking for something new and exciting. For all their tropical embellishments, the creole women staffing Martinique's pavilion were uncannily familiar to a metropolitan audience. In his piece for *L'Illustration*, Arsène Alexander described one of the creole women, Eldja, as follows: "By her physical appearance she was undeniably creole, and by her voice strikingly Parisian—right bank even—and for all that a person of real distinction."[75] In part, this familiarity reflected the fact that few of the creole women had lived on the islands past the age of six or seven and were more acquainted with Paris than with Martinique.[76] According to the Parisian press, those going to the pavilion expected to see elements of the political and labor unrest they had read about in the papers—that is, something exciting and new—but instead they confronted women Parisian in manner and calm in demeanor.

Antilleans themselves participated in, and even encouraged, the glossing over of the Caribbean's colonial status in the French Republic. Mulatto politicians in Martinique politically draped themselves in the garb of the French Republic, while black socialists in Guadeloupe struggled to join arms in solidarity with their brethren in the metropole. In 1908 the Martiniquais section of the League of the Rights of Man and the Citizen—formed by Dreyfusards a decade prior—drafted a letter titled "Republican Martinique to Republican France," indicting the metropolitan government for permitting the *békés*, or colonial white citizens, to attempt to assert political dominance over the island. These *békés*—by and large the owners of the islands' sugar plantations and manufactories—had been fighting against the movement to assimilate Martinique and Guadeloupe into mainland France, instead pushing for more autonomy. Contrary to assimilationist political rhetoric, which portrayed the people of the Antilles as inherently French, the white planter class rejected the inclusion of people of color in their definition of France. Such a sentiment can be traced all the way back to the French Revolution and Haitian independence, when the white planters saw colored republicanism as a threat to their own interests. For instance, arguing that the emancipation of the islands' slaves has led to the "enslavement of the French on their own territory," an angry white planter from Saint-Domingue wrote that to "guarantee the French republic" in the French Antilles, one must champion economics and remember, in the words the Abbé Raynal, that a "colony in the Antilles is an establishment of things rather than of people."[77] That is, it is a colony meant to be economically exploited rather than seen, in the eyes of contemporary republicans, as a colony of settlement.

Therefore, the continued economic dominance of an old white planter class with such backward thoughts caused an outrage among mulatto politicians. Claiming to represent the island's "fidelity to the spirit of the French

Republic" and refusing "to consider as republican those who, contrary to the Declaration of the Right of Man and of the Citizen, make distinctions between humans based on their race, religion, or skin color," the league demanded the removal of the governor of Martinique, Charles Louis Lepreux. The society held him responsible for the assassination on 29 April 1908 of the mayor of Fort-de-France, Antoine Siger—a man of color elected with substantial mulatto backing whose radical socialist leanings upset conservatives on the island.[78] At Siger's funeral, Martinique's representative to the Chamber of Deputies, Victor Sévère, another man of color and a self-avowed socialist, intoned, "The abominable murder that has struck our city hall is not the crime of a single man; it is the crime of an entire party . . . against liberty, against the law, against universal suffrage."[79] In response to the scandal of the assassination, the antirepublican sentiment it uncovered, and the public outrage in Martinique, the ministry removed Governor Lepreux from office.

Whether the aim of redefining the Antilles as colonies of settlement, and therefore to include Antilleans within the conceptualization of the French nation, was noble or hypocritical, the Antilles continued to be economically exploited at the close of the nineteenth century. Antilleans earned yearly salaries roughly half that of their metropolitan counterparts and met discrimination in the legal system, economic market, and popular press. Yet, increasingly, Antilleans began to demand rights and privileges from the French state in the forms of assistance following natural disasters and of wage increases and customs reform following collective action. In response to the driving impetus behind assimilation, Dislère himself recast the citizens living in the old colonies as a new form of leverageable resource. To answer his political opponents who fought against assimilating such old, financially unimportant colonies into the French market—let alone the French nation—Dislère justified assimilating the colonies via a new logic of "civic" extraction from the colonies, arguing that while the average taxpayer in the metropole gives thirty-four days' worth of work to the French government annually, colonial citizens provide far less: twenty-two days' worth in Martinique and fifteen in Guadeloupe.[80] The citizenry was thus seen as an exploitable resource and a source of revenue for the French state—not to mention a nontrivial voting bloc. A similar logic of civic extraction dates to the French Revolution itself, when Sonthonax liberated slaves as military recruits against anti-Republican sentiment in 1793 and Napoleon briefly considered a possible upside of the slave revolt in Saint-Domingue: "They make less sugar than when they were slaves, but they will provide us, and serve us as we need them, as soldiers."[81] Much as it had during the French Revolution, the French state under the Third Republic looked for new ways to extract resources from its Caribbean populations—now recast as colonial citizens—to keep up with the times.

The French educational system instituted in Martinique and Guadeloupe also reflected the ambiguous and rather contradictory conceptualization of the French Caribbean that privileged the notion of inclusion while underscoring the importance of economic extraction. In the jury reports for the Paris Exposition of 1900 officials posited that Antillean public schools needed to focus more heavily on agricultural education than did the metropole to prepare children for manual labor, presumably making them more amenable to menial tasks. This goal was particularly important for placating the mounting socialist sentiment in Guadeloupe, especially the sugar plantations in the north. The report made clear that this instructional regime was to remain differentiated from that instituted in the new colonies, stating that though the educational system would remain along the same lines as that of the metropole, the curriculum would include manual labor due to its ability to make men "more dignified and more moral."[82] In other words, it would make them more docile and willing to accept insufficient pay.

However, although this general idea of manual labor producing societal improvement—the notion of *mettre en valeur*—fit within the larger discourse of the "civilizing mission" meant to elevate populations within the French empire, officials felt the need to stress that Antillean pedagogy would remain distinct from that of the new colonies and similar to that of the metropole. The focus on manual labor producing a demure workforce was one that carried currency within France itself, which was increasingly seeing its share of strikes, and the idea that the old colonies were markedly different from the new colonies was quite pervasive. For instance, Alfred Picard, the general commissioner for the exposition, disagreed with the official jury report slightly, asserting that the colonies of Martinique and

Guadeloupe "do not call for any special guidelines. They have no indigenous peoples to civilize, and the instructional regime must be the same there as that of the metropole."[83] In fact, other contemporaries, such as Bouinais, argued that it would be greatly beneficial to create a national postsecondary school in either Martinique or Guadeloupe on the model of that in Grignon, France's premier agricultural school, which graduated some of France's greatest agronomical engineers and plant scientists.[84] Such reports make clear that the French Caribbean occupied a space apart from the new colonies, though, however French, the colony was still seen as having a primarily economic role within France.

While the economic reality of the French Caribbean was grounded in the extraction of sugar, the place of the Antilles in the nineteenth-century bourgeois *imaginaire* followed cultural and political imperatives, particularly in Martinique, the home of the "Paris of the Antilles," where racial intermixing was common. The metropole itself, as well as the Antilleans, viewed their land as incorruptibly republican and inherently French, even though their inhabitants were nearly 95 percent nonwhite—though this conception often played out in contradictory ways.[85] On the one hand, it played into the racism inherent to the so-called civilizing mission of "new imperialism." On the other hand, as we shall see, it complicated and challenged contemporary understandings of race in interesting and important ways, harking back to the old empire when French officials saw racial intermixture as a positive rather than a negative.

"Old" France with a New Race of Frenchmen

Martinique and Guadeloupe had been French since the seventeenth century, and by the Third Republic the islands were seen as part and parcel of French heritage and often described as a piece of old France itself. For writers of tourist literature, who romantically glossed over the island's history of slavery, the people of the French Caribbean exhibited the old manners and good hospitality of times past:

> Martinique! This name in clear syllables evokes a brilliant past: supremacy of the small island in the 18th century, becoming the first of the Antilles. It

was said then: lords of Haiti, *messieurs* of Martinique and the good people of Guadeloupe. At that time flourished in the island all the graces of a polished and brilliant century of which we can still find a faint echo in the current inhabitants of the Island of Flowers. Customs a bit outdated. Old French politeness. Light preciousness of music and dance. Clothes with affectation. Aged expressions. Gallant and kind memories. Slow and sweet speech.[86]

This conceptualization of the French Caribbean as a piece of old-world France was often coupled with the assertion that Antillean history was French history and that no one could deny the loyalty of the island to France—a loyalty British invasions and subsequent occupations repeatedly tested.[87] As Paulette Nardal explained in her tourism manual, "[t]he history of Martinique, a distinct reflection of that of France, will show him [the tourist], to the contrary, a definitive loyalty among the white French and the African blacks that has been strikingly proven time and time again."[88]

The school system in the French Caribbean supported Nardal's assertion. In his schoolbook *Histoire de la Martinique*, Jules Lucrèce exhibited the cultural conceptualization that will be explored in the remainder of this chapter: that the French Caribbean represented its Frenchness by virtue of racial creolization and acclimatization to a harsh environment. For the Antillean schoolchildren who were learning their history—a history the Ministry of Education framed as inherently French—Martinique represented a space in which European and African heritage combined via French civilization. In the preface to Lucrèce's textbook, Professor L. Achille stated that the book presents a

thrilling history of three centuries during which our ancestors, coming from France or imported from Africa, both confined on the same elemental and fertile soil of Martinique, combined across such obstacles, by the insidious effect of the climate, economic necessities, and social mimicry, to create a complex but well-characterized creole race which increasingly becomes aware of its vigor, of its possibilities, of its land-based solidarity, and which wants to make its small birthplace into a more and more comfortable and attractive place.[89]

The French government received this interpretation of Martiniquais history well. In November 1930, the head of the Department of Public Instruction, A. Fouret, wrote a letter to Lucrèce congratulating him on creating "a practical manual" that gives primary schoolchildren "useful knowledge on the evolution of their *pays*."[90] Unsurprisingly, he appreciated the focus on the democratic reforms of the Third Republic—that is, the reinstitution of universal manhood suffrage, full representation in the national French legislature, the creation of free and public education, and the reintroduction of freedom of the press in the island: in the words of Lucrèce, "the generous efforts of men like Schoelcher, Lamartine, Armand Barbès, Louis Blanc, Ledru-Rollin and others who fought and suffered to grant liberty and raise us to the dignity of citizenship."[91]

Therefore, though it discussed plantation slavery, albeit cursorily, the textbook read as a progression from slavery to liberty, from old regime to republic. Lucrèce characterized Martinique's history, as well as the history of France, from 1870 onward as the product of two forces: "the spirit of conservativism and reactionism loyal to the principles of personal government (monarchy and empire) and the spirit of progress and liberty loyal to republican traditions."[92] The textbook presented events such as the strike of 1900 and the violent response by French troops and the assassination by reactionary whites of the socialist mayor of Fort de France, Antoine Siger, in 1908 not as racial or colonial problems but as symptoms of problems endemic to French society. Claiming that the Caribbean islands had been legislatively and culturally integrated into France, even though they were still nominally colonies, the textbook stated that the people inhabiting these parts of France are "a small people of skin colorations varying from ebony black to alabaster white, but they have the same language, the same interests, the same religious beliefs, the same customs and the same traditions as France."[93]

The painting of the French Caribbean as historically and traditionally French is surprising, given the racial composition of the islanders, the legacy of plantation slavery, and the forced migration of African slaves to the islands. However, it fits hand-in-glove with the assimilationist ideology that characterized French republicanism. After 1848, governmental records no longer tracked the race of the islands' populations, leading Bouinais to divide the populace not by race but by place of origin: creole—all those individuals born in the colony—or immigrant.[94] But despite the lack of official tracking in the *état-civil*, many publications continued to track the racial makeup of the islands, dividing between white, people of color, and black. Nevertheless, metropolitan observers saw the French Caribbean as a slice of a French past—one that was quaint and inviting, whitewashed of its foundational inequity though always under attack from the hazards of the environment. Bouinais, for instance, described the Guadeloupean creole language as "picturesque, colorful, full of finesse," just like French dialects within the metropole itself, and he stressed that traditional French remained the classic language of the island.[95]

Not everyone, however, conceptualized the Antilles as something old and classic; others saw it as a fresh take on French tradition. For instance, in his ethnographic work on Martinique, Louis Garaud—an educational expert and linguist—discussed numerous creole proverbs, explaining both their meaning and their relationship to their metropolitan counterparts. He provided analogs from traditional French proverbs for many of the creole sayings, illustrating that the same ideas permeated both cultures, though he insisted that despite the cultural parallels, these proverbs grew out of creole culture itself:

> Do not believe that these proverbs are flat translations of French proverbs. All the more so when the inspiration for them is sensitive. For I do not believe that these borrowings were premeditated. The people were too naïve and too young to own rags that smelled of centuries' dust.[96]

By innovatively producing proverbs free from the smell "of centuries' dust" that were simultaneously similar to those of French heritage, the creole population—"young and naïve" to Garaud—had invigorated French identity.

This combination of newness with Frenchness extended to the ways in which metropolitan officials understood the French Caribbean's racial dynamics. In the growing intellectual climate of scientism and social Darwinism, Europeans became preoccupied with a hierarchy of races and civilizations, presupposing white people as the most advanced race and colored races as inherently inferior—or, as Garaud's work shows, as younger and less developed than the races of Europe. However, the application of this hierarchical ideology was far from straightforward in the French Caribbean. Hybrid races, like the mulattos of Martinique that constituted roughly a third of the island's population during the Third Republic, challenged this racial hierarchy as a "new race" that had to be fitted into the racial hierarchy.[97] Historians have argued that the mulatto class represented to nineteenth-century Frenchmen a tainted whiteness—that is, a bastard race. As historian and political scientist Mickaella Périna argues, "[f]or the biologists of the 19th century, the hybrid constituted a veritable scandal . . . [, because] 'hybridization' seemed inadmissible when applied to man, in other words, the mulatto was unacceptable."[98] Moreover, some historians have seen this racist ideology, the language of creole whites, as an impediment to assimilation, as well as something that characterized the relationship between the old colonies and the metropole.[99]

Indeed many contemporaries remained wary of republican universalism and the overturning of racial hierarchies. For instance, Armand Corre—a colonial doctor famous for his work on vaccines in West Africa—wrote *Nos Créoles* in 1890, a profoundly racist work highly critical of the imperial project. Corre argued that "principles of race [have been] too imprudently sacrificed for those of lesser value," leading colonial bureaucrats to waste resources in their ill-fated quest to assimilate the old colonies.[100] With an extended culinary metaphor underlying his distaste for the melting pot ideal that underpinned republican universalism, the famed and well-traveled colonial doctor argued that colonial populations could never fully appreciate metropolitan values and the project of assimilation would only unite the disparate races in shared frustration and ingratitude:

> No metropolitan governor will last long in our creole countries. These lands want men of their crude stock capable of blending local rivalries into a sauce of common interest, for which the motherland will provide all the ingredients. Blacks, mulattos, and whites come together in their complaints, reproaches, and sometimes invectives, [all of which they] address to a France that *does not do enough* for the most devoted of its children![101]

Antilleans were participating in French politics and making demands of the French government: black workers lobbying for the social republic, mulattos for increased political and financial enfranchisement of the middle class, and whites for political autonomy. Corre labeled these increasing social demands as ingratitude, and he went on to cite a disgruntled and spiteful metropolitan schoolteacher assigned to Martinique. Complaining that all was in the hands of the Martiniquais—Frenchmen by decree, as opposed to the "true" Frenchmen of France—the teacher lamented in a letter to Cassagnac, Bonapartist deputy of Gers and author of the right-wing, anti-Semitic journal *l'Autorité*:

> Last year, in the full General Council, we were called foreigners, though the word was redacted by the president. . . . The majority of this council has for their motto: "Hate the European, down with whites." And France lets them. And we, the real Frenchmen, we are foreigners, while this band of blacks—more or less dark—are the masters. . . . Tell it in your newspaper, on the grandstand, that in Martinique there's a crowd of Frenchmen of France vexed, tyrannized, pillaged by these blacks and mulattos of the country—Frenchmen by decree, because they are not it in their origin, their language, or their customs. . . . The European, insulted and challenged, is the foreigner, and they, these children of the Congo, call themselves *children of the country*![102]

What we have here are competing visions of what it meant to be French: on the one hand, the republican ideal, outlined in the schoolbooks to which the schoolteacher should be adhering, that said these "Frenchmen by decree" were politically, culturally, and ideologically French. On the other hand, we have a blood and soil tradition—instead invoked by the schoolteacher—that pitted "true Frenchmen" against these Martiniquais doppelgangers. The Martiniquais made claims to being French, and as such, forced metropolitan functionaries to take stock of what it meant to be French. While Corre's work struck a nerve with enough Frenchmen to be republished in 1902, his brand of racism was far from widely accepted under the Third Republic and in colonial circles was politically untenable, at least with regard to the old colonies. In fact, Corre himself asserted that his work had unleashed "great storms" and "brought on [his] person an incredible outburst of anger and manifestations of hatred."[103]

Though vicious racism still plagued these "old colonies," there is something intriguing—and, frankly, downright surprising—in the general application of racial typologies to Martinique. To focus solely on the negative depictions of racial mixing misses something of key importance in the assimilationist ideology. While a number of prominent scientists condemned miscegenation, many French writers lauded the practice.[104] The mixing of European and African "stock" in the context of the Caribbean produced a new and exciting race that combined, to a certain degree, the best of both worlds. These writers also used scientific language to call blackness not a taint on the population but rather a source of strength for the Martiniquais; in their estimation, it gave the civilized and intellectual white race a strength of physique and spirit. While undeniably racist, this understanding complicated the idea of the inherent inferiority of colored populations relative to whites. Although writers like Garaud depicted the Martiniquais as younger than their metropolitan compatriots—and significantly, he did not map this along racial lines but applied it to Martinique as a whole—such youth was often depicted as invigorating to a stale European spirit.[105] In this context, racial mixing was heralded as inherently French and was held up as the civilizing process at work. In fact, the figure of the mulatto woman was often associated with Marianne, the symbol of the French Republic. Posters and popular images following the 1902 eruption of Mount Pelée often depicted Martinique as a mulatto Marianne, complete with a "creolized" stand-in for the Phrygian cap. This imagery attested to the profoundly republican nature of the island—here foregrounded by the tropical environment—as well as the prominence of its mulattos in the French imagination.

The *Grande encyclopédie*, published as a standard middle-class reference book under the Third Republic, echoed this sentiment. It discussed in detail what Frenchmen at the time considered to be the various classifications of the human races as well as the methodological and scientific debates over how to categorize those differences. The *Encyclopédie*'s article on race went on at length about the variations in height, weight, cranial capacity, skin color, hair color, and intellectual and emotional characteristics for each of the "human races." Its only reference to mixed races was to provide a list of the names used to refer to mixed races and to state that racial mixing would not be covered.[106] The article on Martinique, however, attributed the dramatic decrease in the island's white population during the previous century and a half to the greater mortality rate [for whites] than for the African race during yellow fever epidemics, but especially the voluntary segregation of the white from the black who became his equal. However, [eventually] the races founded themselves, mixed with one another with the most diverse nuances, and this resulted in a new race, the creoles of color whose physical and intellectual qualities are remarkable, and to whom the future belongs. The Martiniquais are among the most beautiful of the Antilleans.[107]

As this standard reference book illustrates, the "creoles of color" were seen to possess remarkable "physical and intellectual" qualities, which in turn qualified them to be in possession of the future. Far from degeneracy or decadence, the article suggested the prospect of a positive future in the racially mixed class. The *Encyclopédie* seemed to approve of racial mixing only in the Caribbean context, where, in its imagination, European ancestry had elevated the Martiniquais above their "darker" neighbors. Nonetheless, the fact that colonial circumstances could make *métissage* a virtue rather than the threat it was seen to be in West Africa and Indochina remains astonishing.

Highlighting the positive qualities of the Martiniquais, Louis Garaud introduced his ethnographic book about Martinique by addressing the stereotypes about the islanders, again treating the Martiniquais as naïve and childlike—an idea which, while demeaning, fit with the bourgeois understanding of the mulattos as the future and reflected the broader discourse of the *mission civilisatrice* that saw the need for colonial populations to mature into citizenship. This discourse was in many ways paradoxical, because the people of Martinique were legally full citizens of the French nation rather than subjects of the French empire. Garaud did not specify how the stereotypes mapped onto the island's various races, even stating that the stereotypical "differences between the races which inhabit Martinique are more amusing than true."[108] He elaborated on this idea in the book's preface:

I have wanted to pay to Martinique my debt of knowledge for the charm of its climate, the splendor of its vegetation and the hospitality of its inhabitants whose faults, facts of youth, still seduce more than their [good] qualities.

"What do you think about it?" people say to me sometimes. "The inhabitants of this colony, don't they have intolerable defaults? Aren't they prideful, prodigious, and audacious?"

I respond in this way: "Audacity is the courage that they carry; prodigality is the charity they exhibit; pride would be the most beautiful of characteristics if Christianity had not made it one of the most ugly of the Seven Deadly Sins. For the rest, the starkness of their good characteristics is accented by the shadow of their faults. In fact, can one be astonished that in the land of sun shadows seem more intense?[109]

Garaud's uneven embrace of stereotypes thus included prejudices that were not strictly negative. In fact, he argued that the Martiniquais' "faults" were in fact their strengths: for Garaud, audacity became courage; wastefulness became charity; and pride was a good thing, particularly for a group of people who, in Garaud's eyes, celebrated French culture. This paternalistic description of the people of Martinique clearly reflected the primitivist stereotypes prevalent in colonial discourse, but it did so in a way that underscored the inherent, or rather nascent, Frenchness of the island's population, whose courage and pride ranked among the most emblematic of French virtues.

Garaud also looked at the racial politics of the island. He saw the mulatto class as the impassioned political leaders of Martinique—caught between a laboring black class and an aristocratic, reactionary white class. Garaud found it unfortunate that the white and black residents of the island were mortal enemies and that this new race of mulattos could not reconcile with either one:

People of mixed race or mulattos, which are still called by the euphemism, people of color, are today the leading class in Martinique. They walk at an equal distance between the blacks and whites. Whites sometimes refuse to extend their hand to them; [in turn,] they don't always extend theirs to the Negroes. In sum, they are isolated, and they struggle between the blacks—the rising class, young, inflated with menace—and the whites— the old class that is crumbling and collapsing. It is regrettable that the old masters, the white Creoles, called *békés* in the local patois, have prematurely resolved to live in isolation. This class has closed itself off and left mulattos to struggle. They love their mothers, but they disown their sons. They don't forgive them for having the blood of slaves in their veins.[110]

Garaud's language is highly suggestive here: the blacks are young and on the rise, though menacing, whereas the whites are "crumbling" and "collapsing." In Garaud's estimation, the white planters had forsaken their role as the political elite in the island, leaving the mulattos to lead the island politically—and since they were caught between these two groups, he saw the mulatto class, from which the island's deputies to the French legislature were drawn, as "left to struggle." For Garaud, racial division, and not intermixing, undermined the republican project in Martinique.

Though not interchangeable, race and class were conflated and interrelated terms in Martinique during the late nineteenth century. Governmental officials used a language of racial difference to explain what were essentially class divisions on the island. The direct beneficiaries of the public education system instituted by Jules Ferry in 1881–82, Martinique's mulattos constituted a political class of well-to-do republicans distinct from both black plantation workers and the aristocratic *békés*. Mulattos controlled the island's government and constituted those who represented the islands in the metropolitan government. Therefore, mulattos largely comprised what might be called a bourgeois class of professionals, and as such they readily identified with the bureaucratic makeup of the Third Republic, finding employment as public officials, doctors, lawyers, and teachers, for example. On the other hand, the *békés* were the land-owning class whose plantations predated the First French Republic and recalled the Old Regime, while the laborers, vestiges of the island's cruel slave past, represented the underpaid proletariat that caused so much trouble in metropolitan France over this same period. While the aristocratic whites were seen as a reactionary threat to republicanism, the island's black laborers were associated with socialism and, in general as well as in the case of the strike of 1900, with the mounting labor discontent in the metropole. In this light, it is unsurprising that the Third Republic—pejoratively called by some a republic of lawyers—found its likeness in the island's mulattos. In fact, nearly all thirteen individuals who served as Martinique's deputies during the Third Republic, the majority of whom were mulattos from the 1880s onward, were lawyers or doctors.

One schoolteacher, one notary, one newspaper editor, and a factory owner whose father was a doctor also served during this period.[111]

The writings of Charles Mismer—a soldier who served in the French army for ten years, fought in the Crimean War, and then retired to Martinique to work as a horse groomer—echoed Garaud's frustration with the division of Martiniquais society along racial lines. It did not, Mismer claimed, sit well with his French upbringing. The racial antagonism the white *békés* exhibited surprised him, because he felt that many people of color he had met would fit in well within mainland French society. He went so far as to say that they would not have been out of place in any French salon.[112] For him, therefore, the disdain that wealthy creole whites exhibited toward people of color as well as poor white people—for Mismer, illustrative of the "exclusionary spirit" of the "aristocratic minority"—was characteristically un-French because it threatened republican unity. Not only did it threaten the stability of the island's political and military future; it also violated the "egalitarian ideas with which [Mismer] was imbued from childhood." Viewing himself as a counterpoint to the whites' exclusionary spirit, Mismer, who shared the laborers' pain, stressed that he had "lost no opportunity to stand up for the poor blacks."[113]

Though Mismer traveled to Martinique during the Second Empire, he wrote and published under the Third Republic while working as a sociologist. His understanding of the racial dynamics of Martinique and his condemnation of the exclusionary attitudes of the creole whites illustrate the way in which Martinique's social reality undermined the inclusionary ideals of French republicanism in the eyes of those who traveled there. Mismer was critical of the way in which Martiniquais society limited access to educational and financial resources to whites, seeing those restrictions as threatening to the overall well-being of the island. Nevertheless, Mismer asserted that his time on the island made him "creole of language and cultural mores" to the point that "indigenous" inhabitants of the island would take him for a "compatriot."[114] Both he and Garaud remained optimistic about the possibility that the island's inhabitants could work together in the spirit of republican unity.

The mulattos were well aware of their mixed heritage and of their exclusion from white society, and at points mobilized this heritage for political ends. For instance, at the meeting of the General Council of Martinique on 14 December 1887, one member suggested that scholarships to the colonial boarding schools be reserved for legitimate children of influential colonial personages.[115] Upon hearing this, a counselor general leapt from his bench, exclaiming, "Have you thus forgotten your origin? Gentlemen, we are all bastards here!"[116] This episode calls to mind the political preeminence of the mulatto class and its profound connection to republican-style education, as well as the legacy of plantation slavery—everyone of mixed heritage in the council chamber had as an ancestor an illegitimate child disowned by a slave owner. It also exhibited a political spirit that rejected out of hand exclusionary measures.

In any case, French republicans may have cast "creoles of color" in a positive light, but they nonetheless saw them in racial—and indeed, racist—terms. Indeed, a host of stereotypes, largely founded in the late nineteenth-century racial "scientism" highlighted by Périna, were applied to what Garaud calls the "three colors" of Martinique, a phrase that he used to unify racial mixture and French republicanism by recalling the colors of the revolutionary flag. Though their "faults" were oftentimes spun as positive characteristics that embodied different aspects of Frenchness, blacks were nevertheless seen as inherently lazy and indolent, mulattos as fiery and fierce, and whites as reactionary and resistant to change. This racist discourse, so prevalent in the late nineteenth century, dominated historical accounts of new imperialism, and indeed it saturated a fair amount of writing about the colonial—even the so-called old colonial—world. Although Martinique prominently figured into the foundational myth of the Third Republic and of republican imperialism—that is, the myth of the "liberty, equality, and fraternity" of all citizens of France—Martinique was also colonial in several important ways; it was, after all, founded and maintained as a colony of extraction. However, the island and its mulatto population played into the myth of the civilizing mission, and many saw the bridging of racial differences—a task seen as the responsibility of the mulatto class—as being central to Martinique's prospects of success. And if mulattos could overcome the racial differences plaguing Martinique, then perhaps metropolitan officials might overcome the ever-widening rift between the Third Republic government and its working class.

Problems of Climate: It's Not Like France Here

Although in many ways Martinique and Guadeloupe exhibited their French nature via their language, customs, and republican politics, the tropical environment was undeniably exotic in comparison with the temperate climate of the mainland. Though Antilleans were remarkably familiar in the French imaginary—speaking the same language, often employing the same political precedents, and even drawing on a similar folkloric and literary tradition—the environment in which these people lived remained for many travelers unfamiliar. One writer said that although the island of Martinique "always left [him] with the best memories," he "would not like to live there" because of the exoticism typified when a friend of his visited the island for the first time, and "the emanations of the negro, the cod and molasses odors, which are widespread in the city, made him sick. Two days afterwards, on the open sea, he claimed that his nostrils were still impregnated of this amalgam of perfumes, completely new for him."[117]

As a further explanation of why they would not like to live there, people who wrote about Martinique and Guadeloupe often referred to the perilous nature of the islands' environment and described at length their flora and fauna, the grueling sun, and dangerous natural disasters. In fact, Bouinais wrote more about noisome pests like mosquitos and jiggers, the riches of the tropical countryside, and the dangers of the dreaded Martinican pit viper than he did about Guadeloupe's human inhabitants.[118] The yearly hurricane season posed a perpetual threat to the islands' denizens, and after 1902 the threat of a second volcanic eruption loomed over the Martiniquais. This history has not been lost on the French Caribbean today, where natural disasters remain a real and present danger. For instance, at the base of Grand Soufrière, Guadeloupe's active volcano that last erupted in 1976, is inscribed, "It waits for us . . ." Such arguably justifiable worry characterized understandings of the French Caribbean under the Third Republic. As one contemporary traveler, Henri Monet, disbelievingly explained in his introduction to a diary he wrote and sold for the benefit of victims of the devastating 1891 hurricane,

> There were in total, from 1657 to 1858, in the space of 201 years, 67 disasters. That's one catastrophe every three years. . . .

Sixty-seven disasters! The simple pronouncement of this figure strikes like a hammer, stupefies by its incredibility, troubles like a legend of mythical times.

Sixty-seven disasters! . . .

One asks with an anxious terror if it's really true, if it's possible, that a population could live and prosper under a sun so dreadful, under a climate so terrible.

Sixty-seven disasters!

Nearly one per year. Perpetual suffering, continual panic.

The sword suspended by a thread over the head of Damocles was less terrifying.[119]

Monet's shock at the dangerousness of the islands' climate is palpable. His repetition of the figure "sixty-seven disasters" indicates his disbelief and is meant to strike the reader—most likely someone from metropolitan France, from whom Monet was eliciting money to help rebuild Martinique—"like a hammer." Overall, the French saw the tropical environment of the Antilles as shockingly dangerous. As a French geographer remarked in 1898, the hurricane of 18 August 1891, "the most disastrous in Antillean memory," had ravaged the ports of Saint-Pierre and Fort-de-France, "one of the most beautiful of the Antilles." The hurricane followed a June 1890 fire that had nearly destroyed Fort-de-France. He wrote, "Add to these the bites—nearly always fatal—of the terrible Martinican pit viper, a sad particularity of Martinique and Saint-Lucie, and you will think these wonderful lands have more than their fair share of tribulations."[120]

From a purely environmental science point of view, the Caribbean Basin is indeed a dangerous place. Perpetually besieged by earthquakes, volcanic eruptions, hurricanes, and tropical depressions, the small islands of the Antilles are constantly under the threat of destruction by the natural environment. The entirety of the Lesser Antilles lies along a subduction fault, where the South American tectonic plate is slowly sliding underneath the Caribbean plate, and contains seventeen active volcanoes, of which Mount Pelée and La Grand Soufrière are on Martinique and Guadeloupe, respectively. A large earthquake decimated Fort-de-France in 1839 and killed over fifteen hundred people in Point-à-Pitre, Guadeloupe. Another powerful earthquake struck the region in 1843, and thereafter Martinique's capital, Fort-de-France, was built predominantly of wood to prevent sheering.[121]

In addition to the threat of earthquakes, the Caribbean Basin has had to contend with annual cyclones. Every year from June 1 to November 30, with a massive peak in mid-August, a hurricane season of varying intensity harasses the populations of the Atlantic Basin—from the southernmost part of the Caribbean Sea through Mesoamerica to the northeastern seaboard of the United States.[122] As waters warm along the equator and atmospheric winds rise in intensity, the Earth's own Coriolis effect spawns rotating storms of severe intensity off the west coast of Africa. As these storms feed on the warmer waters of the Caribbean Basin, they gain in intensity before making landfall. This perpetual threat was not lost on contemporaries, and in fact it became one of the defining characteristics of the Caribbean for metropolitan writers. As one contemporary remarked, "Martinique is one of our colonies that has hitherto been strongly distressed by disturbances of nature. The danger menacing it each year is the arrival of a hurricane."[123]

As historian Stuart Schwartz has illustrated, hurricanes are among the unifying environmental factors that overcome the region's insularity, and the storms take a place among other leitmotifs of Caribbean history: race, imperialism, plantation economies, and slavery.[124] Shared by all the islands in the region, the language of meteorological devastation overcomes the linguistic and political boundaries common to the region. According to Schwartz, "Of all the hazards that humans confront in the region, none is more characteristic than the great Caribbean hurricanes that have defined the region and its risks."[125]

This is particularly true in the French West Indies, where thirty storms—either hurricanes or tropical depressions—made landfall over the course of the nineteenth century on either Martinique or Guadeloupe, representing only a subset of the tropical depressions and hurricanes that tore through the Caribbean. When these storms made contact with the built environment, the effects were disastrous. Fort-de-France sits four meters above sea level, placing it at a high risk of flooding in any significant meteorological event. Moreover, it is directly in the path of the trade winds, regularly experiencing high-velocity winds, and the dwellings in which most of its approximately sixteen thousand people lived were weathered and rickety.

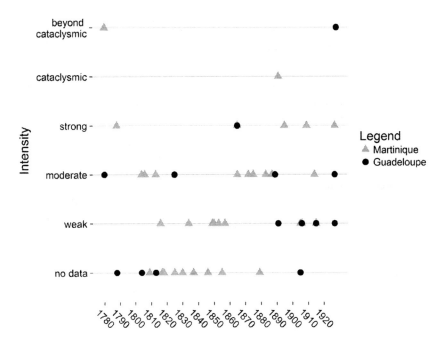

FIG. 2. **Significant meteorological events in the French Caribbean, 1780–1928**
Meteorological events including hurricanes and depressions, with quali-
tative descriptors. Graph created in R statistical package with information
from Saffache, Marc, and Cospar, *Les cyclones en Martinique*, 180–81; Saffache, Marc, and Huyghes-Belrose, *Les cyclones en Guadeloupe*, 259–60.

From a societal point of view, the Caribbean Basin is tumultuous. In
addition to climatic threats, the islands have a human history of disorder
and chaos: brutal war and mass disease came with Europeans' first contact
with the islands' original inhabitants, the Caribs and the Arawaks; forced
migrations and slavery followed as Europeans radically transformed the
Caribbean's political, physical, and economic environment; and then came
civil unrest as the disenfranchised and oppressed struggled for their freedom and equality.

As Schwartz has proposed hurricanes as the unifying factor of the Caribbean, Bonham Richardson has likewise analyzed late nineteenth-century
West Indian history through the lens of fire. In many ways the converse of
natural disasters, which their contact with human society makes unnatural,

TABLE 1. *Deadliest Atlantic hurricanes affecting Martinique and Guadeloupe, 1492–1996*

REGION MOST AFFECTED	APPROXIMATE NO. OF DEATHS	YEAR
Martinique, Saint Eustatius, Barbados, offshore	22,000	1780
Guadeloupe	6,000	1776
Florida, Guadeloupe, Puerto Rico, Turks Islands, Martinique	3,400	1928
Martinique	3,000	1813
Guadeloupe, Martinique	2,000	1666
Martinique	1,600	1767
Guadeloupe, Puerto Rico	1,300	1825
Martinique, Turks Islands, Puerto Rico	700	1891
Martinique, Dominica, New England, Bahamas	700	1788
Offshore Martinique	600	1695
Martinique	440	1766
Guadeloupe, New England, U.S. coast	200	1821
Cayman Islands, Jamaica, Martinique	200	1903
Martinique	100	1713
Texas, Northern Mexico, Martinique	60	1967
Martinique, southwest Atlantic	60	1837
Guadeloupe, Montserrat, South Carolina	60	1989
Martinique, Dominica	50	1970
Guadeloupe, Puerto Rico	30	1956

Source: Rappaport and Fernandez-Partagas, "The Deadliest Atlantic Tropical Cyclones, 1492–1996," http://www.nhc.noaa.gov/pastdeadly.shtml.

fire is nearly always ignited by human sources and has disastrous effects on the built as well as the natural environment. In the Caribbean's post-Colombian history, fire "cleared forests, burned sugarcane, sparked slave insurrections, attracted crowds, lighted streets and houses, and symbolized protest in the region . . . so much so that writers and poets often use 'fire' to signify their discontent with the Caribbean's steeply tiered social hierarchy."[126] Fire is more than just a metaphor for political discontent; with incendiarism as the primary means of protest in the Caribbean, fire was quite literally the embodiment of civil unrest. Moreover, due to past seismic destruction, most Caribbean structures had been constructed of wood by the end of the century, which, with the constant dry rot at the hands of the salty sea air and the brutal tropical sun, provided the perfect kindling for widespread firestorms.

The urban landscape provided little solace against the perpetual onslaught of natural disasters, and some saw the built landscape as a liability rather than a protection. In fact, after a rather small earthquake in 1875, denizens of Martinique's communes—most notably Fort-de-France and Saint-Pierre—deserted the urban spaces for the countryside for a period, feeling unsafe in the built landscape that had collapsed so violently and killed hundreds during the 7.3-magnitude earthquake of 1839.[127] Even today, Guadeloupe's capital of Point-à-Pitre is at an extremely high risk of liquefaction: the process by which the ground, due to soil saturation and its general composition, acts like a liquid during an earthquake.[128] Liquefaction is intensely dangerous, and as a result, Guadeloupe's largest city is at risk of severe damage in the event of an earthquake.

For travelers to Martinique, the wild and dangerous environment of the tropics often stood in contrast to the built and manicured environment of its cultural capital, Saint-Pierre. Some considered the city's appearance inappropriate to Martinique's tropical nature. G. Verschuur, a world traveler and visitor to the Antilles in 1892, for example, wrote that Saint-Pierre's Botanical Garden—with its "symmetrical" and "tidy" pathways—was "much more appropriate to the installation of a European park than to the disordered nature of a tropical country."[129] Regardless of the light in which they viewed it, visitors to the island saw a contrast between the "civilized" nature of the urban space and the "wild" tropical environment. Saint-Pierre's "upper town," the location of the botanical garden, was home to the well-to-do *békés*—the white plantation owners who dominated the island's economic sphere—and wealthy mulattos: doctors, lawyers, clergymen, merchants, and proprietors. By contrast, the "lower town," where the laboring class lived, had a reputation for being far less orderly and sanitary—though it, too, was urban rather than tropical in its appearance.

By contrast to Saint-Pierre, Guadeloupe's principal city, Pointe-à-Pitre, was characterized by European visitors as markedly non-European and unhealthy. A colonial pharmacist and reporter for the French periodical *L'Illustration*, Gilbert Cuzent, complained that the city lacked sidewalks and reliable fresh water, and was plagued by cholera, nauseating smells, and fecal waste from humans and farm animals alike—despite what he saw as the best efforts of colonial administrators to keep the unsanitary habits of islanders in check.[130] While contemporaries saw the climate of the Antilles as potentially life-threatening, as a host of diseases from yellow fever to malaria to typhoid could spell a gruesome death for any who lived there, at particular risk were those who could not afford a living in an environment marked by health precautions and public safety. For instance, Bouinais warned that while Europeans and the wealthy classes could expect to enjoy generally favorable health outcomes, blacks and others who lived in unhealthy environs were particularly susceptible to disease epidemics.[131] Disastrous hurricanes worsened already marginal conditions and menaced islanders' health—destroying homes, pulverizing livelihoods, and drowning mothers and infants alike.[132] European visitors, therefore, saw Guadeloupe's main city—ringed as it was by mosquito-filled marshland and foreign fauna like mangroves—as unruly and potentially dangerous. Their fears of local unruliness would be realized in the fires that plagued the year 1899.

Contrary to the urban threats on Guadeloupe's northern island of Grande-Terre, the islands' southern half—known as Basse-Terre, and today home to a French national park and preserve—was home to thermal springs that colonial physicians thought could rejuvenate mind, body, and spirit.[133] And yet nature provided little respite from the hectic urban climate, as Basse-Terre was also home to the active volcano, La Grand Soufrière, which menaced Europeans all the way back to the island's "discovery," when Dominican missionary Père Breton commented on the turmoil in its entrails betrayed

FIG. 3.   The great palms of Saint-Pierre's Botanical Garden, 1899
André Salles, *Martinique: Les grands cycas du Jardin botanique de St Pierre*
(1899, photograph reproduced by Molténi). Courtesy of the Bibliothèque
Nationale de France.

by its foreboding smoke and fire.[134] Before the twentieth century, La Grand Soufrière's last eruption had been in 1799, though its seemingly constant sulfuric activity, which had resulted in a shower of cinders in 1838, unnerved many visitors to the island. In 1881 Bouinais found the gases released in its fumaroles to produce boisterous detonations and "noises imitating the whistling of locomotives," and he mentioned persistent shaking in Basse-Terre.[135] The volcano's sulfuric emanations continue to threaten the island's inhabitants, who had to evacuate the entire island when it last erupted in 1976.

Writings about much of the French empire reflected a preoccupation with the environment—both built and natural: the *Journal des voyages* is replete with articles about botany, zoology, and climatology from throughout the European empires, and it is full of adventure stories about earthquakes, tsetse flies, and hurricanes. Scientific societies such as the Société Zoologique d'Acclimatation employed the French empire as a laboratory to study ways to habituate organisms to new environments.[136] The re-creation of European styles, as in the case of the botanical gardens of Saint-Pierre, was a characteristic feature of nineteenth-century European colonialism more broadly.[137] What is striking in the French West Indies, however, is the way in which, in many travelogues and guides, the Antilleans stand in for France in a tough, tropical climate. Bouinais, an officer of the marine and a colonial geographer, observed that "despite tests of all sorts—earthquakes, hurricanes, epidemics, fires, . . .—Guadeloupe has never stopped exhibiting the signs of an extraordinary vitality."[138] *The Grand Encyclopedia* echoed this sentiment, adding that the town of Pointe-à-Pitre repeatedly "bounced back and prospered, coquettish and animated, despite repeated disasters: the fire in 1780, the earthquake in 1843, and the fire in 1871."[139] Elsewhere in the empire, colonial narratives typically revolved around the white civilizer-explorer's struggle with foreign atmospheres. In the West Indies, however, the population, in particular the mulatto populace, represented a bastion of French civilization in a tropical setting—though, as Bouinais lamented, a slow-growing bastion that needed familial encouragement to be more like the more sexually active, and in his words "virtuous," Bavarians, whose numerous children heightened natalist fears of a repeat of France's humiliation during the Franco-Prussian War.[140] Accounts like Monet's often juxtaposed the terrifying environmental hazards against French ingenuity and the dedication of the isle's inhabitants. Monet and others charged not the transplanted or errant European but the local "creole of color" with safeguarding French civilization against the onslaught of hurricanes and volcanic eruptions—as the bourgeois *Encyclopédie* stated, the future belonged to the mulatto. Likewise, Bouinais stressed the benefits of the application of universal suffrage and political enfranchisement in Guadeloupe, and in light of such displays of French citizenship, he saw "every reason to have faith in the future of the colony."[141]

In 1875 a doctor named Laurent-Jean-Baptiste Bérenger-Féraud, a member of the French Academy of Medicine and the Society of Surgery, traveled to the West Indies as a chief medical officer of the marine and compiled a treatise on the sicknesses that could be attributed to life in the Antillean climate. His book—*Clinical Treatise on the Sickness of Europeans in the Antilles*—was a grand, encyclopedic collection in two volumes of possible medical afflictions in the Caribbean, and it was meant for white Europeans as a guide to explain the medical precautions necessary for them to survive in the tropics. An advocate of racial purity, Bérenger-Féraud found Martinique's mixed-race population confounding, because despite his expectations, the "health of the father and mother were not added, but multiplied among the mulatto child." Contrary to his deep-seated disdain toward racial intermixture, which he felt would result in unhealthy, infertile populations, Bérenger-Féraud found positive results of racial mixing in the Caribbean's tropical climate:

In Martinique, whites lived next to blacks for a very long time, and the result was, as everywhere, a mélange that produced a variety of shades of those of mixed race. A curious thing is that this mixture seems to have produced children stronger, more vigorous than the parents, and it is undeniable that the traveler arriving in Martinique for the first time is struck by the sight of Europeans of a significantly lower health than they had in Europe, of Negroes who are clearly less beautiful than their counterparts from the African coast, and between them, the most beautiful mulatto came, seeming to have all the attributes of health and force needed to perpetuate their lineage.[142]

Bérenger-Féraud's momentary cognitive dissonance speaks to the specificity of the French West Indies, where mulattos' political and cultural ascendancy lent credence to the notion that their creole nature was well-suited to the tropics. It also explains why, as historian Véronique Hélénon has explained, French officials often looked to West Indians to fulfill the role of colonial administrators in other environments.[143] However, it is important to underline here that Bérenger-Féraud's brief praise of *métissage* applied only to the Caribbean and did little to overturn his conviction that mixed-race populations would rapidly die off should they remain endogamous. In his racially charged discussion of eugenics, Bérenger-Féraud contended that minimal European emigration to the French Caribbean as well as the current political and social divisions between whites, blacks, and mulattos had put a halt to racial mixing, and as a result disease would increasingly wrack the island's population, thus forcing its decline. To avoid this outcome, he claimed, the native mulatto must continue to "bring together in turns white and black blood."[144]

To a certain extent, Louis Garaud echoed this sentiment, seeing cooperation, not necessarily intermarriage, as essential to the prosperity of Martinique. Garaud ended his ethnographic travelogue with a description of the effects of hurricanes—most recently, that of 1891—on the small Antillean island. He lamented the hardships thrust on the people, but given the lushness of "this green, fecund land" he was confident that all "vestiges of the disaster will have disappeared within a few months." In short, in the tropical environment he located the perpetual promise of rebirth. More interesting, he identified the need for the population to work together within this hostile—yet "fecund"—environment:

> Ah! If in this sorry land the men of color wanted, in contact with this generous earth, to replant, to rebuild, and to recover, they would need above all to come together with the whites and blacks who are their brothers, uniting their hands and joining forces in the same efforts and the same progress, without antagonism, without resentment and without reservation.
>
> Following the example of France, Martinique finally unites its three colors. In closing this book, I can make no better wish for the prosperity of the most beautiful and the most unfortunate of the Antilles.[145]

It is noteworthy that he saw the "men of color" as those with the agency to rebuild and unite Martinique along the lines of the French Republican model. In adversity emerged the three colors of France—here, Garaud was referring both to the tricolor flag, the symbol of the French Republic, as well as the three races that make up the island's population. Thus the Frenchness of the island's inhabitants—or at least, the potential thereof—stood in stark relief in this inherently un-French environment. In Garaud's terms, the shadows in the tropics (i.e., the perilous climate) made the light (i.e., republican French civilization) seem that much brighter. For the French, mulattos represented a branch of the French race that had been grown in the tropics and was thus suited to its environment in a way that Europeans and Africans were not.

Conclusion

Though the French Antilles were grounded in a strictly colonial economic reality, the islands served as a success story for the longevity of French civilization abroad in the cultural *imaginaire* of the Third Republic. Though sugar was no longer being extracted from Martinique and Guadeloupe in its earlier quantities nor bringing its earlier windfall profits, French republicans were now able to extract ideological fuel for their civilizing mission. What is interesting is that the defenders of republican French civilization were not the whites who were transplanted long ago under the Old Regime but a new race of mulattos, created out of the colonial experience, who were capable of protecting French values against the onslaught of a hostile tropical environment. For Louis Garaud, the mulatto mediated between the outdated and aristocratic white planter class and the laboring black majority. In fact, the irony is that the minority settler population is not the success story but the antagonist in these travel narratives. Observers like Charles Mismer were unable to reconcile their French values with the white exclusionism of the *békés* and in fact felt the need to defend the honor of the colored populations on the islands. For many who saw them as vestiges of the Old Regime, the white planters—economically empowered but politically isolated—were anathema to the ideals of the French Republic.

The islands of Martinique and Guadeloupe fit into a unique space in French colonialism. In an environment characterized as un-French, the citizens of these "old colonies"—in particular, their nonwhite population—were seen to represent the success of French universalism by embodying "tropical" Frenchness—a version of French identity that was simultaneously viewed as new and adapted to the natural environment, particularly through racial mixing, as well as old and rooted in French traditions. This dichotomy suggests that racial politics on the islands, as well as between the French Caribbean and the mainland, cannot be boiled down to the "triumph of whiteness" typically associated with commonplace narratives of social Darwinism and the civilizing mission. The bizarre way in which social Darwinism was translated by French republicanism in the case of the Caribbean, as well as the colonies' special designation as *ancien*, highlights the instability of the division between the metropole and the colony during the Third Republic. The Caribbean's longstanding relationship with France, both culturally and racially, coupled with the complex way in which the Antilles fit into both the imagination of and the class tensions within the French Third Republic, sheds light on the paradoxical status of the islands, of the oft repeated slippage of the distinction between metropole and colony.

2

The Language of Citizenship

Compatriotism and the Great Antillean Fires of 1890

In the rising swelter of the tropical summer, a fire rampaged through the heart of Martinique's capital city, Fort-de-France. The trade-wind-fueled blaze incinerated sixteen hundred homes, destroyed 1,018 nonresidential properties, killed thirteen people, and left six thousand people—half of the city's population—without food, water, shelter, or clothes. Nearly three-quarters of the city lay in ruins.[1] In addition to the human and physical costs, the economic costs were staggering. With the total damage estimated at between fifty million and sixty-seven million francs, the destruction was more than ten times Martinique's yearly budget, and the blaze consumed all the capital and assets that kept La Société Mutuelle—the city's primary insurer—solvent. The homes alone were valued at over fifteen million francs.[2] Guadeloupe's governor, Antoine Le Boucher, exclaimed a day later, "Fort-de-France no longer exists! A terrible fire has completely destroyed it."[3] The embers in Martinique had not yet cooled when the town of Port-Louis on Martinique's sister island of Guadeloupe went up in flames a week later, destroying sixty-eight homes, burning down three-quarters of the town, and, according to the French National Assembly, "plunging another 4,000 inhabitants into misery."[4]

These fires—along with a litany of hurricanes, earthquakes, and disease epidemics, as well as the catastrophic eruption of Mount Pelée in 1902—furthered the commonplace French view that the Caribbean was a volatile, exotic environment that perpetually threatened to annihilate those living there. Nevertheless, this distant and dangerous locale held a special place in the French imagination. Not only had it been under French control since 1635—longer than many parts of the metropole (Nice, Savoy, and Alsace, to name a few)—the ideal of colonial assimilation had been made good in the form of full citizenship rights. As a result, French Antilleans demanded a quality of life equal to that of their metropolitan counterparts.

Given the sad social conditions of so many French people within the metropole, Antillean citizenship may have been worth little. A governmental report in 1881, for instance, demonstrated that 85 percent of Frenchmen in the Haute-Loire department were either indigent or completely destitute.[5] Meanwhile single parents headed more than one-third of all French households in 1900, as late industrialization dislocated communities and debased workers in an inequitable labor market.[6] The republican universalist virtues of liberty, equality, and fraternity projected the battle cry of a French Republic that sought to rectify inequality in all its forms, but they also conjured the sarcastic lament of a citizenry that, in its endeavor to create a social republic where one did not yet exist, experienced what Eugen Weber described as the "internal colonization" of a nation being knitted together by railway lines and coal mines—the groan of a citizenry under the yoke of unfair labor practices, dangerous working conditions, and a destitute standard of living. As full French citizens, Antilleans should be situated as active participants in the social and cultural developments of a turn-of-the-century France riddled with social cleavages, labor unrest, and, to some extent, a delusional sense of optimism undercut by a pervasive fear of cataclysm on the horizon.

The great fires of 1890 and the French government's relief campaign illustrated to contemporaries the French state's need to safeguard its Antillean citizenry. In exploring the duty incumbent upon the state to safeguard the French citizenry at large, including those living in the remarkably un-French environment of the tropics, this chapter examines the way in which the 1890 fires in the Antilles resonated throughout the metropole. Viewing the people living there as inherently French—"more French than the French," as many say today—Frenchmen met the dire situation following the great fires of Fort-de-France and Port-Louis with an outpouring of public support from all across France and a call for everyday compatriots to open their wallets to their brothers in peril.

This chapter begins with a discussion of the Fort-de-France and Port-Louis fires, their causes, and the way in which contemporaries in the press and government interpreted the virtual annihilation of Martinique's capital city and Guadeloupe's plantation town. Then it describes the subsequent relief campaign orchestrated by the French government, with an eye toward what that campaign tells us about the cultural place of the French Antilles in the French Republic. The third part of the chapter looks at a disaster within the metropole itself—a mine collapse at Saint-Étienne—that was not only contemporaneous with the fires of Fort-de-France and Port-Louis but also analogous in many ways. Analysis will show that victims on both sides of the Atlantic occupied similar places in the French imagination. While racism undeniably underlay the French understanding of these great disasters, classism and elitism were just as important to understanding how the French treated their Antillean compatriots. By looking at a mine collapse at Saint-Étienne in southeastern France, we can see that race was mapped onto class, and that class was understood as a racial concept.

Fort-de-France: "A Town of Silent Ashes"

The geography of the Caribbean presents a unique confluence of dangers. It is atop an active plate boundary, riddled with volcanoes, perpetually menaced by hurricanes and tempests, and characterized by a built environment that seeks a compromise with the multitude of dangers and, in the manner of compromise, is summarily compromised. As Marie-Sophie Laborieux remarks in Patrick Chamoiseau's *Texaco*, "Whoever feared earthquakes, would erect a house of wood. Whoever feared hurricanes or remembered fire, erected a house of stone."[7] A governmental report echoed such a sentiment in 1897, when an earthquake shook Guadeloupe: "Originally built of wood, Point-à-Pitre burned down once. Reconstructed of stone, it crumbled in 1843. Rebuilt of wood, the fire of 1871 destroyed it."[8] In short, it was impossible to build a city to withstand the elements in the West Indies.

Since the earthquake of 1839, which wreaked devastation on Fort-de-France, and that of 1843, which decimated Pointe-à-Pitre, the majority of the islands' homes had been rebuilt as single-story units made entirely of wood.[9] Those that were not made entirely of wood had a stone base with wooden upper stories. Using wood rather than brick or stone allowed load-bearing walls to flex during tremblors, thus preventing the home from collapsing during the region's prevalent earthquakes. For instance, between 1839 and 1900, there were 1,075 known seismological events in the Caribbean Basin, of which 48 had epicenters in Martinique and 438 in Guadeloupe.[10] Lumber construction posed a new hazard, as repeated droughts had dried out the wooden structures, and in incendiary conditions, the homes' construction allowed fires to easily jump from house to house. Given the threat of earthquakes on the one hand and fire on the other, Caribbean citizens were stuck between a rock and a hard place.

The Caribbean islands were not new to fire. Four-fifths of the principal town of Guadeloupe—Pointe-à-Pitre—had burned down in two back-to-back fires in 1871.[11] The city was subsequently rebuilt with more sound building codes, only to burn once more in 1879.[12] Fire was simply a matter of life in the Antilles. The use of coal and kerosene lamps to light and heat homes had risen along with the flammable, earthquake-resistant housing, increasing the region's vulnerability. As historian Bonham Richardson has pointed out, poor members of the black working class could not afford proper glass lanterns or globes, and thus home-made, jury-rigged lanterns became commonplace throughout the Caribbean. Moreover, since the cost of proper kerosene was so high, many filled their improvised lanterns with unstable, highly flammable low-grade oil.[13] Urban fires throughout the region increased dramatically as the nineteenth century marched on. While many journalists faulted Fort-de-France's disaster preparedness and organization, arguing that the prevalence of water and the availability of a sizable firefighting force should have minimized the devastation, the volatile fuel, the ad hoc lighting, the ferocity of the region's trade winds, and the aftermath of a prolonged drought combined to set the stage for a disastrous fire outbreak.[14] The same held true for Port-Louis, where aging wood houses provided ample kindling and an underperforming water pump hampered firefighting efforts.[15]

Early Sunday morning on 22 June 1890, a resident in a small cabin on rue Blenac in Fort-de-France left a teakettle heating over an open flame, precariously perched over a vase of kerosene used for lighting and heating the home. At around 8 a.m., the stove tipped, the kettle fell, and the floorboards ignited.[16] The kerosene exploded, and the small wooden house burst into flames. The Lesser Antilles had been in a massive drought for nearly eight months, and June was in the middle of the windiest time of the year. The fire could not have found more favorable conditions as it jumped from wooden structure to wooden structure, devouring the entire downtown area and chasing people from their homes.[17] As dazed firefighters and citizens converged on the scene, they realized that the fire originated in a part of town that had an insufficient water supply with weak pressure, so the pumps could not provide enough water fast enough to slow the pace of the fire. Moreover, since it was Sunday, many of the stores in the commercial district were closed and locked up tight, so access to fire axes was limited.[18] Firefighters eventually resorted to demolishing homes in the path of the blaze to create a fire barrier, sundering the air with detonations that sounded to observers like "lugubrious cannon fire."[19] Observers remarked that it was as if the town were "under siege," which, according to the press, put the citizenry into a panic. As the denizens of Fort-de-France watched their homes and livelihoods go up in flames, they created refugee encampments in the sprawling nearby park known as La Savanne and sought sanctuary in the hills at Fort Tartenson.[20]

Strong winds from the northwest and the inaccessibility of enough water held firefighters at bay until nightfall, when help arrived from Saint-Pierre and the fire was finally extinguished. In the words of an observer,

[The fire] lasted, it can be said, all day and all night, fostered by a combination of unfortunate circumstances, supported and driven by fate, finding everywhere boons for its destructive work, taking advantage of all: the lack of water, the lack of pumps, the wind which seemed to blow expressly to expand it in all directions, the late arrival of relief, the panic that never fails to occur in such cases and against which only an extraordinary firmness can respond, the absence of authorities, etc., etc. Rarely has one seen a disaster occur in rescue conditions so defective.[21]

Devastating both the city's rich commercial center and the poor workers' district, the fire completely decimated much of the heart of Fort-de-France, burning through major boulevards and small side streets alike.[22] Only one house in the path of the fire was saved, and the fire destroyed much of the city's infrastructure. Though the Palais de Justice and the Direction of the Interior were spared, the fire destroyed the sugar factory at Point-Simon, the hospice, the postal and telegraph offices, the Saint-Louis Cathedral, the customs house, the contributions house, and the Schoelcher Library.[23] In short, many of Fort-de-France's key cultural and administrative buildings had been lost in a matter of hours.

Although Fort-de-France was the administrative capital of the island and France's military headquarters in the West Indies, it was neither the island's chief economic port nor its cultural heart. This was not lost on the French press, who, just days after the catastrophe, were quick to point out that the economic hub of Saint-Pierre was doing quite fine.[24] Official press releases assured the French population that the sugar plantations and refineries, far from Fort-de-France and its environs, were safe and that Martinique's faith and credit with foreign and national banks remained sound.[25] While the local Caribbean press underscored the scope of the devastation, Parisian papers trivialized the damage to some extent to assuage investors and prevent more capital from being withdrawn from the island. Therefore, while the sugar refinery at Point-Simon in Fort-de-France was indeed important for financial investors and its loss marked a significant blow to Martinique's already suffering sugar industry, papers hungrily proclaimed that sugar production remained on target at the island's other refineries, and that investors had little reason to pull their money from their Martiniquais investments.

Contrarily, when the Parisian paper *Le Temps* reported the subsequent fire in Port-Louis, Guadeloupe, where the fire's cause was similarly accidental and its progression eerily similar, the paper highlighted the fact that vital sugar factories were in the town's vicinity and that the fire threatened the local economy.[26] The fire's origin had set some on edge, as it had begun on the night of 28 June in the bedroom of two married servants of a local merchant, Léo Dufau, and from there spread throughout the entire town to destroy its wealthiest quarters.[27] With the damage valued at roughly 1.5 million francs, the press highlighted the fact that "the entire commercial and wealthiest part of the town was destroyed."[28] Alarmed that sugar output might dwindle as a result of the fires, some worried that malfeasance by the laboring class had sparked the fire in Port-Louis and perhaps in Fort-de-France as well.[29] To allay their fears, Guadeloupe's private council to the governor put the gendarmerie on high alert and resolved to allocate special funds for merchants' lost merchandise and industrialists' equipment not covered by insurance to "help them regain their proper means, their commerce and their industry."[30] Port-Louis' victimized population of about fifty-eight hundred inhabitants took second billing to economics.

FIG. 4. Popular illustration of downtown Fort-de-France engulfed in flames
L'Univers Illustré, 5 July 1890, cover.

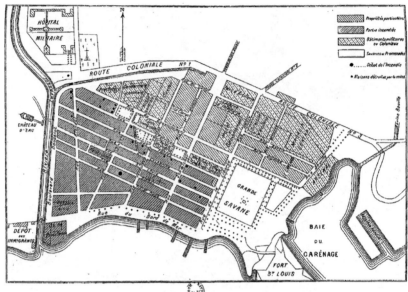

PLAN DE FORT-DE-FRANCE APRÈS L'INCENDIE DU 22 JUIN 1890

MAP 1.   Fort-de-France after the fire of 22 June 1890
The destroyed section of the city is darkened to heighten the contrast.
Garaud, *Trois ans*, 231. Courtesy of the Bibliothèque Nationale de France.

The Commission de Secours in Martinique and the Comité de Secours in Paris

While deprivation, starvation, and confusion followed in the aftermath of the fire, insurance provided no relief. The fire destroyed the financial capital of the Société Mutuelle, a mutual insurance agency that had insured Fort-de-France and garnered capital from its population, and according to press reports, foreign insurance companies agreed to pay only an infinitesimal portion of the total damages, leaving charity the sole recourse of Fort-de-France's populace.[31] In fact, of the 1.8 million francs held in insurance policies, a mere ninety thousand francs, or 5 percent, had been paid out.[32] To rebuild Fort-de-France, the French people—Antilleans first among them—really needed to pay for it themselves. Appealing to the hearts and minds of Martinique's citizens, the press pleaded,

Creole hearts, open yourselves to your unfortunate brethren. Inhabitants of Saint-Pierre and the suburbs, direct to Fort-de-France your devotion, the tireless testimony of your charity. Give to the unfortunate as much as you can. They are ruined but will not die if you feed them. Feed them, in God's name, in the name of charity, [and] on behalf of compatriotism. In short, bread, rescue, life for compatriots who demand and expect it from you.[33]

In recognition of Martinique's help following the 1871 fire in Pointe-à-Pitre, one of the earliest sources of aid to Martinique was its sister island of Guadeloupe.[34] Within days Guadeloupe began a public subscription campaign, loaded two cargo ships with food destined for Martinique, and replaced its Bastille Day celebration, this year a costumed gala, with a benefit and raffle for the fire's victims.[35] But a fire devastated Guadeloupe within a week—reflecting the same factors that had enabled the fire in Fort-de-France—and no further help came from this source. In fact, the governor of Guadeloupe opined that this "acknowledgment of debt" had strained its resources now that Port-Louis had gone up in flames.[36]

Governor Germain Casse created a local relief organization for the establishment of shelter, the distribution of food, and the distribution of clothing the day after the fire in Fort-de-France. On 24 June, Casse established the ten-member Commission de Secours over which Martinique's bishop, Monseigneur Julien-Francois-Pierre Carméné, presided.[37] Such governmental relief commissions had a precedent in earlier disasters, most notably the fires that raged through Pointe-à-Pitre in 1871 and 1879.[38] In addition to raising funds from the parishes and municipalities on the island, the commission was charged with documenting, allocating, and distributing all donations received locally and from the metropole.[39] Collections began in Martinique's parishes and townships, raising over one hundred thousand francs (24,415 francs from episcopal and 79,650 francs from municipal donations).[40] The governor himself provided a credit of one hundred thousand francs to be distributed among Fort-de-France's victims, equating to ten francs per victim. Given the price of manioc at the time, this would have paid for nearly two weeks of food.[41] A second such credit was opened in August. Within days of the fire, the mayor of Fort-de-France, Osman Duquesnay, created squads of workers to clear the rubble from the city, offering a pay rate of two francs per day supplemented with food rations.[42] Support arrived from Saint Thomas, Trinidad, and Demerara, and since Fort-de-France's most immediate need was food, Jamaica sent three hundred barrels of flour and three hundred bags of rice.[43] It was rumored that the U.S. government had planned to donate seven hundred thousand francs, though there is no evidence that this ever came to fruition. In fact, foreign aid to Martinique amounted to only thirty-seven thousand francs.[44] Under the urgent conditions, however, the intake and distribution of foodstuffs was not subjected to any form of systematic accounting, which colonial investigators later identified as a "willful ignorance" on the part of both the French military and the municipal government.[45]

Ultimately, local support was not enough. In a letter from 8 July 1890, just two weeks after the fire swept through Fort-de-France, Governor Casse warned the colonial undersecretary of state that once aid from Martinique's neighboring cities and islands is exhausted, "the most terrible misery will reign if Parliament and the Metropole do not come to our aide. . . . Without you, we would be lost. . . . We have confidence in France and await full of gratitude."[46] He argued that there was a real danger that public disorder and chaos would ensue if the central government did not intervene. He called on Martinique's General Council to engender sympathy from the metropole in the name of the victims: "put aside your divisions, your grudges, your hatreds, if you don't want to paralyze the goal of solidarity that leads the Metropole toward you." In response, the General Council sent photographs documenting Fort-de-France's devastation to Paris in an effort to further demonstrate Martinique's dire need for support.[47]

However, information was slow in reaching Paris, because the capital's postal and telegraph offices were lost to the fire. All correspondence had to be rerouted using English telegraph lines through New York via Saint-Pierre, thus drastically slowing communication between the administration in Martinique and the central bureaucracy. Consequently, few realized the full extent of the devastation wrought in Fort-de-France. The entire city west of rue Schoelcher, as well as the section between rue Saint-Louis and rue Saint-Laurent, was destroyed. In fact, journalists lambasted Governor

Casse for failing to supply sufficient and timely information regarding the postincendiary conditions of Fort-de-France.[48]

Relief efforts for Port-Louis were folded into those for Fort-de-France. A month after the two fires, an official centralized relief effort in Paris was led by the "Comité de secours aux Incendiés de Fort-de-France (Martinique) et de Port-Louis (Guadeloupe)," directed by Alexandre Peyron and coordinated by Eugène Étienne. A vice admiral, recipient of the Legion of Honor, former commander of the Antilles naval commission, and former minister of the marine and colonies, Peyron was an irremovable senator—that is, a senator for life—from the center left in the French legislature, while Étienne was an opportunist who received support earlier in his career from ardent republicans like Jules Ferry and Leon Gambetta.[49] These two political figures represented the heart of republican empire, and their fund-raising campaign brought people together from across the political spectrum, successfully bridging the gap between assimilationist republicans and socialist deputies. In December 1890, when the Comité had decided to formally disband, Undersecretary Étienne thanked its members for the hard work of dedicated individuals like Admiral Peyron and those he represented. At the behest of Admiral Peyron, Étienne officially commended M. Bertin, the Comité's accountant and second-in-command, and even formally recognized the work of M. Gerville-Réache, the socialist legislator from Guadeloupe.[50]

The Comité de Secours carried out a nine-month fund-raising campaign to help the victimized populations of Martinique and Guadeloupe. The Comité sent out two-sided sheets to all the French communes: one side had a description of the disaster written by Admiral Peyron and signed by the committee, and the other side was a form for taking donations. Individuals, business owners, and municipal officials collected signatures and donations, each carrying out their own miniature fund-raising campaign. Oftentimes the activity was conducted at a local event, such as a gala or banquet, or at the local school. The local fund-raisers then turned over the subscriptions to the Comité directly by mailing them to the colonial undersecretary of state or indirectly via the military or local treasurer, who then turned them over to the Comité. Everyone who donated money and signed the subscription paperwork had his or her name published in the *Journal officiel de la République française*.[51]

The central government initiated the campaign to raise money, but departmental prefects, mayors, townships, and schools executed it. Thus the fundraising took a variety of forms. At one point, the prefect of Seine-Inférieure and the president of the local charity committee in Le Havre joined forces to stage a *kermesse*—a traditional charity celebration in northern France and the Low Countries—designed to raise money for their *concitoyens*, or fellow citizens, in Martinique and Guadeloupe. The centerpiece of this event was to be a "reconstituted" Martiniquais village built under the direction of a "worker familiar with the assemblage of the pieces [of such displays]." In the organizers' estimation, this reconstituted village would give "more flair and local charm to this event" and thereby encourage attendees to donate to the cause. The organizers requested materials to build this mock village from the minister of the marine, though they were ultimately denied access to the necessary supplies.[52] Nonetheless, several such local fund-raising events took place across France.

Soliciting donations from the press, prefectures, schools, organizations, and individuals within the metropole—while receiving donations from foreign governments as well—the Comité de Secours raised over six hundred thousand francs within the first few months of its operation (by November), and at that point planned to disband.[53] This is a substantial amount of money, given that the average yearly wage for a French worker in the metropole during the 1890s was 1,080 francs, paid at 35 centimes per hour.[54] In addition to the Comité's fund-raising, the central government had already allocated two hundred thousand francs to Martinique on 24 June, and proposed a contribution of an additional three hundred thousand francs to Martinique and one hundred thousand francs to the newly burned Guadeloupe on 8 July.[55] Annotated "colonial service" under the financial law of 17 July 1889, this money was earmarked for reconstruction and individual aid in order to stave off what officials feared would be inevitable starvation and disorder.[56] The law contributing four hundred thousand francs, about 10 percent of Martinique's annual budget, to the Antilles passed unanimously—511 votes for and zero against.[57] The Comité decided on 25 July 1890 that it would apportion the donations received between Martinique and Guadeloupe. Based on an approximation of the losses within each affected city, the Comité decided to apportion 90 percent of the funds to

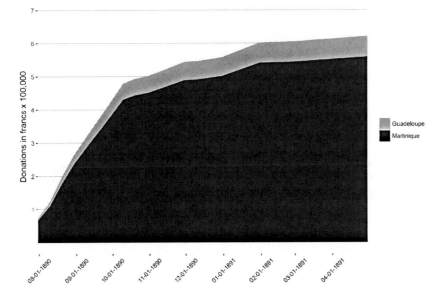

FIG. 5.   Comité de Secours donations as distributed
to Martinique and Guadeloupe
"Secours aux incendiés de la Martinique et de
la Guadeloupe: Liste des souscriptions," *Journal
officiel de la République française,* 13 August 1890–
30 April 1891, FM 2400COL, carton 92, ANOM.

Fort-de-France, Martinique, leaving 10 percent for the town of Port-Louis, Guadeloupe.[58] Though the Comité de Secours had officially dissolved by December 1890, donations continued to trickle in from all over France and its empire until April 1891.

Between the metropolitan relief campaign and the local fund-raising efforts, 1.7 million francs were deposited into the treasury of Martinique, with roughly half being received by the end of July 1890.[59] While some of the funds went to fill budgetary shortcomings, the bulk went toward direct dispensations to the afflicted populace. When the governor opened a credit of one hundred thousand francs on 27 June to be distributed to the population at the rate of 10 francs per victim, the administration divided the city up by roads and appointed a ten-person subcommittee to decide how to distribute the funds. Some of the money was used to create shelters for the neediest families, while the rest was distributed to the populace on 4 July. The fire's victims presented themselves to the treasury or the revenue office, signing off on the allocated amount of 10 francs. A second credit of 122,320 francs was opened in the same fashion on 21 August, and a third credit of thirty thousand francs provided assistance for previously undiscovered indigents at the rate of 36.80 francs per victim.[60] The bulk of the Comité's funds, however, went toward compensating victims for their structural, property, and commercial losses from the fire at a rate of 10 percent. Distributing 1.3 million francs by the end of 1891, the local Commission de Secours—the organization tasked with distributing the nationally raised funds—paid out a tenth of the declared value of an individual's losses, which, according to official reports by colonial investigators, privileged small proprietors over the large.[61]

Due to the overwhelming devastation caused by the 1890 fire, as well as the hurricane that followed on its heels in 1891, it took over a decade to rebuild Fort-de-France. Nevertheless, by 1903, nearly seven-eighths of the city had been rebuilt. The U.S. Bureau of Foreign Commerce described it as a "pretty and interesting town" that was "vastly improved" following the devastation of the 1890 fire. In addition to the funds provided by the Comité, the government of Martinique awarded homeowners 50 percent of the market value of their burned-down homes in order to encourage reconstruction, paying out a total of eight hundred thousand francs to help defray the costs of rebuilding the city's housing.[62] Moreover, Martinique's General Council provided a credit of three million francs through three-hundred-thousand-franc annuities over a ten-year period to homeowners who lost their homes in the fire.[63] By 1 January 1892, the General Council had already used 260,000 francs of those funds to rebuild forty-nine homes, and though the 1891 hurricane had significantly slowed reconstruction and posed a host of new problems, colonial investigators acknowledged that the reconstruction of Fort-de-France was proceeding "at great steps."[64] Following the 1890 fire, officials acknowledged the riskiness of the Caribbean's built environment. In their reconstruction efforts, officials mitigated the dangers of earthquakes on the one hand and fires on the other by establishing new regulations that required new wooden homes to be built with a metal framework. Similarly, the town of Port Louis in Guadeloupe revised its construction standards to make homes more resistant to fire.[65]

Laicization: Religious Fund-raising in
Martinique, Lay in the Metropole

Catholicism played an important part in the relief effort, as Martinique had been integrated into the French Catholic Church during the Second Republic, becoming part of a diocese that included Guadeloupe and Réunion. This diocese was attached to Bordeaux, largely due to the close commercial relationship with the city that began during plantation slavery. In a world often characterized by metropolitan Frenchmen as *ancien régime*, Catholicism played a large role in the everyday life of the denizens of the French Antilles. According to one American priest, "Martinique forms a striking contrast with some parts of France. The Lord's day is well kept, the churches crowded at every religious function and the sacraments are observed frequently."[66] Unlike the new colonies, where French administrators felt strongly that "anticlericalism was not for export," however, Martinique was not free from the French state's push for laicization and the culture wars that came to characterize the Third Republic.[67] The government nominated its bishop, and the Church approved the nomination. The 1880 laws that secularized instruction in the metropole were also extended to the old colonies, and secular instructors replaced the Frères de Ploëmel, the religious order from Brittany tasked with restructuring the school system in Martinique and Guadeloupe after emancipation in 1848.[68]

The management of donations reflects this division between religious adherence and mounting republican secularism. The Catholic Church oversaw the local Commission de Secours, while the metropolitan Comité de Secours was purely a secular organization. The sources of the donations also reflect this division: religious organizations accounted for a very small percentage of total donations collected by the metropolitan Comité de Secours, whereas much of the Commission's fund-raising took place in parish churches. That is, while virtually all local donations were filtered through the church in Martinique, religious donations raised by the Comité de Secours in the metropole accounted for only 0.26 percent of all money raised for Martinique and Port-Louis. By contrast, municipal and communal collections in the metropole accounted for nearly 20 percent; banquets for 11 percent; educational institutions for 10 percent; and commercial institutions for roughly 6 percent. While donations originating from metropolitan religious institutions were likely filtered through the municipal, communal, and public collections, it is nevertheless significant that they were not counted as distinct and were instead folded into the secular metropolitan bureaucracy.

The distinction between a Catholic colony and a secular metropole engendered disputes over what the state was obligated to repair. In 1892, when colonial investigators reopened an examination of the distribution of funds and supplies for the victims of the 1890 fires, they were insistent that the state not pay for the reconstruction of religious buildings on the islands following the 1891 hurricane. The investigatory commission believed that "the state is not fairly obligated to contribute with the communes to such costly expenses for the exercise of religion," but instead should only fund the reconstruction of buildings that serve a "necessary and incontestable public utility."[69]

Although "secularism was not for export" to the colonies at the end of the nineteenth century, the struggle between secularism and Catholicism came to characterize local understandings of the fires in Fort-de-France and Port-Louis and their significance. The disagreement over whether the French Antilles were a secular or religious space was encoded in the way in which the local press covered the disaster, split between conservatives who saw the fire as an act of God that societal charity and individual faith could rectify, and republicans who viewed the entire catastrophe as the machinations of local politics and governmental malfeasance. The ashes of Fort-de-France, the administrative hub of the island, were a backdrop to divergent political views—conservatives evinced a strong allegiance to an old-fashioned understanding of Martinique as a relic of a Catholic *ancien régime* France, while republicans framed the disaster in the context of an ongoing political war between leftists under Deproge and centrists under Hurard. Calls to aid from the population were framed in very nationalistic language: those who donated were true patriots, while those who did not contribute were "anti-patriots" who did not hold true to their republican values.

Nearly an Algeria: The Cultural Significance of Antillean Citizenship and Disaster Relief

Public relief was intricately tied to the legal and cultural incorporation of the French Antilles into the Republic, as well as the extent to which Antilleans were seen as equals to their metropolitan counterparts. Germain Casse's position at the head of the local relief effort ensured the connection. As the appointed governor of Martinique from 1889 to 1890 and a longtime advocate of equality for French Antilleans, Casse was a creole born of an emigrant Frenchman and a local woman in Pointe-à-Pitre, Guadeloupe. As a mixed-race man who spent much of his early life in Paris, where he attended grade school and later earned his law degree, he was an outspoken supporter of full assimilation of the French Antilles, and writers like Armand Corre described him as "at the helm" of the mulatto politicians.[70] Under the Second Empire, Casse fought for the establishment of a republic, and during the siege of Paris commanded the 135th battalion of *francs-tireurs*, or irregular troops who used guerilla tactics against the Prussian army. As a Blanquist socialist who expressed his sympathy for the French Commune and later attended the First International Workingmen's Association, Casse sat on the extreme left of the French National Assembly during the early years of the Third Republic, first as the deputy from Guadeloupe and then as the deputy of the Seine.[71] As a radical, he fought to abolish the presidency and secularize the republic, though he became tempered in his radicalism in his later years and sought a rapprochement with parliamentary moderates and opportunist republicans. As a mulatto from Guadeloupe at the center of Parisian politics, he embodied the republican ideals of colonial assimilation, as well as the Third Republic's penchant for parliamentary dilettantes. As the following caricature by André Gill from the irreverent *Les Hommes d'aujourdhui* demonstrates, Casse's contemporaries saw him as a champion for combining the Antilles' African heritage with French culture during his time in office. *Les Hommes d'aujourd'hui* described him as follows: "His revolutionary temperament, his spirit of independence, his love of liberty, his conscience which clerical education could not diminish, his just sentiments led him to seek emancipation in the Republic and freedom of thought."[72] However, due to his political leanings and, probably, his mixed heritage, many in the financial world did not like him, viewing his focus on Antillean citizenship rights as an impediment to their interests in the Antilles. The *Gazette agricole* unfavorably described Casse as a "journalist without talent" whose governance in Martinique had demonstrated "incapability without equal," and others criticized him for his political "zigs" and "zags."[73] In 1886 he was even the target of an unsuccessful assassination attempt by Jean Baffier, a deranged nationalist sculptor who followed the infamous anti-Semite Edouard Drumont and saw Casse as an impediment to the reawakening of Gaul.

The cultural importance of the relief campaign, and its connection to Antilleans' citizenship rights, was not lost on the Comité's membership, who were interested in bringing relief to the Antilles precisely because they were French and republican. In fact, the "honorary president" of the Comité was Victor Schoelcher, the French statesman who championed slave emancipation and black citizenship in the Caribbean.[74] Making his call to the French population's generosity in the Comité's official press announcement, Admiral Peyron expressed his certitude that everyone would give generously, "for, it is never in vain that one calls upon the sentiments of solidarity that unite all members of the French family."[75]

The Comité successfully appealed to Frenchmen's shared citizenship with their compatriots in Martinique and Guadeloupe. The Parisian newspaper *Les Tablettes Coloniales* exclaimed that "the call for help addressed to us by our Antillean compatriots . . . will be heard, this cry will not stay without echo. All that is possible to do to help the numerous unfortunate people, France will do without hesitation, bringing to [the task] full alacrity and heart."[76] The newspaper went on to assert that "this is not only a humanitarian question, but a patriotic duty that everyone in France will be able to understand. . . . It is incumbent upon all of France, and by that we mean not only the metropole, but also all its colonies, to come to the aid of this dignified population."[77] Likewise, imploring fellow citizens to remember "the links which unite you with our colony of Martinique," Bordeaux opened its own subscription campaign and called upon its citizens to help "your unfortunate compatriots without respite or food," for the people of Martinique "wait for the *mère-patrie* to lift them from the ruins and assuage the miseries accumulated by this terrible catastrophe."[78]

This familial language certainly conveys the sort of paternalism many historians of French colonialism have highlighted. Martinique was indeed still a colony, though one with a special place in French culture, and as such it was still subject to the eugenic and paternalistic mindset prevalent in turn-of-the-century France. Martinique was described as a tropical version of *ancien régime* France, and most descriptions of the fire were rife with discussions of coconut palms, brightly colored headdresses full of bananas and

3ᵉ volume. — Nᵒ 133.   10 c.   Un an : 6 fr.

LES HOMMES D'AUJOURD'HUI

DESSINS DE GILL

BUREAUX : 48, RUE MONSIEUR LE PRINCE, PARIS

GERMAIN CASSE

FIG. 6. Caricature of Germain Casse holding a
white French child and an African child
Illustration by André Gill, *Les Hommes
d'aujourd'hui* 3, no. 133 (1881), Paris.

other tropical fruits, and traditional dances with untraditionally mixed-race peoples.[79] Few articles in Parisian papers, particularly those dealing directly with colonial issues like *Les Tablettes Coloniales*, neglected to append racial typologies to the end of their articles on the Fort-de-France fire: images of the prototypical creole woman, the *mulâtress*, or the Negress stood side by side with images of the island's devastated capital city.[80]

Nevertheless, several metropolitan cities like Bordeaux underscored their linkages to the island—which, granted, had been forged through chattel slavery and the exploitation of forced sugar cultivation—and the duties incumbent upon citizens to help one another. While ultimately Bordeaux was not among Martinique's primary benefactors, the origin of the donations received by the Comité demonstrated the more general linkages between the metropole and Martinique. Most of the donations received over the course of the Comité's nine-month campaign came from public and communal collections, banquets, and educational fund-raising (figure 7)—in short, from everyday Frenchmen, women, and children.

While the majority of funds came from Paris itself, home to the financial institutions and the largest population in France, the spread of donations across France reveals the breadth of the fund-raising campaign (map 2). In part, this widespread participation likely reflects the minister of the interior proclaiming an official subscription in the school system, as well as a testament to the interconnectedness of France by the close of the nineteenth century. The bulk of donations came from public collections, which shows that knowledge of the disaster, as well as an interest in the well-being of the victims, extended across the metropole. According to *L'Illustration*, the news of the fire "caused a commotion in France, because, more than any of our other colonies, Martinique is in constant contact, familial relations most of all, with the mère-patrie. There are few Martiniquais, few families of settlers established there, who don't have very close relatives here. It's nearly an Algeria, if not by extent or proximity, at least by links of the heart."[81] The *Journal des Voyages* echoed this very sentiment for its readership in France, supporting their involvement in the fund-raising campaign.[82]

The regions of France that were the most ideologically invested in the well-being of their *concitoyens* in the Caribbean were also the least invested financially—discounting Paris, through which all money in France ulti-

mately flowed. The largest donations came not from the mercantile powerhouses of Marseille, Bordeaux, Le Havre, and Nantes that had close
economic ties to the Antilles dating to the islands' slave past, but from the
fringes of the French nation that had little to no financial connection to
Martinique and Guadeloupe (see maps 2 and 3, figure 7). Of the total tonnage of goods arriving in the metropole from Martinique in 1892, 26 percent
went to Marseille, 34 percent to Bordeaux, and the remaining 40 percent
was split between Le Havre and Nantes. In fact, nearly a third of sugar from
Martinique, and a quarter of all commerce, went through Marseille alone.[83]
While they accounted for roughly two-thirds of all trade with the French
Antilles, Marseille and Bordeaux combined donated a total of 0.5 percent
of all money raised for Martinique and Guadeloupe, with Marseille itself
falling just behind the far distant Pondicherry, a French colony in India until
1954. In fact, the Gironde department (Bordeaux) was ranked among the
lowest donors per capita, while Loire-Atlantique (Nantes) and Bouches-
du-Rhone (Marseille) were in the class of second-to-lowest donors. One
exception to this rule was Le Havre, which held a special charity event
for which they requested materials to "reconstitute" a model Martiniquais
village. Seine-Maritime/Seine-Inférieure (Le Havre) ranked among the
tier second from the top.

The region of Lorraine, specifically the department of Meurthe-et-
Moselle, had by far the largest donations per capita, at ten centimes per
inhabitant (maps 3 and 4; figure 8; tables 2 and 3—101.25 francs per thousand; median, 22.5; average, 83.3). This department represented the remnants of what Germany had seized in the Franco-Prussian War from the
former departments of Moselle and Meurthe. Its rate of donation exceeded
that of the far wealthier and business-oriented department of the Seine,
which included the financial powerhouse of Paris. Perhaps this generosity reflected the region's own *revanchisme*, or its need to prove Lorraine's
Frenchness after the disaster of the Franco-Prussian War, but the disaster
in Martinique clearly resonated in Lorraine, which was rural yet industri-
alizing. Lorraine was France's primary iron-ore mining region, and figures
from 1896 put Meurthe-et-Moselle as, by far, France's leading provider of
cast iron.[84] The department mined and smelted over 1.4 million tons (62
percent of France's total output)—1.2 million more tons than the next

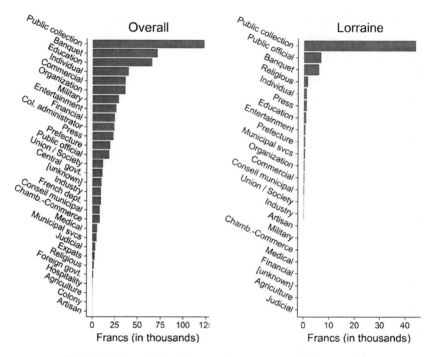

FIG. 7. **Donations by origin and sector, Lorraine versus France, 1890–91**
Overall donations (*left*) versus donations in Lorraine (*right*) received by the
Comité des Secours, broken down by sector. Graph created in R statistical
package with compiled donation data from FM 2400COL, carton 92, ANOM.

highest producing department in France, Le Nord.[85] Though fairly well-
off, with a well-balanced economy split between agriculture and industry,
Meurthe-et-Moselle was far from fabulously wealthy, lagging behind the
Seine with regard to the percentage of rentiers comprising the department's
population. Only 3.61 percent of the department's population could sustain
itself from income earned from investments, while 5.54 percent in the Seine
and 6.71 percent in Seine-et-Oise could. In this Meurthe-et-Moselle fell in
the seventy-fifth percentile among French departments, which suggests
that its donations did not impose hardship as it might among citizens of
departments like Le Nord (1.19 percent, tenth percentile).[86]

Nonetheless, the coverage of donations from Lorraine is astonishing (see
map 2). While public collections and relief banquets held in Nancy gener-

MAP 2. **Donations within France, 1890–91**
Geo-located donations plotted within France with Gephi. All nodes are
the same size and represent a donating commune. Donation data from FM
2400COL, carton 92, ANOM.

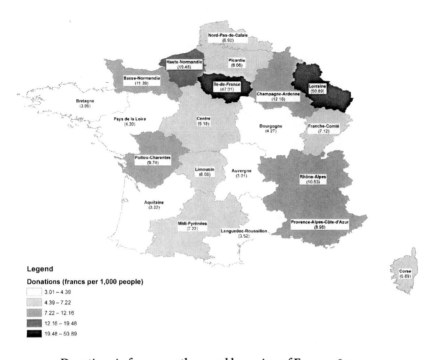

MAP 3. Donations in francs per thousand by region of France, 1890–91
Note the high number of donations in Lorraine. Map created in ArcGIS
with five natural breaks (Jenks). Population statistics from *Social, Demographic, and Educational Data for France, 1801–1897*, ICPSR00048-vol. 1.
Donation data from FM 2400COL, carton 92, ANOM.

ated the bulk of donations, nearly every commune in the region donated to
some degree. The nationalist campaign in Lorraine likely drove this coverage;
the "civilizing mission" had sent a legion of cultural ambassadors through
the school system to heighten awareness of Lorrainers' French nationality. The French government used the public school system in Lorraine to
acculturate what it saw as a backward and fairly autonomist peasantry to
the mores of the French urban centers, heightening this attempt following
the loss of Alsace-Lorraine to Germany during the Franco-Prussian War.
As historian Stephen Harp has shown, the French government believed
that Lorrainers had to "learn to be loyal" to the French nation, and with
the goal of nation building from 1850 to 1871, the government sent a veri-

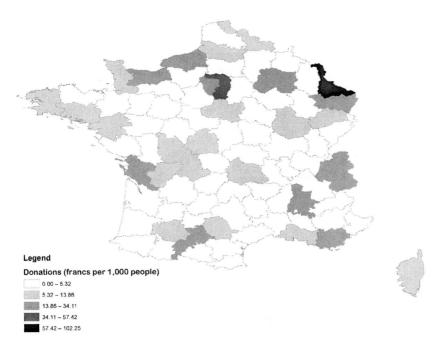

Legend

Donations (francs per 1,000 people)

- 0.00 – 5.32
- 5.32 – 13.86
- 13.86 – 34.11
- 34.11 – 57.42
- 57.42 – 102.25

MAP 4. **Donations in francs per thousand by department of France, 1890–91**
Note the high number of donations in the department of Meurthe-et-Moselle, in the Lorraine region. Map created in ArcGIS with five natural breaks (Jenks). Population statistics from *Social, Demographic, and Educational Data for France, 1801–1897*, ICPSR00048-v1. Donation data from FM 2400COL, carton 92, ANOM.

table army of French schoolteachers to the region to teach French history, culture, and language.[87]

The widespread support for the French Antilles was connected to the growth of the republican public education system. Schools made up one of the primary donors to Fort-de-France and Port-Louis, because the minister of public instruction authorized collections in all public schools in France.[88] Yet even more important was the schools' role in acculturating the populace and encouraging them to donate. The education system's role as a vehicle for republican values was strongly felt in Lorraine as in Martinique, where middle-class mulattos were both the island's leading republicans and the primary beneficiaries of a public education system modeled more closely

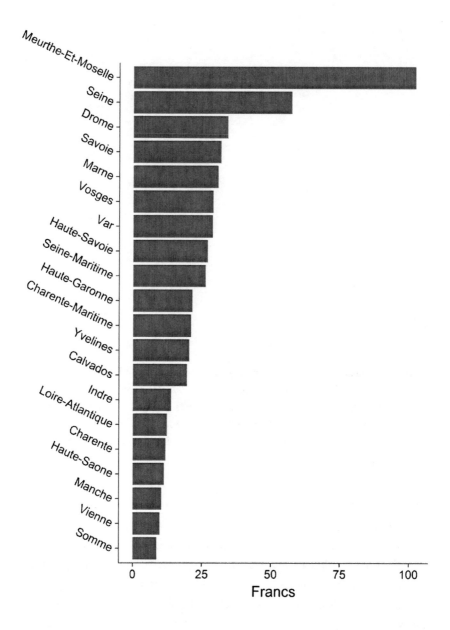

FIG. 8. **Top twenty donating departments, 1890–91**
Francs per one thousand people. Graph created in R statistical package
with compiled donation data from FM 2400COL, carton 92, ANOM.

TABLE 2. *Top twelve donating departments and amounts donated, 1890*

DEPARTMENT	FRANCS
Ville de Paris	167,849
Meurthe-et-Moselle	45,507
Seine-Maritime	21,857
Nord	13,747
Marne	13,398
Yvelines	12,840
Vosges	11,803
Drôme	10,391
Haute-Garonne	9,966
Charente-Maritime	9,527
Calvados	8,395
Savoie	8,292

Note: Meurthe-et-Moselle had the second-highest contributions.
Source: FM 2400COL, carton 92, ANOM.

on that of rural regions like Lorraine than on the colonial education system found elsewhere in the French empire.

Lorrainers' donations reflected a strong impetus to prove their republican convictions. As historian Mark Sawchuk has shown with respect to Nice and Savoy, those regions within France that had to prove their Frenchness were the most invested in French republicanism. After hearing the final sum donated by Meurthe-et-Moselle, colonial undersecretary Étienne wrote to the prefect at Nancy, "I would congratulate you especially for the remarkable results that you have achieved in this charitable work, and to heartily thank you for the momentum you've given to this movement of sympathetic commiseration that has manifested itself in Meurthe-et-Moselle in favor of our unfortunate compatriots of the Antilles."[89] The

TABLE 3. *Top twelve donating departments and donations per thousand, 1890*

DEPARTMENT	FRANCS
Meurthe-et-Moselle	102.25
Seine	57.42
Drôme	34.11
Savoie	31.71
Marne	30.64
Vosges	28.84
Var	28.67
Haute-Savoie	26.97
Seine-Maritime	26.18
Haute-Garonne	21.46
Charente-Maritime	20.93
Yvelines	20.42

Note: The donations from Savoie and Haute-Savoie reveal their strong commitment to French republicanism and strong distrust of monarchism and Bonapartism based at least in part on their recent incorporation into the French nation, in 1860, and their deep Italian republican heritage.
Source: FM 2400COL, carton 92, ANOM.

resonance of this disaster in Lorraine demonstrates the extent to which Lorrainers internalized republican ideals, most notably those of cultural and political assimilation.

Aside from Paris, in which all economic, financial, and bureaucratic functions were centralized, the largest donations came from those regions with the weakest financial ties to the Antilles, as well as the weakest connection to the traditional conceptualization of France. Those departments that donated the most were precisely those that had to prove their French national identity.

Embers in the Ashes: Looters, Brigands, and Smoldering Political Differences

The day after the fire in Fort-de-France, a disgruntled man was arrested in Saint-Pierre near several barrels of oil outside a storefront, shouting, "Down with the 18th of July! Long live the fire!" Though the press labeled him a crackpot, monomaniac, or hoaxer, it admitted that there was a palpable— and in their view, justified—fear that the Fort-de-France fire would not be an isolated incident, for "every misfortune that erupts soon finds its counterpart somewhere else."[90] The press and authorities anticipated that someone might rekindle the fire in Fort-de-France—or perhaps even spread it to Saint-Pierre—or that panic would throw the entire population into violent pandemonium. In light of fears of disorder and widespread panic, therefore, gendarmes patrolled Fort-de-France to prevent looting, particularly of the storehouses of food at the unburned military base at Fort Louis. In fact, a destitute group of fire victims—whom the press labeled an outside influence—attempted to procure supplies from that military storehouse, where gendarmes intervened with bayonets.[91]

The city was placed under siege, and as the press put it, "Military surveillance is ceaselessly very active and severe in Fort-de-France. It's necessary. Bands of looters, rogues, vagabonds—those birds of prey that one meets after any tempest, feasting among the debris, those foxes and jackals who live on spoils—are beginning to infect Fort-de-France, certainly looking to, it is said, revive the fire."[92] In the wake of any natural disaster, the fear of looters and brigands typically emerges—a fear thoroughly laced with racism and classism stemming from political tensions that predate the disaster. Recent sociological studies have shown that social identification, racial prejudice, historical memory, and media attention heavily influence how survivors, governments, first responders, and the public make sense of disasters.[93] The threat of looting and panic following a natural disaster is rarely a reasonable concern, and when looting does occur in a disaster—or perhaps, to be more accurate, is perceived by authorities—it is often intimately tied to political stresses.[94] In a world turned upside down one person's "survivalist" is another's "looter," and the distinction nearly always reflects race, class, or politics.[95] Synthesizing sociological findings across numerous disasters in the United States and several abroad, Thomas

Drabek has found that "[w]hen victimized by a disaster—be it a flood, tornado, or earthquake—most individuals evidence behavioral continuity and remarkable composure."[96] Rather than falling into pandemonium as contemporary news reports cautioned—as they have recently in the wake of Hurricane Katrina (2005), the Haitian earthquake (2010), and the Japanese tsunami and nuclear meltdown (2011)—disaster survivors typically evidence "constructive, goal-directed behavior" and acts of selflessness and community.[97] While panic is possible, it is not common enough to merit the attention the media gives it, and it represents the extreme end of the spectrum of human responses to disaster situations.[98] Even today, however, the mass media and official discourse continue to promulgate ideas proven to be false by years of empirical research, and these "disaster myths"—most notably the panic myth—have real consequences for how disaster survivors behave and how official authorities respond.[99]

To temper, or perhaps to mask, the grievousness—or rather, the baselessness—of "blaming the victim," the French press tried to paint the "pillagers" as an outside influence disrupting the otherwise tranquil Fort-de-France population.[100] Martinique's republican newspaper, *Les Colonies*, vociferously opposed this assertion, claiming it was an unfair attempt to off-load responsibility onto the rest of the island.[101] Instead, it pinned responsibility on the elected mayor of Fort-de-France, Osman Duquesnay, because he was the leading political opponent of the newspaper's editor, Marius Hurard. The newspaper summed it up as follows: "A city burned with 35 million lost and 5,000 people without respite . . . is certainly a beautiful trophy in the arms of M. Duquesnay. . . . Can we at least hope that this will be the last, and that our population, so cruelly struck, will finally open its eyes to the acts of this scoundrel and understand his immorality."[102] The great fire, as well as the public's perceived incompetence of Duquesnay's response, fed into the ever-growing rift in Martinique's Republican Party after 1885. At the time of the fire, wealthy middle-class mulattos dominated *Les Colonies*, and their largest political opponents came from the far left: the socialist republicans led by Ernest Deproge who had split from the Republican Party five years earlier. Though *Les Colonies* framed the disaster in terms of its human costs, its calls for charity revolved around political patriotism and were predicated on party allegiance.

Tensions flared between Mayor Duquesnay and Governor Germain Casse, who shared no love for one another. Casse threatened to imprison Duquesnay at Fort Desaix if any further misfortune, fire or otherwise, befell Fort-de-France.[103] Undoubtedly a hollow threat, it nevertheless illustrated the level of discord between the municipal and colonial governments—one that continued through the relief effort to follow. In a broadside posted throughout the city, Duquesnay's political opponents accused him of incompetence and political maneuvering in the face of real disaster.[104] Duquesnay argued that Casse had overstepped his legal authority in creating the local Commission de Secours, and he was disgruntled that his name came below that of the mayor of Saint-Pierre in the commission's roster. For center-right republicans, the true culprit was not Casse but Duquensay himself and the political infighting he incited in Fort-de-France by being a political opportunist.[105] In fact Les Colonies ran for several months and in very large letters a quote from Victor Schoelcher, who in 1884 lambasted Duquesnay for his political opportunism. The quote painted Duquesnay as an unworthy politician whose place in Martiniquais politics was not only a great shame but also shameful.[106]

While Les Colonies considered the entire catastrophe a result of Duquesnay's blunderings, the conservative Catholic newspaper Les Antilles treated the fire as an act of God that the charity and faith of the good parishioners of Martinique should alleviate (figure 9). The conservative paper was geared toward the island's white plantocracy, and as such it held a strong association with an ancien régime France characterized by centralized government. Therefore, it focused much more heavily on the metropolitan government's response, as well as the role played by the appointed governor. It underscored the inequities prevalent among the people of Fort-de-France, even discussing the event as an opportunity for Fort-de-France to mend its ways and stop the persistent political infighting that had come to characterize the island's locally elected assembly.

A telegram from Saint-Pierre to Paris was quick to put the fire in the context of the political battles and social tensions of the late 1880s, casting the fire as further proof that Martinique—"with its discord, hatreds, and excessive ardors"—is like "an overheated machine threatening to erupt."[107] Some Catholics saw the fire as a form of divine retribution, for "God has his designs . . . and Fort-de-France had wrongs to right," and they considered

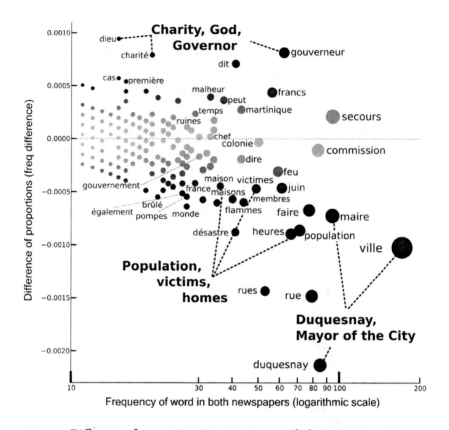

FIG. 9. Difference of proportions in newspaper vocabulary, 1890
Frequently used words appear larger and farther along the x-axis. Words
associated with *Les Antilles* (*top*), the conservative religious journal,
appear higher and are colored darker, whereas words associated with
Les Colonies (*bottom*), the centrist republican journal, appear lower and
darker. Words shared by the two newspapers appear in the center in light
gray. We can see that "governor," "god," and "charity" are more closely
associated with *Les Antilles*, while "population," "victims," "homes," "city,"
and "duquesnay" are more closely associated with *Les Colonies*.

the fire a means of setting the wayward Fort-de-France on the proper path.[108]
The biggest wrong in their eyes was impiety and the declining importance of
Catholicism—something which, by the 1890s, was felt all across France—
but religious conservatives also saw Fort-de-France as filled with excessive
emotions engendered by political discord—namely due to the 1885 split

in Martinique's Republican Party between Marius Hurard's Progressives and Ernest Deproge's Radical Socialists—and the economic downturn.[109] Labor unrest in Martinique continued to rise in the 1890s due to the volatile world sugar market, eventually culminating in the Antilles' first general strike in February 1900, covered in chapter 4. The press coverage betrayed a primary concern for the financial solvency of the city, especially losses to the businesses, docks, and sugar refinery at Point-Simon.

French officials took upon themselves the responsibility of protection and relief, reflecting their own societal and political visions in the reconstruction effort. As journalist Naomi Klein demonstrated in *The Shock Doctrine*, the growth of liberal, free-market economics fit hand in glove with what she terms "disaster capitalism"—or the use of cataclysmic moments to reshape the economic and political world of those affected.[110] In the view of Martinique's conservatives and their counterparts in Paris, the denizens of Fort-de-France needed to align themselves with "calm, order, and tranquility" in recovering from the disaster and rebuilding the city. The first wave of donations came from financial and commercial powerhouses in Paris, many of whom had financial investments in Fort-de-France.[111] Perversely hoping that the fire had "consumed the discord, hatred, and excessive enthusiasm that boiled over there [in Fort-de-France] as if in a furnace," conservatives in Saint-Pierre argued that while atrocious, the burning of Fort-de-France presented an opportunity for rebirth:

> We'll see if, with a change in material situation, it'll bring about change in ideas and feelings. . . . City of Fort-de-France, sister city of ours, we take part in your grief; we share, as brothers, your affliction, and we wish to lift you up from your ruins. We will help you even. But lift yourselves up in wisdom. Lift yourselves up with sane ideas, lift yourselves up in right sentiments, lift yourselves up with noble resolutions, lift yourselves up with a greater faith, lift yourselves up with all the elements of a true and solid prosperity.[112]

By mid-August, conservatives in Paris began a racially charged diatribe against the victims in Martinique, asserting that the fire in Fort-de-France was the machination of a corrupt elected official who wanted to win over a disgruntled black population. A sensationalist article in *La Paix* asserted that the fire was an act of political vengeance wherein "a man occupying an elected position set fire to the city with the certainty of being approved by the black population. Negros repeatedly blocked the efforts of the fire fighters, and Negresses propagated the fire." The article continued that "this explosion of animosity toward France manifested itself in the same conditions in Port-Louis [Guadeloupe] where the fire was equally set by a criminal hand."[113] *Les Antilles* lambasted the article as inaccurate, ridiculous, and absurd, framing its sensationalism as evidence of Martinique's strained relationship with France.

The knowledge that the governor of Martinique, Germain Casse, was himself a person of color did little to assuage the alarmed Parisian press. The *Journal des fonctionnaires* accused Governor Casse of malfeasance, arguing that he delayed in responding to the fire, showed insensitivity by strolling through the still-burning streets with a lit cigar hanging from his mouth, and diverted relief funds from the victims to his political allies. Such negativity toward officials was commonplace at the close of the century, becoming a hallmark of parliamentary politics under the Third Republic. Alleging a track record of "the illegal suppression of the local government, the impoverishment of the colony, . . . [and] his heinous and passionate politics that have furthered divisions," the *Journal* implored the colonial undersecretary of state to remove Casse lest he siphon off the remaining funds destined to rebuild the city.[114] Casse was reassigned as the treasurer of Guadeloupe on 24 August 1890 and replaced by his own minister of the interior, Delphino Moracchini, who had been instrumental in distributing fire relief supplies.[115] Prompted by Duquesnay and the newly appointed governor, the local government conducted an investigation into the appropriation of the relief funds to see if money had been embezzled. The investigatory commission found no malfeasance, identifying only a few negligible irregularities in the distribution of foodstuffs and supplies to the fire victims.[116]

The French press and authorities underscored the threat of looting in disaster situations, deploying the military for the dual purpose of providing relief and ensuring security and public safety throughout the Third Republic. The *béké*-dominated conservative press on the island was overwhelmingly fearful of mass panic and looting, and though they were quick to emphasize that the victims were not the perpetrators—that outside elements were exploiting the poor and the indigent—they nevertheless underscored the perpetual threat of criminal activity. This desire to safeguard public tranquility against the threat of civil unrest—whether real or imagined following natural disasters—had very real consequences for the population of Martinique. It was this strong desire to keep order during the days before the eruption of Mount Pelée, for instance, that kept so many within harm's way.

At the same time, the French press also underscored similarity between the victims of the Antillean fires and metropolitan republicans. On the one hand, the citizens of Martinique and Guadeloupe were *concitoyens* in need, while on the other hand they represented the most radical elements of the French left—"pétroleuses" (the politically motivated female arsonists who had come to characterize the Paris Commune), socialists, and malcontents—as well as the worst that parliamentary government had to offer—electoral fraud, administrative corruption, and embezzlement. The right's unfounded concerns over looting and the general unruliness of the unwashed masses in Martinique and Guadeloupe echoed those leveled by the French right within the metropole against their political opponents in the French legislature.

In any case, the parallels drawn with Algeria, which held a similarly impactful and problematic place in France's understanding of itself, as well as the depth and breadth of donations received from everyday Frenchmen, suggest we must take seriously the Comité's appeal to the French citizenry on the grounds of compatriotism and the duty to help beleaguered *concitoyens* of the Antilles. The reaction in the French press to a disaster within the metropole itself employed the same kind of paternalistic, racist dialogue that underlay public discussions of the great Antillean fires. Comparing depictions of "colonial citizens" to what I call "metropolitan colonials" reveals that the dynamics and paradoxes found in colonial citizenship also apply to denizens of the mainland itself. Late nineteenth-century colonialism cannot be understood strictly in the straightforward geographic terms of "here" and "there."

From Colonial Citizens to Metropolitan Colonials: The Saint-Étienne Mine Collapse

Coal mining is a notoriously dangerous enterprise, and the dramatically increasing demand for coal in the late nineteenth century compounded the danger as coal miners felt the pressure to maximize production at the expense of safety. Like the constant threat of hurricanes, fires, and earthquakes on the faraway islands of Martinique and Guadeloupe, the persistent risk of mine accidents—explosions, floods, and collapses—haunted the small town of Saint-Étienne in the heart of France. This town along the River Furens in the department of the Loire had a long history of mining disasters. The town was constructed above coal deposits, and the numerous nearby coal mines had undermined it with passages, so the threat extended beyond the miners themselves to their family and friends in the village above.[117] Moreover, Saint-Étienne's officials resembled Martinique's and Guadeloupe's in their concern for economics over human safety; just substitute coal for sugar.

Near midday on 3 July 1889, over two hundred miners were buried alive at a coal mine in Saint-Étienne when a gas pocket known as a firedamp exploded. Within minutes, four thousand of the town's nearly 111,000 inhabitants had rushed to the nearby mine, along with the police and the mine company's personnel, but given the gruesomeness of the explosion, the main task in the aftermath was not to rescue survivors but to excavate bodies from under four hundred meters of earth.[118] For those not killed in the immediate blast, asphyxiation quickly set in, and only a very small portion of the victims was ultimately saved. At least 162 cadavers of the trapped miners were recovered, and of the 213 miners who were trapped within the mine that day, only six survived.[119] The disaster presented a mortal danger to the rescue crews as well. Of the forty-nine rescuers who had been working in the nearby Saint-Louis pit, only two survived. In fact, four rescue workers passed out on entering the mine—three were revived in open air, one fell to his death—and one rescuer suffocated in a pit that was eighteen hundred meters from the explosion's point of origin.

The 1889 disaster was the largest mining catastrophe in France until the Courrières accident of 1906, and the danger persisted long after the initial explosion. Fires continued to rage in the damaged mines, and the gas pocket remained to menace the workers. For instance, two days after the disaster, at least sixty miners at the Rimbaud pit rapidly evacuated upon noticing an irregularly large flame in their safety lamp.[120] It took until August 1890 to drain the Saint Louis mine pit after the explosion in July 1889.[121] But before the wreckage of the previous catastrophe had been cleared, disaster struck again on the night of 29 July 1890, when over 150 miners working for the Villeboeuf company fell victim to poor ventilation in the Pélissier pits.[122] An explosion ripped through the night air when volatile gases collected once again into a firedamp.[123] Enveloping miners in what one reporter called "a hurricane of gas," this tragedy, which killed about 120 miners and wounded roughly thirty-five, represented the town's fifth major mining accident in thirty years: an explosion in the Jabin pits killed seventy-two miners on 9 October 1871 and then another two hundred one month later on 8 November 1871.[124] Another explosion in the Jabin pit in 1875 killed approximately 226 people, with only one hundred bodies of the deceased recovered for burial.[125] A collapse at Chatelus killed ninety miners on 1 March 1887, and the disaster at the Verpilleux pits in 1889 had killed over two hundred.[126]

The place of the miners at Saint-Étienne in French society was in many ways analogous to the place of the Antillean fire victims. Aside from being in a perpetual state of disaster, sitting under Damocles' sword, as it were, they were also at the bottom of the social ladder within France, and, as Eugen Weber has shown, had only been recently integrated into the Parisian-dominated French nation-state. As the image from *L'Illustration* shows (figure 10), race and class were inextricably intertwined in the French imaginary. Not only were the workers dispossessed of rights, property, and safe living and working conditions, as were their compatriots in the Antilles, they were racialized in a similar fashion. The authors of *L'Illustration* explained that the workers' lips were swollen and their bodies charred from the fire, and that their artist's engraving tried to replicate the, in the author's words, "blackened" nature of the corpses.[127] Though undoubtedly the miners would have been horrifically disfigured and burned, the artist's rendition of the cadavers replicates far more than mere disfigurement. Nineteenth-century viewers would have readily seen in the image the racial typologies prevalent in France at the time, for the miners had been "blackened" in more ways than one. In fact, the trope of washing the blackness away from the African saturated soap advertisements at the start of the twentieth century in the francophone world.[128] Running alongside this trope in some advertisements, such as that for Le Savon Dirtoff printed here, was the notion that one's labor blackened his skin. In such cases, only the soap and cleaning products

FIG. 10. **Rescuers discovering victims at Saint-Étienne, 1889**
An image of the mining disaster's victims racialized as black colonials, with a rescuer entering from the right. The miners have blackened skin, pronounced lips, and short, curly hair—all characteristics of contemporary black stereotypes. "La Catastrophe de Saint-Étienne," *L'Illustration: Journal universel,* 13 July 1889.

FIG. 11. **Rescuers discovering victims in the Verpilleux pits, 1889**
An alternative image of the mining disaster's victims, with rescuers entering from the right. "L'Explosion de Grisou au Puits Verpilleux, à Saint-Etienne," *Le Petit Parisien,* 14 July 1889. Courtesy of the Bibliothèque Nationale de France.

FIG. 12. **Miners at work in Saint-Étienne, 1890**
In this postcard (circa 1890), what was omitted from the artist's rendition found in *L'Illustration* (see figure 10) is plain to see—pants, shirts, boots, and helmets. Courtesy of the author.

FIG. 13. Racist soap advertisement for Le Savon Dirtoff, circa 1930
This poster shows the racist trope that a strong enough soap
can cleanse a person of his or her blackness. The soap is specifically targeted at those of the laboring class, namely mechanics
and housekeepers. Courtesy of Harry Proctor.

afforded by modernity and progress could bring the laborer from savagery back to civilization.

According to historian Dana Hale, the most common image of "black-ness" during the Third Republic was that of a "black head in silhouette, full view, or profile on trademarks and advertising." The most prominent features were lips, teeth, and hair, features that Europeans saw as distinct from their own, and the most recognizable "African characteristic" was that of overly exaggerated lips. In many scientific circles, eugenicists used Africans' pro-nounced lips as "evidence" that they were morally deficient and less evolved than Europeans.[129] In the image from L'Illustration, the "blackened" miners' lips are pronounced, and their hair is short, receding, and curled (figure 10). They bear a closer resemblance to African caricatures (figure 13) than to either the French rescuer with the lantern entering from the right or the same miners as drawn by an artist from another French paper (figure 11). A comparison with another contemporary image of the same rescue found in Le Petit Parisien makes apparent the host of racial and class-based stereotypes informing the image in L'Illustration. Unlike the miners in the image from Le Petit Parisien, those in L'Illustration are shirtless, barefoot, and bereft of any safety gear, suggesting the miners' inability to take care of themselves as well as their savagery and stupidity. As Dana Hale reminds us, nudity and near-nudity represented African savagery in the press, scientific journals, travel books, and commercial advertisements. The racialized image from L'Illustration, therefore, would have reminded nineteenth-century viewers of the racist caricatures found in bourgeois encyclopedias and advertisements, as well as the common depictions of the mulâtresses and négresses found in colonial periodicals like Les Tablettes Coloniales.

A month after the explosion, writers in L'Illustration were calling for a continued parliamentary inquiry into the causes of the explosion, with the hope that better safety precautions could be taken to prevent another catastrophe. The victims could not recall what had sparked the explosion, so investigators resorted to interrogating workers on their daily routines to ensure that proper safety protocol had been followed. The subtext was that the workers had brought it on themselves—as evidenced by the lack of safety gear, let alone clothing, on the workers in the drawing from L'Il-lustration. A similar sentiment echoed throughout the metropole regarding the Fort-de-France fire, for many saw Fort-de-France as underprepared and full of civil and political unrest, and some went so far as to claim that the Martiniquais helped the fire along, acting, in a sense, as the *petroleuses* did during the Paris Commune.

Just like the French Antilles, Saint-Étienne experienced a large disaster at a time when it was declining in relative economic importance. As the French Antilles were once the primary producer of French sugar, Saint-Étienne was once France's premier coal-producing region. Both gave way to newer, less expensive production (figure 14). Sugar production shifted from cane plantations in the Caribbean to beet sugar refineries in Europe (figure 15). And though coal production and consumption were on the rise at the close of the century, the locus of the coal industry had relocated from the Centre region to collieries in the Nord region, particularly at Pas-de-Calais.[130] Prior to 1863, Saint-Étienne and the nearby Rive-de-Gier had been the primary coal fields in France, but by 1903, 64.5 percent of all coal production in France was coming from the Valenciennes fields in Pas-de-Calais.[131]

Donors in metropolitan France connected the events and began to send money for Saint-Étienne to the committee tasked with fund-raising for the Antilles. Unfortunately, it is impossible to track the money through the archives, since relief aid for Saint-Étienne was outside the mission statement of the Comité and the accountant, M. Bertin, forwarded along the money without recording it in his registers or publishing it in the *Journal officiel*. However, surviving letters from donors reveal that many saw the two events as related national incidents. For instance, the Society of Harmony of the Familistère of Guise—a social, cooperative commune modeled on the ideals of Charles Fourier—held a benefit concert in December 1890 explicitly for the victims in both Fort-de-France and Saint-Étienne.[132] Similarly, a republican Corsican newspaper—the *Monitor of Corsica*—sent money raised by an artistic youth organization sponsored by the paper "for the benefit of the fire victims of the Antilles and for the victims of the catastrophe in Saint-Étienne." In Paris, twenty authors, among them the moderate republican politician Jules Simon and the celebrated playwright Ludovic Halévy, compiled and sold an anthology of poems and short stories titled *Faisons la chaine*, which raised twenty-five hundred francs for victims of the catastrophes.[133] The book's preface drew a direct connection between

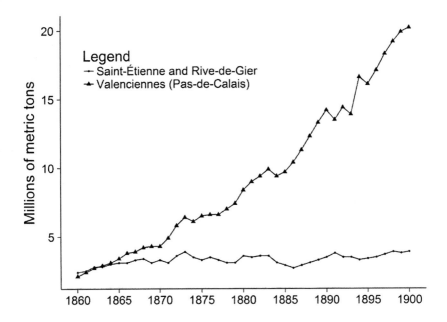

FIG. 14. **Coal production in Saint-Étienne and Rive-de-Gier versus that in Valenciennes, 1860–1900**
This graph shows the declining importance of Saint-Étienne's coal production in comparison with that of the Valenciennes region. Graph created in R statistical package with information from Wright, *Twelfth Special Report*, 186–87; Hitier, *Plantes industrielles*, 13–15.

"the fire in open air that devoured a city in a single night and the fire under the earth that asphyxiated workers in a single minute."[134] Consequently, the authors' publisher insisted that half of that sum go to the Caribbean and half to Saint-Étienne. Moreover, the towns of Valenton, Garches, Saint-Gervais, and Villiers-en-Arthes, among others, all collected money specifically designated for both Antillean and metropolitan victims.[135] Even expats in Yokohama, Japan, and colonial subjects in Senegal sent money earmarked for all three disasters. Unprompted by the Comité, therefore, individuals and organizations within France and its empire began sending money with enclosed letters referencing their suffering "compatriots" in the Caribbean and in Saint-Étienne, equating the two.[136] In effect a fund-raising

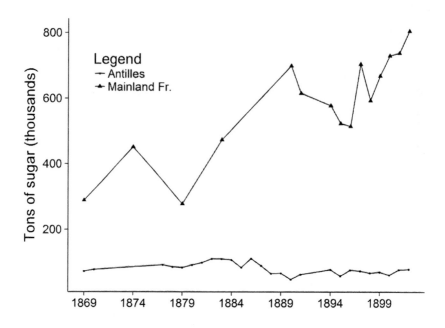

FIG. 15. **Sugar production in the Antilles versus that in the metropole, 1869–1902**
This graph shows the declining importance of sugar production in the
French Antilles in comparison with that on the French mainland. Graph
created in R statistical package with information from Rolph, *Something
about Sugar*, 242; Chemin-Dupontes, *Les Petites Antilles*, 241–42; Hélot, *Le
sucre de betterave*, 214.

committee created out of various offices within the French colonial bureaucracy began handling money for metropolitan victims in Saint-Étienne as
well as colonial ones in the Antilles.

An outpouring of public support from across France, as Frenchmen
heeded the call for Martinique and Guadeloupe's compatriots to open their
wallets to their brothers in peril, met the dire situation following the Great
Fires of Fort-de-France and Port-Louis. Those regions that had the most
tenuous connection to the "French tradition" were precisely the places that
donated the most money to help their "compatriots in peril." Moreover,
French citizens drew little distinction between a coal mining village, whose
inhabitants were themselves struggling for social welfare and work safety,
and two of France's economically exploited colonies. As everyday people

began sending in money to help their beleaguered *concitoyens* in both Saint-Étienne and the Antilles, the colonial committee that had been created to raise funds for the fires in the Caribbean inadvertently began raising money for a metropolitan disaster. Therefore, we must take the donors' choice of word—"compatriots"—seriously; reexamine the weight of republican universalism and how it played loose with geography, in both a positive and a negative way; and view both the metropolitan coal miners and the Antillean colonial citizens as part of a larger entity: what historian Gary Wilder calls the "imperial nation-state." For at the height of "new imperialism," France had "colonial metropolitans" within its borders and "colonial citizens" outside them.

Conclusion

The Fort-de-France and Port-Louis fires illustrated the ambiguous, contested place of the Antilles within the French imagination. On the one hand, requests for national aid from local officials demonstrated Antilleans' desire to be afforded their rightful place in the French nation. The republican myth of assimilation hinged upon satisfying these demands, and to some extent, these demands were heard and heeded. The national reach of the government's relief campaign clearly showed its ambition to safeguard a French citizenry far removed from the metropole, which for some was the catastrophes' silver lining. As the republican paper in Guadeloupe put it, "The disastrous events of Fort-de-France and Port-Louis which we deplore have nonetheless permitted us to appreciate the zeal, the heart, and the character of the men in whose hands our country has been entrusted. We are very proud of them and ourselves."[137] On the other hand, political infighting at the local level and accusations of malfeasance and agitation at the national level betrayed colonial prejudices that highlighted the West Indies' otherness and precluded their incorporation into the French nation.

The tension between inclusion and exclusion, however, must be understood within the political processes of national integration, as those with the most to gain by asserting their Frenchness were often the most vulnerable. The Lorraine region of France donated disproportionately to the victims of Fort-de-France and Port-Louis, because they saw this action as their opportunity to put questions of their loyalty to rest. Moreover, many within

France's traditional borders faced similar issues when asking for aid from the national government, pointing to the importance of considering both race and class in any discussion of the political and social divisions of fin-de-siècle France. The plight of Saint-Étienne's miners makes it clear that the issue of national integration was not strictly a colonial issue. Whether fires in the West Indian colonies or a mine collapse at home, France was dealing with a disenfranchised citizenry seeking a political voice and social welfare. And yet ever looming in the background was the importance of monocrops from these at-risk regions—whether sugar or coal—to the national interest.

3

The Calculus of Disaster

Sugar and the Hurricane of 18 August 1891

Famous Antillean writers such as Daniel Maximin and Patrick Chamoiseau have described life in the Caribbean as shaped by the environment: the tropical sun, cyclonic winds, and torrential downpours have had very real consequences for Caribbean life and society. Not only did the yearly rhythm of hurricanes shape life on the islands, but it also influenced the islands' political and economic development. French officials at the turn of the century viewed the Antilles through the lens of natural disasters, seeing a foreign tropical environment that perpetually threatened French civilization in the Caribbean. Moreover, the French legislature predominantly focused on economic extraction, describing the effects of natural catastrophes in terms of lost harvests and damage to public infrastructure, all the while trumpeting the extension of French citizenship to those living there.

The Antilles' position as more than colonies but not quite departments, as well as French officials' erroneous conception of them as colonies of settlement, created a tension between the realities of economic investment and the ideals of cultural and political incorporation. To the chagrin of assimilationist politicians fighting for Antillean political rights, the islands' Frenchness hinged on their economic utility. Tabulating data with respect to the islands' natural environment and monocultural economy, officials subjected them to financial profit-and-loss analyses and economic valuations as they quantified human suffering in charts, graphs, and tables. Numbers mattered in the nineteenth century, when the advent of censuses and statistical measuring encouraged officials to comprehend their world through faceless numbers.[1] In the case of the Caribbean, it permitted the French state to translate centuries of exploitation and racism into a seemingly more benign language of financial feasibility, sound investments, and economic measurement.

The tension between economic measurement and political ideology came to a head in 1891 in the aftermath of the largest hurricane to hit Martinique in several generations. The hurricane came on 18 August, one year after the 1890 fires when the capital city was still in the process of being rebuilt, and killed seven hundred people.[2] While it was nowhere near as deadly as the Great Hurricane of 1780—the deadliest hurricane in recorded history, which killed around twenty-two thousand people throughout the Atlantic coastal region, with at least seven thousand deaths on Martinique alone—or even the hurricane of 1813, which killed three thousand people across the Caribbean—the 1891 hurricane was the forty-fourth most deadly Atlantic hurricane in the period from 1492 to 1996.[3] It concentrated its fury almost exclusively on Martinique, and the island suffered more than five hundred deaths and two thousand wounded.[4] Combined with the destruction from the year prior, the island's distress was overwhelming. One contemporary observed that "the shock [on the night of the hurricane] was such that most women who were pregnant gave birth to stillborns."[5] While likely an exaggeration, this contemporary's assertion nevertheless elucidates the truly strong emotional and physical ordeal experienced by Martinique's population—an ordeal that did not end once the storm had passed. The hurricane continued to claim victims over the following months: from 18 August to 31 December 1891, 1,120 people died as a consequence of the cyclone, largely due to poor hygienic conditions.[6]

With the amount of damage to the economy taken into account, the 1891 hurricane caused more devastation spread more widely on Martinique than the 1890 fire. However devastating the fire, damage had been contained in Martinique's administrative capital. Most important to French officials, who by this point had begun to feel disheartened by what seemed to be an endless supply of Caribbean catastrophes, the hurricane had much farther-reaching consequences for the island's plantation economy. At the opening of the extraordinary session of Martinique's General Council, the minister of the interior focused on the economic toll of the storm, exclaiming that "prosperous days before, [Martinique] is now more beaten down, more ruined than at any other time in its history."[7] In the words of Martinique's governor, "Since 1817, we haven't had a disaster so lamentable."[8]

The previous year's fire amplified the relative damage and sense of danger the hurricane had caused. In the island's capital, a tornado had torn through the city's recently rebuilt urban landscape, causing over four million francs in damage to Fort-de-France alone.[9] And in the days following the hurricane, the undersecretary of the colonies cabled Martinique's governor, Delphino Moracchini—a Corsican-borne career functionary who had served as the organizer of the 1890 relief campaign under Governor Germain Casse—to inquire whether any funds and foodstuffs remained from the previous year's relief campaign.[10] In response, the governor requested that the central government send as much flour, salted cod, dried legumes, potatoes, and salted meats as possible, for of the 1.7 million francs raised for relief after the 1890 fire, only seventy-five thousand francs remained.[11] In fact, by the end of 1891, the General Council of Martinique had voted to use some of the money received for hurricane relief to instead rebuild some of the buildings that had been destroyed in the 1890 fire, and to use the "relief measures" from the 1891 hurricane to assist the fire victims who were still struggling.[12] Facing financial instability, the government requested a prorogation of all debts for three months, and the undersecretary tried to arrange a one-million-franc loan to keep the colony solvent, though the finance minister summarily denied both measures.[13] In short, the 1891 hurricane had put the island under water literally as well as figuratively.

Instead of providing a million-franc loan and suspending the colony's debt, the central government once again drew upon the patriotism of the French population and international sympathy to come to the aid of Martinique. Over the next few months, workers' organizations, Martinique's local government, the central French government, concerned individuals, and particularly other Caribbean islands all donated to help the 1891 hurricane victims. By December 1891, over 791,000 francs in financial and in-kind assistance had been provided "in favor of the victims of the Cyclone of 18 August."[14]

Yet, while an outpouring of public support and an overt—if at times, qualified—display of shared compatriotism between metropolitan France and its "colony of citizens" in the Antilles had met the 1890 fire, economic concerns constrained relief efforts and undercut aid distributions after the hurricane, despite the damage being far more widespread. Though the rank and file in France heeded the call for compatriotism once more, and the international community opened its wallets in sympathy once again, disaster fatigue had set in among French officials who saw all the work rebuilding Fort-de-France literally washed away overnight. Therefore, in contrast to the previous year's fire-relief campaigns, the hurricane inspired an economic calculus that French officials couched in racially coded terminology and phrases, all the while disregarding the history of slavery that had shaped Martinique's monocultural economy and placed it in such a financially vulnerable position. As the French government took stock of the 1891 hurricane, its conceptualization of Martinique's "Frenchness" and the island's belongingness suggested the Martiniquais were responsible for the very socioeconomic circumstances that French colonialism had helped to create.

For instance, just days after the hurricane, Martinique's appointed governor invoked the ideals of French ancestry in a press release. Moracchini glossed over the island's complicated history of plantation slavery, saying Martiniquais should "imitate our ancestors who never new discouragement," suggesting Martiniquais should emulate either "the Gauls" or the founders of the French republic. Beyond merely imposing an inaccurate historical narrative onto the island, Moracchini's address implied that Martinique's lazy black workers were not doing enough to rebuild and that they needed to be more "Gallic" or French in their approach. Such a prejudice was held by many during the Third Republic who criticized the island's working class as plagued by an "incurable laziness."[15] Dating to the days before emancipation, this racist trope undermined slaves' bids for freedom by pinning the islands' profitability on their unfree status. Although abolitionist Victor Schoelcher had railed against such commonplace prejudices fifty years earlier, explaining that the black man "is lazy because his work is not paid, because he does not receive the fruit of his labors," they were given new life under the Third Republic as an explanation of the islands' declining economic relevance.[16]

Despite being devoid of any explicit references to race, therefore, the implication of Moracchini's address, effectively an exhortation to work, was not lost on contemporaries. In response, the island's republican paper, *Les Colonies*, pointed out that the ancestors of the Martiniquais were not Gauls but hardworking slaves who had rebuilt the island following major hurricanes in 1723, 1724, 1756, 1758, 1766, 1779, 1786, and 1788 by force. These slaves had become republicans themselves, despite lacking a Gallic ancestry, and would rebuild the island again, but not under duress. Now that slavery had been abolished, the free market established in the colony, and a class of free and independent workers had been created, Martinique's laborers would work hard to recover, but like everyone else in France, they would do so for pay and could not, as citizens, be forced to work without compensation. Therefore, the republican mouthpiece on the island contended that the French government needed to put its money where its mouth was and inject capital into Martinique to improve laborers' employment prospects, lest class warfare threaten the stability of the island. Having merged the legacy of slavery with demands for financial assistance from the central government, *Les Colonies* invoked the Frenchness of Martinique in its turn, asserting that at this juncture it was all the more important that the metropole not "leave its oldest colonies in the Antilles to perish—these old colonies, so devoted and patriotic, that form in reality French departments on the American continent."[17]

The Howling Wind: The Events of 18 August 1891

Around 6 p.m. on 18 August 1891, the most powerful hurricane to hit the French Antilles in over a century made landfall on the eastern side of the island of Martinique. The hurricane was compact, powerful, and fast, crossing the island's seventy kilometers in a matter of hours. The tempest had picked up speed as it strengthened over the warm waters of the Caribbean, and Martinique lay in its direct path, receiving the brunt of the storm's most powerful winds along what meteorologists call the storm's eye-wall. The destruction was overwhelming. Counting on the "generosity [of the] Parliament and *concitoyens* [of the] *mere-patrie*," the governor of Martinique telegraphed the colonial undersecretary:

> Colony ravaged; towns completely destroyed; plantations[18] annihilated; sugar cane, colonial services ravaged, foodstuffs disappeared; factories half-demolished; village, rural buildings razed; 50 million in losses; population without respite, without food; famine menaces; aid urgently needed, in food and in money.[19]

While it is impossible to know the exact strength of the hurricane, eye-witness accounts and contemporary measurements suggest that the storm was small in diameter but intense. Modern meteorologists since 1969 have rated hurricanes and their damage potential according to the Saffir-Simpson hurricane scale, which ranks hurricanes on a scale of one to five.[20] They consider anything category three or above to be a major hurricane due to its potential for substantial property damage and the risk of a significant loss of life. The scale's damage estimates are not linear, as the damage potential of a major hurricane is exponentially greater than that of a minor one. In fact, while only accounting for 24 percent of yearly land-falling storms from 1900 to 2005, major hurricanes category three and above caused roughly 85 percent of all hurricane damage in the United States.[21]

The reported barometric pressure in Fort-de-France at the time of the storm's landfall was 28.35 inches (720 millimeters) of mercury, and the pressure at the eye of the storm had dropped to 27.95 inHg (710 mmHg).[22] According to the Saffir-Simpson scale as well as modern meteorological data, the storm was at least a category-three hurricane with sustained winds of 111 to 129 miles per hour, and may have been a category-four storm, with sustained winds of 130 to 156 miles per hour. The Saffir-Simpson scale states that a category-three hurricane causes "devastating" damage to well-built homes constructed according to twenty-first-century standards. The scale rates a category-four hurricane as causing "catastrophic" damage, with large numbers of buildings sustaining severe structural damage or being destroyed.[23] Thus, the 1891 hurricane certainly caused devastating damage; it was very likely catastrophic.

A great deal of the damage caused by hurricanes comes from the storm surge, or the difference between the normal tide and the storm's tide. In other words, the storm surge is the amount by which the sea level rises as the hurricane makes landfall, and it depends on the hurricane's wind speed, among other factors like its forward speed and heading with respect to the shoreline. Although the storm's small diameter mitigated the likely damage—storms with a larger surface area produce more significant storm surges—the island's topography made it ripe for flooding. With the copious rainfall that accompanies hurricanes, flooding typically becomes concentrated in the low-lying areas, and therefore the shape and composition of the shoreline largely determines flooding. Though Martinique is mountainous, much of its farmland and urban space is in low-lying coastal areas, ravines, and valleys. As the runoff from the higher altitudes collected in areas of lower elevation, the hurricane's rainfall and storm surge utterly destroyed Martinique's urban and agricultural landscape. As an observer of the 1891 hurricane remarked to the Chamber of Deputies, during that "horrible night" of 18 August, "water penetrated everywhere, flooding everything."[24]

Stone or concrete would have afforded some protection against gale-force winds, but the earthquake-tolerant wood homes popular in the nineteenth-century Caribbean had little chance against the hurricane. Weathering by the unforgiving Caribbean elements compounded the problem. While the walls of most structures remained, the roofs were often lost and the interior destroyed.[25] On the one hand, the undulating roofs of the island's urban structures made with corrugated steel or overlapping tiles were quite susceptible to uplift from the pressure differential caused in gale-force winds, easily blowing off and leaving the interior exposed. On the other hand, the homes of the island's rural peasantry had roofs made from cane stalks, which had no hope of withstanding sustained winds. Few urban dwellings remained intact, and almost none of the island's many rural and isolated dwellings could withstand the hurricane.[26] In the countryside where the homes had weak foundations and poor construction, several homes completely inverted, while others rolled through the fields spurred along by the winds.[27]

In correspondence to table 4, "Hurricane damage by commune, 1891," map 5 shows the distribution of damage across the island normalized by population. Communes that sustained less damage per capita are shaded a lighter color than those with heavier losses. By cross-checking eyewitness reports with a geospatial map of the damage sustained from the hurricane, we can estimate the storm's path. The hurricane made landfall at the communes of La Trinité and Le Robert. Over the course of approximately three hours, with a brief twenty-minute calm as the storm's eye passed, the hurricane successively destroyed the communes of Gros-Morne, Le Lamentin, Le François, Saint-Joseph, and Fort-de-France on its way westward. Reports state that Saint-Joseph, Duclos, Le Vauclin, and Gros-Morne suffered total devastation.[28] Those areas with higher populations, such as Le Robert and Le François, and those with large swaths of low-lying and beachfront dwellings,

TABLE 4. *Hurricane damage by commune, 1891*

COMMUNE	FRANCS
Saint-Pierre	12,191,800
Le Lamentin	6,569,658
Le François	5,665,200
Le Robert	5,407,100
Fort-de-France	4,392,320
La Trinité	4,166,756
Gros-Morne	2,903,266
Le Marin	2,658,720
Le Vauclin	2,386,000
Le Morne-Rouge	2,357,000

Source: Based on the reports from communal commissions, September 1891, FM SG MAR 72, d. 581, ANOM.

like Saint-Luce and Le Marin, felt the brunt of the storm. Halted by the heights of Mount Pelée, the hurricane paused as its powerful winds batted the communes in the valley below: Saint-Pierre took the heaviest damage on the island, both overall and per capita, because the heavily populated city sat directly under the hurricane as it perched itself on Pelée's southern slopes. Meanwhile, the mountain shielded the communes of Le Marigot, Lorrain, Basse-Pointe, and Macouba on its far side. The storm then headed westward from Saint-Pierre, leaving Martinique and continuing its march through the Caribbean.

All told, the storm ruined countless cash and subsistence crops, and early reports warned of an oncoming famine.[29] For example, the cacao plantations of Le Precheur, as well as the cacao and coffee plantations and subsistence farms of Le Vauclin that had existed for generations, were totally leveled. The sea level rose substantially, hammering ships docked at Saint-Pierre's port and completely flooding the commune of Le Robert. Schools, churches, city halls, roads, bridges—that is, public infrastructure of all kinds—were

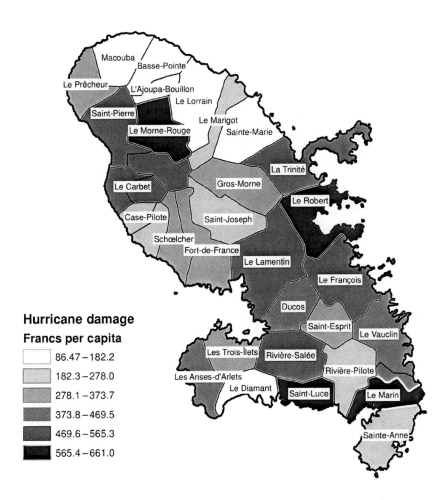

Hurricane damage
Francs per capita

- 86.47 – 182.2
- 182.3 – 278.0
- 278.1 – 373.7
- 373.8 – 469.5
- 469.6 – 565.3
- 565.4 – 661.0

MAP 5. **Total hurricane damage in Martinique by commune, 1891**
Normalized per capita with six equal interval breaks. Map created in
ArcGIS. Shape file of Administrative Communes: The GADM Database
of Global Administrative Areas, version 2, January 2012. Retrieved 12
December 2012 at http://www.gadm.org/. The 1891 population figures are
estimated from two censuses: Lanessan, *L'expansion colonial*, 773; *Annuaire
de la Martinique: 1901*, 142–45.

completely obliterated in under three hours. Lines of communications between Fort-de-France and the rest of the island, including Saint-Pierre, were interrupted, and the town of Le Lamentin, which sits at sea level, was completely destroyed. In Le Morne-Rouge, where picturesque and isolated homes dotted the mountainous landscape of the slopes of Mount Pelée, the tempest destroyed every single "vacation villa" of Saint-Pierre's wealthy elite. Because the destruction was limited to Martinique, commerce minister Jules Roche and finance minister Maurice Rouvier observed that "it seems to have concentrated and exhausted on our unfortunate colony all the rage and destruction that nature holds in reserve."[30]

The government of Martinique—left insolvent by the previous year's fire, initial relief efforts, and the complete destruction of its sugar crop—requested a prorogation of all public debts by three months immediately following the hurricane. The French minister of finances, who himself admitted that the hurricane was one of the "most gruesome in its effects . . . ever unleashed on the sea of the Antilles," denied the request, citing the need for a special law passed by the National Assembly to allow the measure.[31] The ministry also denied a follow-up request for a loan of one million francs, made on behalf of Martinique by Undersecretary Étienne, on similar grounds. The minister of finances argued the specter of human suffering and the nobility of relief did not obviate the need for the National Assembly to deliberate about the loan and pass it as a budgetary law.[32] In other words, the state needed time to ensure that the terms of the loan would permit a timely financial return and that the colony would not default on its debt. Ultimately, the Chamber of Deputies did provide one hundred thousand francs in immediate assistance to supplement the remaining seventy-five thousand francs from the 1890 fire relief, levied from the state's reserve funds.[33] However, in light of the devastating consequences of the storm and the longer legacy of environmental destruction, as well as the state's reluctance to embroil its finances in Martinique's economic recovery, this sum was far from enough to bring the island out of insolvency. With disaster fatigue setting in amidst a collapsing sugar economy, as Martinique scrambled to provide the state with damage estimates that would justify the requisite budgetary laws to alleviate the island's fiscal troubles, France's central government began to question whether the juice was worth the squeeze.

The Road to Economic Recovery: A Calculus of
Human Suffering and Colonial Belonging

Randomly selecting members from among its assembly, the General Council of Martinique formed a commission the day after the hurricane to estimate the losses it caused. After an investigation, which Martinique's Senator Vincent Allègre described as "meticulous," the General Council calculated that the storm caused nearly eighty-nine million francs' worth of damage. The average yearly wage for a French worker in the metropole during the 1890s was 1,080 francs, paid at 35 centimes per hour, making the storm's costs equivalent to the yearly wages of approximately 82,000 metropolitan workers.[34] Martinique's entire male population likely numbered around 82,000, and its working population earned less than its metropolitan counterparts. Sugar workers, for instance, earned between 1.50 francs and 2 francs per day in 1884, while miners earned about 3.8 francs per day.[35] To put it simply, the storm had brought the island's economy to a grinding halt. But the eighty-nine-million-franc estimate was seen as extreme by the Parisian business elite and the central government. On 25 August, the governor's minister of the interior, Maurice Fawtier, created the "Central Aid Commission" to handle all food and monetary assistance, national and foreign, to Martinique's population. Governor Moracchini presided over this commission, while Carméné, Martinique's bishop, and Fawtier carried out its day-to-day tasks, which included enumerating the hurricane damages in greater detail than the initial commission had. On 5 September it solicited evaluations of communal damage and individual losses, as well as substantiation from each local commune. The minister of the interior asked communes to detail the following losses in francs: colonial works, roads, bridges, and buildings; communal works, roads, and buildings; factories; homes and plantation dwellings outside towns; individual homes in the towns; home furnishings and other such property; merchandise; sugar harvests as a percentage loss based on annual yields; food harvests, and all others; and finally, total losses of all other sorts.[36]

Each commune created a local commission consisting of the mayor, the director of the civil engineering service, and the receiver-general (a tax official) following protocols that had been established for earlier natural disasters, such as the 1875 hurricane.[37] Supplementing property evaluations from the Banque Coloniale, the commission surveyed the towns and countryside; visited agricultural fields and subsistence plots; and consulted administrative and financial documents to arrive at their figures. Inhabitants of the various communes were also encouraged to come forward to report their own losses, which delegates of the commission then verified by surveying the damage for themselves. The commission reserved editorial control and lowered or raised the figures as they saw fit.[38] Most of the reported losses were ruined harvests of sugar, tafia (a cheap rum consumed locally), and foodstuffs, as well as damage to plantations and factory equipment. The communes also reported the loss of homes and public infrastructure (roads, bridges, and municipal buildings), but commercial casualties largely overshadowed these losses in terms of the attention commanded in the official reports.[39]

Faced with the lack of food, water, and shelter, the Central Aid Commission set about distributing foodstuffs and supplies to the populace, using the government's advance and the remaining 1890 fire-relief funds. Due to the damage to the island's infrastructure, as well as the virtually complete destruction of the island's shipping capacity, the commissioners looked to neighboring islands, such as Saint Lucia and Guadeloupe, to provide supplies. But the storm and a protracted economic downturn had limited the capacity of local islands to provide aid, particularly in Guadeloupe, where the collapsing sugar market had left many destitute. When the governor of Guadeloupe pledged fifty thousand francs in food aid to Martinique's victims, Guadeloupe's irritated labor class asked, "Where are we going to find 50,000 francs' worth of food? Who has that? Our markets are empty; our boutiques, our stores are poor. Our fields no longer produce anything."[40] While the local islands could not provide substantial financial and material aid, they could provide stop-gap services such as shipping. Therefore, the commission ceded shipping rights to foreign governments to get food to the worst-afflicted areas. The hungry population needed food, so the commission resolved to secure foodstuffs, some of which they distributed free to the designated needy. They also distributed money and sold foodstuffs to the general population at a fair price. They determined that if local vendors were suspected of price gouging, municipal stores would be set up as an alternative.[41] Local mayors were tasked with distributing both the food and the funds, though they found their role in bureaucratic oversight a burden on their local personnel and budgets.[42] Once the reports came in from the local commissions by the end of September, the governor believed that food aid was under control and turned his attention to repairing the island's infrastructure, particularly that involved in agricultural output.[43]

The impact of the storm on the economy was of major concern not only to the business elite on the island but also to the laborers they employed. The scope of the disaster necessitated a substantial rebuilding effort, a fact not lost on the socialists of Martinique's sister island of Guadeloupe. The socialist newspaper *Le Peuple* called on workers to come to the aid of Martinique, not through finances—the workers were themselves destitute—but through their labor: "Let's go, therefore, workers! En route! To Martinique! There is the work you need. Go there, therefore, and you will have paid your part of the common debt of charity for which we are all creditors to one another."[44] While the gesture was largely symbolic and there is little evidence that Guadeloupean workers did in fact travel to Martinique to help rebuild, the symbolism highlighted the human misery and economic despair in the minds of the working and capitaled classes alike. For the workers, employment was a result of the catastrophe. For the plantation owners, sugar production would get back on track. The initial press reports, ministerial letters, administrative circulars, and communal reports emphasized the inundation of sugar plantations and the destruction of fruit orchards, as well as the destruction of rum distilleries, sugar refineries, and shipping ports, over the more human consequences of lost homes and ruined subsistence crops, by and large. The images that accompanied the news reports (figure 16) as well as the reports themselves reveal this preoccupation. The conservative, *béké*-dominated paper, *Les Antilles*, reported the following on its front page just days after the hurricane, when people were still without food, water, or shelter:

> As for the large sugar mills and distilleries that are the powerful lever of our agricultural production—the instrument without which our agriculture would be sterilized—they are deeply affected, some completely destroyed. We know the huge capital allocated to these large industrial facilities—capital exceeding 24 million francs. A small part of that capital has been annihilated, and the rest has been immobilized until the power plants can be restarted after painful repairs.[45]

LE CYCLONE DE LA MARTINIQUE. — Des navires échouent au mouillage de l'Anse. (Page 335, col. 2.)

LE CYCLONE DE LA MARTINIQUE. — Ruines de l'usine Dillon, près de Fort-de-France. (Page 335, col. 1.)

FIG. 16. **Damage following the 1891 hurricane**

Shipping was a major concern after the hurricane, but so was humanitarian relief to the populace. Images accompanying news reports, however, typically focused on the commercial rather than human losses. B. Guliet, "Le Cyclone de la Martinique," *Journal des Voyages et des aventures de terre et de mer*, no. 750 (22 November 1890), 335.

Though many viewed the hurricane through the lens of human suffering, many others saw it in terms of realpolitik. As a writer for the colonial paper, the *Journal des Voyages*, wrote, "with the local resources lacking, there is no doubt that the metropole will come to the aid of this old colony so cruelly afflicted, in order to permit it to [once again] fulfill its strategic function in the Atlantic."[46] Since Martinique served as an important entrepôt in the Caribbean with a nontrivial sugar industry, the local press shared this faith and repeatedly asserted its belief that the French government would come to the aid of "one of its most loyal children" if for no other reason than to safeguard the sugar industry.

While the business elite were concerned about lost capital and the damage done to the sugar harvest, the island's workers were concerned about lost wages, property damage, and where their next meal might come from. In the aftermath of the hurricane, the island's working class experienced a heightened concern about competition in the labor market, since the diminished sugar harvest offered few jobs, and they expressed a growing animosity toward foreign workers from the neighboring British West Indies as well as toward indentured servants. Following emancipation, plantation owners imported approximately 25,700 indentured servants from South Asia to Martinique, particularly to keep labor costs low and black laborers disenfranchised.[47] As one observer remarked in 1886, "without immigration, the plantation owner is at the mercy of the blacks, and a single strike of a few weeks could ruin a plantation."[48] With immigration, however, plantation owners could sidestep laborers' agitation by supplementing the workforce with indentured servants under low-cost, mandatory contracts. Given that many of these workers had signed labor contracts before the hurricane struck and therefore were already part of the job market pool, the resentment was based not strictly on newfound competition after the hurricane but on longer-term labor shortages, xenophobia, and a postcatastrophe closing of the ranks on those whom laborers saw as belonging in Martinique.[49]

Tensions reached a high point as the local government began trying to take stock of the damage that the press had deemed "incalculable." While the local General Council had reported damages totaling almost eighty-nine million francs to the central French government, Governor Moracchini's Central Aid Commission calculated only seventy-two million francs based on the reports of the local communal administrations. Outraged, Senator Allègre complained to the undersecretary of the colonies and began petitioning the Chamber of Deputies. The nearly seventeen-million-franc difference between the cabinet and the General Council reflected the General Council's inclusion of the impact of the hurricane on successive harvest seasons in its estimate. The gubernatorial commission had accounted for only the impact on the immediate growing season, perhaps because the metropolitan officials did not understand that planters used cane stubs left from the previous year's harvest to plant the next. The disputes over the damage estimations did not end there. The governor himself guessed that there was only thirty-five to forty million francs' worth of damage, much lower than either the estimates by the General Council or the local communes. This tension strained relations between the island's elected representatives and the national leadership, and local legislators feared that this number would continue to fall.

Local legislators proved prescient. By late January 1892, the figure dropped further, to fifty million francs, following an administrative report by colonial inspectors sent to Martinique to look into the impact of the hurricane on sugar harvests, the living conditions of the population, and the overall property and structural damage caused by the hurricane. Led by Émile Chaudié, a long-time colonial administrator who would eventually become the first governor general of West Africa in 1895, the investigatory commission traveled the island, retraced the steps of the local commissions, and cross-checked figures from financial annuaries and property evaluations. According to investigators, the earlier reports by the local communes could not be trusted: they were "exaggerated" and "fanciful," and, in the case of the communes of Le Francois, Le Vauclin, Sainte-Marie, and Saint-Esprit, guesstimates of the total damage submitted in lieu of in-person inspections and concrete valuations.[50] Though the investigators did see the situation as desperate, they nevertheless believed that emotion had driven the initial estimates, and they scrutinized every expense and aspect of the island's relief effort. They could not understand why each commune reported wildly different amounts of damage, because all had been equally decimated, and each commune's property should have roughly the same value.

One aspect of the relief campaign that was subjected to the colonial investigator's scrutiny was the arrival of food aid. In the month follow-

TABLE 5. *Enumerated hurricane damages from Martinique's General Council, 1891*

ENUMERATED DAMAGES	COST (IN FRANCS)
40 percent of a harvest of 40,000 tons of sugar and 10 million liters of alcohol	8,400,000
Loss of the harvest of 1893 affected by the destruction of the cane	5,000,000
Food-producing habitations (plantations) employing 70,000 people at 200 francs per person	15,000,000
Buildings of 540 sugar establishments	13,500,000
Buildings and machinery of 25 factories	2,500,000
Damage to the ceramic industry	400,000
Industrial, commercial, property, and national (direct and indirect costs)	44,000,000
Total	**88,800,000**

Source: Compiled by Special Commission, Saint-Félix, *Rapport de la Commission spéciale du Conseil Général sur le cyclone du 18 août 1891*, FM SG MAR 72, d.581, ANOM.

ing the hurricane, food assistance arrived from Barbados (15,135 francs), Saint Lucia (12,791 francs), Guadeloupe (52,178 francs), and metropolitan France (158,162 francs). Since so much of Martinique's food crop had been destroyed, local officials argued that sustained foreign assistance was necessary. Consequently, Saint-Pierre and Fort-de-France requested an additional 1.8 million francs' worth of food from the central government. But colonial investigators claimed that the food aid already received—a total of 238,266 francs—should have sufficed to feed the island until it could sustain itself, and that communal administrators had given food to the capable as well as the needy to secure their own reelection. Inspector Chaudié criticized the island's laborers for working the system, traveling great distances to the island's urban centers to receive aid that they did not really need. He accused them of self-interest, sloth, and greed, because the state assistance was worth more than their salaries. Though he refrained from referring to

TABLE 6. *Enumerated hurricane damages from gubernatorial Central Aid Commission, 1891*

LOSSES TO	COST (IN FRANCS)
Colony	854,507
Communes	2,797,110
Factories	4,644,650
Rural homes and estates	19,443,086
Urban homes	15,534,475.5
Property/furnishings	6,254,514.5
Merchandise	2,080,397
Cane harvest	10,315,833
Food harvest and orchards	10,100,858
Total	**72,025,431**

Source: Letter from governor of Martinique Moracchini to undersecretary of the colonies, 30 September 1891, FM SG MAR 72, d.581, ANOM.

the laborers' race, Chaudié leveraged age-old stereotypes against the islands' black laboring class, wrapping them in an economic justification centered on salary-to-assistance ratios, to justify lowering the amount of state aid.

The Central Aid Commission echoed Chaudié's concern about the misuse of materials—or the "mob of abuse in the Communes," in the words of Bishop Carméné—as well as the waste that accompanied the relief effort's lack of organization. To combat the alleged abuse by those who "do not really need it," the Central Aid Commission demanded the local commissions create registers with the names of the neediest, which it would have to approve prior to the distribution of aid. Though the governor insisted that the secular local commissions distribute aid, it was decided that religious charity institutions would verify and distribute the aid only to those named on the approved list.[51] But the Central Aid Commission experienced extreme difficulties coordinating the relief effort with the various mayors on the island, many of whom declined to cooperate, and the Commission's efforts were poorly organized. In a deposition to investigator Chaudié, the mayor of Gros-Morne admitted to having received but ignored the instructions from the island's minister of the interior, refusing to restrict access to foodstuffs to only those designated as the "most needy."[52] Instead, the mayor gave food to anyone who presented himself at the town hall, determining how much to give by the individual's outward appearance of poverty. Officials charged him with favoring his own daughter, in the process, and although he was cleared, the charge reflects the distrust common at the time. It also highlights the widening divide between locally elected officials, most of whom were people of color, and the appointed colonial officials performing the evaluations. In fact, several other mayors never even convened their local commissions, completely flouting the regulations imposed by the metropole, while the commissions of other towns remained deadlocked in deciding how to apportion the aid to their constituents and whether to follow the state's instructions.[53] Compounding the lack of adherence to the directives, communication between the central and local commissions repeatedly broke down. For instance, the town of Le François continued to receive food assistance long after the mayor had requested that it cease.[54]

After reviewing the manner in which aid was distributed, the colonial investigators reiterated the Central Aid Commission's concerns about assistance going to those who do not "merit" it, and they even characterized the lack of coordination as a form of malfeasance. Claiming that such "abuse and waste" constituted "economic and social peril" to the "great detriment of the interests of the treasury," inspector Chaudié argued that "thinking the hurricane brought famine" constituted "a grave error." Investigators insisted that only those whom the cyclone left with "neither bed, nor linens, nor rags" merited assistance, while all others had "lost nothing but their jewels" and would "get over it, like those who never had any."[55] Although Chaudié profoundly distrusted the hurricane victims and saw many of them, particularly men of working age, as having cried wolf to obtain state funds and sit back on their haunches, he did criticize the Central Aid Commission for dragging its feet in distributing the funds and supplies to those he saw as truly needy: the sick, old, and utterly destitute.[56]

In general, however, the inspectors were eager to set aside their own sympathy in the interest of fiscal accountability. Though they did underscore the suffering of the population in their report to the colonial undersecretary, they nonetheless insisted that estimates of damage were elevated. Since poor populations have little to begin with, their losses do not represent high financial stakes. Moreover, the lure of financial assistance promoted abuse, waste, and laziness—all racist criticisms from a bygone error, though absent of explicit reference to race and heralded in the name of equity. Ultimately, the investigators saw the suffering of their Martiniquais compatriots in financial terms—that is, as part of what Chaudié called an "evaluative work that is not personal, but based on statistical givens"—and concluded that the assistance had heretofore been a poor investment. Pointing to the uncultivated land and abandoned dwellings around La Pagerie and Les Palmistes, the investigators argued that "the losses caused by the hurricane cannot include the value of structures that have none."[57] Moreover, given that public buildings had already sustained damage in Fort-de-France for reasons other than the hurricane (i.e., the previous year's fire, as well as neglect), the official assessment of hurricane losses should not include those damages (even though some of the funds dedicated for hurricane relief had initially been designated for fire relief), inspectors claimed. They insisted that the damage estimates should not reflect the costs necessary to completely renovate the damaged structures and homes, restoring them to a like-new condition but rather to return them to their—in their eyes—often dilapidated state prior to the arrival of the hurricane. In all, they cut the damage estimates nearly in half, lowering the overall property damage of urban homes from nearly 15.5 million francs to 8.4 million francs.

Laden with implicit racism and classism that denigrated the island's class of black laborers, the investigators' skeptical and miserly report superseded both the damage estimates by the General Council and those proposed by the local communes, and the calculations done by the investigators were not only precise but also manufactured to lower the damage estimates.[58] For instance, Chaudié figured that since the costs of recently imported zinc, tiles, and other roofing materials amounted to only six hundred thousand francs, the estimates of structural damage in Saint-Pierre of 2.4 million francs were felonious. Slashing the original estimates by as much as 75 percent in some cases—such as the loss of merchandise in Gros-Morne, a town that inves-

TABLE 7. *Reported hurricane damages from gubernatorial Central Aid Commission, 1891 (estimated)*

LOSSES TO	FRANCS
Colonial roads, bridges, and buildings	854,507
Communal roads, bridges, and buildings	2,797,110
Factories	4,644,650
Rural homes and estates	19,443,086
Urban homes	15,534,475.5
Property/furnishings	6,254,514.5
Merchandise	2,080,397
Cane harvests	10,315,833
Other agriculture (food/orchard)	10,100,858
Total	**72,025,431**

Source: Letter from governor of Martinique Moracchini to undersecretary of the colonies, 30 September 1891, FM SG MAR 72, d.581, ANOM.

tigators had identified as one of the most afflicted by the hurricane—the investigators eventually lowered their estimate even further, to forty-three million francs, its final resting place.

While the investigators claimed to touch the estimations of the losses felt by sugar cane growers and manufacturers "with the most extreme reserve" and insisted on the urgency of getting the sugar factories running as soon as possible, they nevertheless slashed the local estimates in half. Though Chaudié added a million-franc "coefficient" in the budget for the dashed expectations of an exceptionally bountiful harvest, the inspectors' valuation paled in comparison to that of local sugar growers. In addition to lowering the losses felt by big industry, the investigators made extensive cuts across the board: homes, communal structures, colonial infrastructure, and personal and public property.

During their inquiry into the use of relief funds following the 1891 hurricane, the investigators even returned to the distribution of food and

TABLE 8. *Accepted hurricane damages from colonial investigators, 1891*

LOSSES TO	FRANCS
Colonial roads, bridges, and buildings	618,038
Communal roads, bridges, and buildings	2,123,500
Factories	3,146,700
Rural homes and estates	12,931,000
Urban homes	8,467,550
Property/furnishings	3,619,000
Merchandise	1,904,500
Cane harvests	5,691,915
Other agriculture (food/orchard)	4,754,800
Total	**43,261,000**

Source: *Annales de la Chambre des Députés* 38:76–77; M. Chautemps, Report No. 2125, FM SG MAR 72, d.582, ANOM.

monetary relief after the 1890 fire, looking for a long history of wasted funds and foodstuffs. The mayor of Fort-de-France, Osman Duquesnay, vociferously denied such allegations, pointing to the investigatory commission that cleared his name in December 1890. However, colonial inspector Blanchard concluded in his report of February 1892 that municipal officials wantonly distributed the public monetary and in-kind assistance with a "general tendency to be ignorant of the individual character of the charitable acts" and to dole out assistance to any "beggar" who presented himself. In large part, the antagonism toward Duquesnay owed to the fact that he was himself a mulatto and his municipal government was staffed by people of color, whom colonial administrators did not trust. Frustrated with the general lack of accountability, Blanchard asserted that municipal and military authorities refused to take responsibility for the distribution of donated foodstuffs and supplies, and that these supplies were sold on the black market in some cases.[59]

In the aftermath of the 1891 hurricane, investigators from the colonial undersecretary's office reevaluated the efficacy and honesty of the distribution of aid by the municipal government of Fort-de-France and, as a result, concluded that national aid from the central government should not come in the form of direct monetary or in-kind relief. They believed that the local government, made up of citizens of color, could not be entrusted with direct funds—though they never explained it in such terms—and that direct aid to the suffering would do little to get the economy back on track. Rather than thinking of the individual needy, therefore, authorities concerned themselves with economics in the abstract, deciding how they should intervene strategically to jump-start the crashing Martiniquais economy to help the hurricane's victims indirectly and thereby line the coffers of financiers in the metropole. For example, with regard to the sugar and tafia industry, the government used tax breaks to the planter class to revitalize the economy and thereby recuperate industrial losses, and colonial officials tied economic assistance to specific and quantifiable property damage. For instance, cocoa and coffee farmers would be compensated one franc for each destroyed tree that was six to eighteen months old.[60]

Overall, the investigators found that the hurricane caused the most harm to the islands' *cultivateurs* and small planters who worked subsistence and small cash-crop plots, as well as the urban population of the sick, old, and young. But Inspector Chaudié had little sympathy for the male and healthy. In his eyes, while the urban factory workers sustained heavy losses, they were part of a prosperous industry that paid them for their labor rather than the fruits of that labor, which in turn shielded them from the overall impact of the hurricane on their industry. In fact, he reasoned that their salary would double or even triple in the aftermath of the hurricane, because restoring the beleaguered sugar market would create a high demand for labor. In Chaudié's view, wage earners' suffering paled in comparison with that of small farmers—whom he romantically referred to as the "peasants of Martinique"—who had little to begin with, whose very survival depended on their daily toil, and whose crops of manioc, yams, taro, and fruits had been decimated.[61] Although tuberous plants like yams and manioc can withstand the uprooting gale-force winds of hurricanes far better than their aboveground counterparts, they remain particularly vulnerable to heavy rains that saturate the soil and lead to rot.[62] Tubers are also exceptionally susceptible to salt spray, which chemically burns the crops, and to being washed out by floods.[63] In the case of the 1891 hurricane, it is possible that the high rainfall and the subsistence plots' proximity to the ocean led to a combination of flooding, crop burn, and rot that decimated the harvest. In any case, following the hurricane, the price of manioc nearly doubled, straining the population's limited resources to find food.[64]

While the inspectors criticized doling out unneeded assistance to the urban or working poor, their rose-tinted view of the countryside encouraged them to provide direct assistance to the Martiniquais peasantry. Inspector Chaudié recommended that the Chamber of Deputies attribute a fixed sum of 150 francs for the estimated ten thousand owners of rural homes, while the governor's office estimated that ten thousand subsistence farmers should each receive fifty francs in direct aid (for a total of five hundred thousand francs) as well as a grant for 6 percent of their total losses of ten million francs (which would amount to six hundred thousand francs). The Chamber of Deputies accepted Chaudié's conclusion, resolving to distribute the bulk of its direct aid to the population (the *paysans* of Martinique, as he called them) and give to only the neediest urban populations.[65] For the neediest urbanites, Chaudié recommended that the chamber allocate an as yet undetermined indemnity for those "inhabitants of the villages and towns whom the hurricane left without shelter."[66]

Chaudié's awkward glorification of the so-called peasants of Martinique—completely incongruous with his thinly veiled prejudices against the black laboring population of the island—reflected a French drive to recast Martinique as a colony of settlement as opposed to a colony of extraction, perhaps in part to assuage republican guilt about the history of plantation slavery while at the same time being able to figure Martinique into the republican myth of assimilation. This motif—that of the poor, hard-working "small planter" from the countryside suffering at the hands of Mother Nature—not only figured prominently in the ministerial reports following the 1875 hurricane sixteen years prior but also typified a vision of rural Martinique as populated by willful migration and thereby overlooked the legacy of forced migration and unfree labor.[67] Though an Antillean sugar-growing peasantry did not exist in the classic sense of the term, contemporaries nevertheless uncritically and inaccurately applied the term to all black agricultural workers outside the islands' cities and larger villages.[68] As one historian wrote in 1904, "Blacks remain the base of the peasantry. They live in the countryside, in the prairie, as it's called."[69] They lived off the land and grew subsistence crops, as well as small cane crops sold to local sugar refineries, but did not become large-scale growers themselves.[70] Even though they spoke Creole and not French, republicans like Chaudié felt compelled to cast them as French peasants, perhaps because they inhabited rudimentary dwellings known as *cases-nègres* that differed little from those of the early colonists or perhaps because they were themselves sugar growers of color who seemed to belie the racism inherent to the plantation economy.[71] Even the Creole language was cast as peasant-like, as Louis Garaud had described the hybrid language as a form of French patois akin to that spoken by peasants in the metropole.[72] Moreover, colonial bureaucrats led by Paul Dislère at the École Coloniale, as well as cultural commentators like August Terrier and Albert Bouinais, had referred to the Antilles as the exemplars of French assimilation, as "settlement colonies" where the people were inherently French and their politics coincided with that of the metropole.[73] As historian Elizabeth Heath has shown, republican officials were ideologically drawn toward creating an economy centered on small-scale farmers in southern France as well as Martinique's sister island of Guadeloupe. Consequently republican officials saw in the Martiniquais *paysans* the potential for the small-owner agricultural class that they idealized in metropolitan agricultural schools during the Third Republic.[74]

The fact remained, however, that the French Antilles were not settlement colonies. Colonization had completely eradicated the islands' indigenous populations, supplanting them with forcibly migrated slaves. Frenchmen migrated to the Antilles not for settlement but to invest their money in slave economies of sugar, amassing fortunes from extracted resources and labor. This elision—the reconfiguring of Martinique as a settlement rather than an exploitive colony—permitted officials, in part, to look past their own participation in creating the problems that investigators now used as evidence against Martinique's local damage valuations. To some extent made obsolete by advances in beet sugar production, the plantations abandoned prior to the hurricane, such as La Pagerie, which Chaudié saw as valueless and thus excepted from the official damage valuations, bear testament to that exploitive past.

If Only We Were a Department: Martinique's Demand for Aid

In addition to debating the merits of direct versus indirect assistance, officials considered the impact of Martinique's status as "not quite" a department. Martinique's General Council foregrounded the quasi-metropolitan status of the island in its demand for national relief, arguing that while national support mitigates the distress of a department, a colony is typically completely on its own and must pay all its own expenses. Therefore, the Council argued that it behooved the government to grant Martinique national assistance, because the alternative would be to allow the island to collapse. The Council contended that "[f]or a French department struck as cruelly as Martinique, rebuilding would be impossible without the powerful and effective help called for by the governor. But for a colony, the state's help is that much more indispensable, not only to rebuild, but also to survive."[75] Faced with a budgetary deficit of 870,000 francs in 1891 and over one million francs in 1892, the colony demanded direct national aid and tax relief as if it were a department—arguing that Martinique should be a department—because the colony lacked the necessary money and credit to rebuild its devastated economy, referring to the Martiniquais as "175,000 Frenchmen."[76]

The discrepancy between the two relief commissions, as well as the fear of an ever-dropping damage estimate from the colonial investigators, was not lost on Martinique's Senator Allègre. In a letter to the undersecretary of the colonies, he argued that the inspectors—because they were born in mainland France rather than "in the province itself," that is, Martinique—could neither appreciate nor fully comprehend the losses experienced by Martinique's "energetic population who, in trying to lift itself up, will use up its last resources and count on the future as well as the goodwill of the mother country."[77] To underline the "desperate calls" of France's "unfortunate compatriots" and to express their dissatisfaction with the colonial investigation carried out by the undersecretary's office as well as the disparity between their estimates and those of the governor's office, members of Martinique's General Council signed on to Senator Allègre's letter to the colonial office of the Ministry of the Marine.

Both the Council and Allègre focused on the economic impact of the disaster, depicting financial recovery as the best path forward to restoring a sense of normalcy on the island. To this end, they demanded from the central government a tax exemption on Martiniquais sugar and an annual grant accorded to the colony to help balance its budget. With the backing of the governor, the General Council of Martinique requested a total of 7.6 million francs from the central government, which included three million francs to balance the budget, eight hundred thousand francs in tax and customs relief, and two million francs in agricultural allocations.[78] Compared with the forty-three-million-franc estimation made by the colonial investigators—a substantial reduction from earlier estimates—in the end the central government offered only three million francs to balance the colony's budget, which would be provided as an advance that would ultimately have to be reimbursed beginning on 1 July 1898 in ten annuities of three hundred thousand francs each.[79] It was further recommended, though not legislated, that the money from the budgetary advance be distributed as follows: 550,730 francs for tax relief via customs duties on sugar and tafia, 449,250 francs toward the restoration work necessary to repair the damage caused by the hurricane, and finally, two million francs as allocations (primes) to small planters.[80]

While direct aid would help tremendously in rebuilding public infrastructure and homes in the island's cities and towns, it would not be enough to help the island's rural "peasant" population of subsistence growers nor the large industrial cane growers, insisted representatives from Martinique in a presentation to the Chamber of Deputies. They asked for an exemption on property taxes and export duties on both sugar and tafia to help the large plantations, and that the state provide assistance to the island's peasantry with the tax revenue left to the cane planters, for "[i]n this manner we will stop the culture of death, that is to say, we will save Martinique itself."[81] Referencing the precedent of relief from custom duties and taxes following the 1817 hurricane in Martinique and various others afflicting Réunion, they pointed out that the state would not hesitate to provide such relief to metropolitan departments, such as those grape-growing regions plagued by phylloxera. The planter lobby even used their relatively small impact on the metropolitan market as ideological leverage: since they produced only thirty thousand to forty thousand tons normally, they figured, relaxing the tax duties would negatively impact neither the domestic beet sugar nor the colonial cane sugar markets. Rather, the representatives claimed that the state had a moral duty to help Martinique's sugar economy, which in turn would help the island's peasantry—again, a slippery term contemporaries used to refer to the islands' black agricultural laborers. Ultimately, however, the state denied both these proposals, because the colonial investigators had deemed that the hurricane's impact did not extend beyond the 1892 sugar harvests and thus there was no need to grant a five-year exemption.[82] In light of the inspectors' reports, the chamber decided that a tax exemption would be unwarranted, because the crops, which Chaudié had said "suffered little," would rebound quickly. Therefore, the only measure proposed to assist what the chamber had acknowledged were "the unfortunate *concitoyens* in Martinique" was a loaned budgetary advance of three million francs to be distributed as Martinique's General Council saw fit.[83]

Referencing the privilege of departments compared with colonies, Senator Allègre demanded a law identical to that which provided aid to Nice following a large earthquake in February 1887 that was centered in the nearby Italian Alps. The earthquake in the Alps had incurred costs in Menton of about seven to eight million francs and damages in Nice of about 1.5 million francs. By the law of 22 July 1887, the central government had borrowed 4.6 million francs from the Crédit Foncier de France to help the region rebuild. The central government took responsibility for three-fifths of the loan and left two-fifths for the department to repay. Much like investors' concerns about the economic impact of the hurricane in Martinique, both the Crédit Foncier and the central French government were aware of the financial necessities and risks of rebuilding the towns of Menton and Nice in the metropole. In 1887 the government found such a deal to be feasible, citing that since the Crédit Foncier had "considerable engagements" in the department of Alpes-Maritimes, lending money for reconstruction would be to the bank's benefit.[84]

In response to pressure from Senator Allègre and Martinique's General Council, both of whom deemed the central government's response underwhelming two and a half months after the hurricane, Colonial Undersecretary Étienne argued that the government's response would be "analogous" to the aid it gave to the Alpes-Maritimes department, including a grant to help meet local budgetary shortfalls.[85] Senator Allègre had emphasized that departments in France had access to support, supplies, and funds unavailable to colonies, which in his estimation were expected to stand alone with only a yearly budgetary allowance as assistance. Therefore, he put pressure on Undersecretary Etienne, who in turn conceded the argument and agreed to find support equitable to that given to departments in emergency situations.

On 25 November, the Crédit Foncier responded to the central government's request for a loan on Martinique's behalf, agreeing to provide the funds at an interest rate of 4.1 percent if the state were to authorize the loan with a law and guarantee its repayment.[86] The terms would require the state to repay the entirety of the loan, rather than splitting the loan between the colony and the state. The undersecretary intervened, claiming that the rate was too high, and that he expected the Crédit Foncier to accept terms analogous to the agreement made with regard the 1887 earthquake in Alpes-Maritimes. In response, the Crédit Foncier insisted that such terms were impossible, because it was authorized to loan only to departments. In fact, the only colony it could loan money to was Algeria, and beyond that, the bank had no organized service or presence in Martinique. The bank did agree, however, to lower the interest rate to 4 percent.[87]

The undersecretary of state of the colonies then turned to the Caisses d'Amortissement, the governmental body in charge of public debts, to see if it could intervene or lend the money to Martinique on behalf of the central government. After a meeting of the board, the general director of the Caisses d'Amortissement informed the undersecretary that lending money to a foreign entity—in this case, a colony—would be a "difficult accomplishment" that would violate the organization's traditions, and thus it would be impossible.[88] Under pressure from the undersecretary to circumvent "the difficulty," the Caisses responded by agreeing to lend the money directly to the colony rather than to the affected proprietors like the Crédit Foncier had done in the Alpes-Maritimes.[89] This move would allow the state to guarantee three-fifths of the loan, as it had in Alpes-Maritimes. But the deal would be contingent on the proof of the loan's importance, an agreement on the amortization schedule, and the strength of the guarantees provided by the state.[90] In short, obtaining the loan for Martinique on terms equitable to those provided to Alpes-Maritime was unlikely.

Both the hesitation on the part of the Crédit Foncier and the Caisses d'Amortissement, as well as Colonial Undersecretary Étienne's insistence on an agreement analogous to that made for the Alpes-Maritimes, speak to the incomplete integration of Martinique into the domestic sphere in 1891. While the language the colonial undersecretary used emphasized compatriotism and Martinique's General Council underscored the island's "near departmental" status, both financing institutions shied away from breaking with their "tradition" of lending only to full departments and resisted giving money to a colony on such lenient terms.

Arguments against Considering Martinique a Department

The Crédit Foncier was not the only significant actor to argue the French legislature should not treat Martinique as an afflicted department. The Chamber of Commerce of Bordeaux insisted that though Martinique was "one of the oldest and most loyal overseas possessions," it was nonetheless a colony. Pointing to Martinique's status as a colony of extraction characterized by a monoculture of sugar cane, the chamber argued that investing in a colony with a bleak economic outlook was bad business:

> It would be a mistake, ahead of the planned assimilation, if we considered Martinique to be a French department, ignoring the profound divergences created by its geographical, physical, and agricultural situation. French Departments form a whole—if not uniform, at least almost homogeneous. Their extent, the variety of their cultures, their many industries, their intimate union, the proximity of communal assistance, the flexibility and multiplicity of mechanisms of public credit—all of these allow for a speedy recovery in a community struck by an event of major force. Moreover, [when such an event strikes in the metropole, which isn't economically reliant upon a monocrop] all the means of public wealth are not extinguished in one fell swoop. Martinique, like all the West Indian colonies, is isolated at a large distance from the mother country: deprived of industry, Martinique has only agriculture and its trade closely depends on agriculture. . . . All the means of livelihood

in the country, all means of existence therefore, for both the poor as well as the rich, for the proletarian and proprietor, depend solely on sugar cane.[91]

Bordeaux's economic calculus applied to Martinique's well-being stood at odds with the general outpouring of "patriotic" support during the fires the previous year; though we must recall that Bordeaux was among the bottom tier of donors, and even during the height of public support for the fire victims, in the background we heard the concerns of agitated investors fearful that the Martiniquais sugar economy would falter. In the case of the 1891 hurricane, commerce and agriculture—in other words, sugar production— were at the forefront of the minds of many. As Bordeaux asserted, it's not personal; it's just business. Although racism most likely tinted Bordeaux's hard-nosed attitude toward Martinique, the Chamber of Commerce cast its hesitation not in racial or cultural terms but in purely economic ones. In other words, though shared culture and the myth of assimilation might compel France to treat Martinique as a department—or at least, a "near department"—Bordeaux's Chamber of Commerce provided a calculated reminder that economics trumped culture, that giving Martinique aid as if it were a department would be a fiscal blunder.

The solution put forth by the Chamber of Commerce of Bordeaux asserted that the best and most direct avenue toward recovery—that is, the best way to ameliorate the destitution of the island's denizens—would be to grant a tax exemption on sugar and tafia.[92] The Chambers of Commerce of Le Havre and Marseilles, supported by the local General Council of Martinique, echoed this statement, and even Senator Allègre advocated for this solution. In the words of Martinique's General Council, "What industry has created, it's up to industry to recreate. . . . It's through the import tax, the most powerful social agent there is, that we must ask the state to save us."[93] Faithful that "the metropole will not leave her loyal Martinique to die," the General Council asked for a complete prorogation of all taxes (import, export, rent, property, etc.) for the year of 1892, and a successive reinstatement of taxes in 20 percent intervals for the five years after that (i.e., taxes attenuated by 80 percent of their pre-1891 amounts in 1893, 60 percent in 1894, 40 percent in 1895, 20 percent in 1896, and 0 percent in 1897).

In drafting their response to the hurricane, the Chambers of Commerce referenced the government's response to the sugar crisis of 1884: keeping cheap German beet sugar out of French markets by introducing foreign tariffs and a taxation scheme that encouraged better mechanization by taxing sugar yields in relation to the number of beets grown. With tax breaks and taxation schedules set in 1884, governmental intervention favored the producers of domestic beet sugar rather than the consumers.[94] Following the hurricane, the metropolitan Chambers of Commerce proposed similar protections for Martiniquais cane sugar, asking for a significant reduction in taxation for Antillean sugar that would effectively increase production.

To secure the assistance of the metropole, Martinique's sugar planters in Saint-Pierre sent a joint letter to the undersecretary on 2 March 1892 outlining the dire situation of the island's economy, the key importance of sugar cultivation, and the breadth of the devastation following the 1891 hurricane.[95] Asserting that the situation in Martinique was direr than that of the Alpes-Maritimes region four years prior—that the Alpes-Maritime agreement Etienne had sought was actually too little rather than too much assistance to the island's economy—the planters of Martinique, with the backing of Martinique's Chamber of Commerce, the agricultural syndicate, and the manufacturing syndicate, made the accusation that such "assistance has never been refused in the metropole to industries that have never experienced suffering as terrible as what we've just experienced." Dissatisfied with the reports the colonial investigators had made, the planters and the syndicates claimed that official reports overlooked the indirect effects of the hurricane. For example, they alleged that electrical storms desiccated the sugar crop, which lowered crop yields by at least 25 percent and in turn affected molasses production. Since the sugar crop represented 97 percent of the colony's economic production, the agricultural and manufacturing syndicates purported that the livelihood and well-being of everyone in the colony—not just the wealthy landowners, but everyone from "city workers, to *cultivateurs*, to merchants, to proprietors, to manufacturers"—was at stake, because no secondary crops stood in line to replace the devastated sugar economy.[96] In their estimation, the moral and "democratic" thing to do would be to support Martinique's decimated sugar production through tax relief and assistance in the amount of thirteen to fourteen million francs, far more substantial than proposed, and that an agreement analogous to that made in Nice would actually privilege the urban spaces over the rural and do little to jump-start the sugar economy. The sugar planters on the island underscored the preeminence of the island's sugar monoculture, viewing tax and customs relief rather than direct public assistance as the true way to alleviate suffering on the island.

However, although inspectors Chaudié and Blanchard had thoroughly slashed the original damage estimates by submitting Martinique's suffering to an impersonal calculus, they nevertheless supported a direct loan to the colony as a means to rebuild the island's colonial and communal buildings.[97] Chaudié explained that the reconstruction must be warranted, however: "the metropole can only make financial sacrifices in favor of a department or a commune insofar as the expenditures for which it loans its aid are put toward buildings that serve a necessary and public utility." Therefore, he argued that the state should not rebuild the island's many churches and rectories, which only serve a religious function, and should instead only fund the reconstruction of the vital communal buildings that serve a secular or administrative function. This ran counter to the interests of the Central Aid Commission in Martinique, which not only had the Bishop of Martinique on its governing board but also did not distinguish between private, public, and religious institutions. For instance, in November 1891, the commission allocated three thousand francs to assist the Nuns of the Déliverance from Le Morne-Rouge.[98]

By May 1892, Undersecretary Étienne had abandoned the plan to secure a loan on terms analogous to those the department of Alpes-Maritimes had received, even under the conditions of the state treating the colony itself as the borrower rather than those afflicted citizens who lived there. In light of the colonial investigation, the Chamber of Deputies decided that the damages did not warrant the degree of assistance Étienne sought, and that the lure of two million francs' worth of direct subsidies would engender far too much corruption.[99] While the sugar industry was pushing for more aid than was originally proposed, the central government was only willing to grant less. Ultimately the colony received only the aforementioned loan of three million francs, and it would have to pay it back in full in installments of three hundred thousand francs beginning in 1898.[100] The president of the Republic, Marie François Carnot, signed this loan into law on 20 July 1892.[101] All the valuations—by the General Council, the municipal commissions, and the colonial investigators—were irrelevant to the final decision. That is, the investigatory work Chaudié had done, his willingness to slash valuations throughout his endeavor to lower the estimated damages from eighty-nine million to forty-three million francs, had no ultimate impact on the aid Martinique received.

The Méline Tariff of 1892

With the rise of empires and the return of protectionist economies, the close of the nineteenth century saw the sunset of what historian Eric Hobsbawm deemed "the age of capital"—that "enlightened, sure of itself, self-satisfied" age when governments had an unshakable faith in free market economics, state nonintervention, and aggregate statistics.[102] Though the sun was slow to set, France had lost its faith in the international free market by the 1890s. Officials' economic calculus of disaster and recovery ran side by side with debates throughout 1891 and 1892 about the passing of a new customs law that would reconfigure tariffs between France's colonies and the metropole, effectively bringing the Antilles and France into the same tax zone. The law of 11 January 1892—named the Méline tariff after its champion, Jules Méline—was designed to protect national agricultural interests, stabilize domestic prices, and safeguard the French domestic market from external threats; the Méline tariff ended France's thirty-two-year flirtation with free trade following the Cobden-Chevalier Treaty of 1860.[103] At the same time that the metropolitan agricultural sector was floundering in the international market, the Martiniquais economy was struggling due to widespread agricultural devastation.

That the 1892 customs tariff folded the old colonies into the domestic market demonstrated that they were economically considered part of France, as were all of France's colonies under this law.[104] But as historian Christian Schnakenbourg has pointed out, while the tariff proclaimed the principle of "customs assimilation into the metropole," it was only an inequitable half measure that created a new form of subordination within the metropolitan economy.[105] Since the Antilles were economically considered part of the metropole, they now paid metropolitan duties for imported staples but still had to pay a customs tariff when selling goods to mainland France, albeit at a lower rate than foreign companies.[106] The Méline tariff was an important, if highly problematic, step toward the old colonies' eventual integration into the French nation as departments in 1946, but it imposed discrimination in the domestic French market on Antillean industry and substantially increased the cost of living in the French Caribbean. This situation caused political fallout in the colonies that had come to a head by 1899, when prices for Antilleans reached new heights within the French customs zone. For instance, factory owners by the close of the century were attacking those representatives who had voted to pass the Méline tariff, mostly on ideological grounds.[107]

The customs law, as well as the governmental response after the 1891 hurricane, reflects the split—or rather liminal—nature of France's oldest colonies: not really a colony but not yet a department. Schnakenbourg's assertion rings true, given the dual-edged nature of the metropolitan response. Oscillating between a near department and an extractive colony, Martinique met an underwhelming amount of support, as those financial heavyweights with the strongest economic ties to Martinique—Le Havre, Marseille, and Bordeaux—weighed in and demanded a way to get the most money out of Martinique while putting the least money in. It was on the basis of arguing that Martinique was a full department that Martiniquais politicians petitioned to receive aid analogous to that the Alpes-Maritime department had received following the earthquake in 1887. Moreover, Martinique's business elite, along with the agricultural and manufacturing syndicates, advocated for a five-year tax relief plan that would jump-start the flagging sugar economy.

Ultimately, however, negotiations with respect to both these plans broke down, and while Martinique was in fact folded into the French customs zone following the Méline tariff, it remained on unequal footing with metropolitan beet growers and received little in the way of substantial aid. Beet sugar continued to outstrip the production of sugar cane, and by 1895, the land cultivated for sugar cane dropped to half of what it was in 1889 (from roughly twenty-one thousand to ten thousand hectares).[108] The value of Martinique's commerce dropped precipitously, cut nearly in half from its high-water mark of seventy million francs in the early 1880s to roughly forty-five million francs a decade later.[109] Over this period, Martinique's trade with foreign nations took the largest losses.[110] Consequently, real wages for Martinique's sugar workers continued to fall over the course of the 1890s, precipitating the island's first general strike in 1900 which, as we will see in the following chapter, nearly toppled the metropolitan administration as parliamentarians and activists argued over the relationship between the state and its labor force.

As the sugar industry collapsed from natural disasters, market forces, and political neglect, Martinique was denied the tax relief departments afflicted with phylloxera in the metropole had received, and colonial investigators were questioning the efficacy of direct governmental aid to the island's suffering populace. Sidestepping Martinique's slave plantation past by focusing on the island's unstable monoculture as if it emerged of the victims' own volition, French officials, the Chambers of Commerce, and the financial system all refused to acknowledge their own role in Martinique's market instability. That is, at the same time that France's colonial empire was being folded into the metropolitan market, politicians were figuring out a way to keep Martinique from receiving the same sort of national assistance that regularly went toward departments.

Conclusion

Overall, in their response to the 1891 hurricane French officials displayed their economic motives, as they depicted humanitarian aid as nothing more than, in the words of Émile Chaudié, "evaluative work that is not personal, but based on statistical givens."[111] Though the real economic aid proposed by the chamber had no relationship to this evaluative work, the work itself nevertheless reflects an ideological approach to disaster relief. As historian Joshua Cole has pointed out, social science, censuses, and statistical measuring rose in the nineteenth century, and consequently officials retreated to the comfort of faceless numbers to describe French society, in many cases quantifying human experience in the name of scientific endeavor and justifying policy decisions and cultural prejudices with tables, charts, and aggregate statistics.[112] Faced with two back-to-back disasters, the colonial investigators, as well as the Chambers of Commerce of Le Havre, Bordeaux, and Marseille, crunched the numbers to find and thereby avoid the point of diminishing returns, all the while either ignoring or glossing over the societal inequities at play. For fear of providing too much and thereby engendering waste and abuse, "to the great detriment of the interests of the treasury," officials sought a way to restore the economy, restart the sugar factories, and recuperate their losses, all while injecting the least amount of capital. A far cry from the outpouring of support the previous year, this calculus—which even reevaluated the 1890 fire-relief campaign—dashed Martinique's hopes to receive money on par with those afflicted departments that sought governmental aid. The cold calculus performed by colonial investigators reflected—implicitly, if not overtly—racist and classist stereotypes of indigent and lazy black laborers.

Owing to the Antilleans' status as citizens and their legal, albeit uneven, incorporation into the metropole, as well as the prohibition of officially tracking or addressing the race of French citizens since 1848, official documents on the hurricane never spoke outright of race. But systemic racism predicated on economic inequity and rooted in the legacy of planation slavery faced Antilleans, as officials like Chaudié couched their discriminatory rhetoric in the language of good finance. As investigators slashed the damage estimates and emphasized Martinique's economic instability, they in turn sidestepped race altogether—including the legacy of slavery, the inequitable market forces at play, the history of inequality between the wealthy white elite and the black labor force, and the perennial underfunding of public infrastructure. The investigators even glorified a mythic island peasantry to justify keeping money out of the hands of the afflicted urban spaces, and they performed a calculus meant to inject the "appropriate" amount of capital for maximum economic effect, which they assured a disaster-fatigued administration would be to the benefit of all. In subsuming humanitarianism into economics, Chaudié and his colleagues relied on a longstanding republican tradition dating to the French Revolution, when, with their hands tied by the Declaration of the Rights of Man and Citizen, advocates for slavery couched their arguments as good economic sense rather than prejudice.[113]

But Martinique's elected representatives and their assimilationist allies pushed back. Regrettably, assimilationists' plans for substantial governmental assistance to Martinique never materialized. And yet their insistence that

Martinique receive the sort of aid that had previously gone toward metropolitan departments, which they grounded on cultural imperatives as well as economic justifications, and the brief moment for which Undersecretary Étienne entertained and even advocated for the Alpes-Maritime plan, highlighted the way in which Martinique was always almost a department—or at the very least, "nearly an Algeria"—and that its colonial citizenry was constituted by, in the words of Frantz Fanon, quasi-metropolitans. Unfortunately it also meant that Antilleans, though heralded as compatriots who embodied the myth of assimilation, were nonetheless treated as second-class citizens.

4

The Political Summation

*Incendiarism, Civil Unrest, and Legislative
Catastrophe at the Turn of the Century*

At the close of the nineteenth century, the French Caribbean's black labor-ing class chafed under the control of colonial bureaucrats ever preoccupied with the bottom line in the islands. Even the islands' minor products (fruit, cocoa, coffee, and tafia) gained more attention than human suffering in the face of natural disasters, and reasonable and fair wages merited still less attention. Many in the French bureaucracy shared the disdain and disregard that colonial inspectors like Chaudié displayed toward the island's black laboring class. Whereas metropolitan officials had couched their racism in economic language during the 1891 hurricane, many now explained away the islands' political strife as outright racial conflict, owing to the large entry of black citizens into the political sphere and the rising specter of socialism in the years following the hurricane.[1] The international decline of the cane sugar market worsened standards of living and lowered wages for the islands' workers, who had begun to form labor unions and mutual aid societies following their legalization in 1884. For instance, Martinique's first union formed in 1886, while Guadeloupe's first socialist paper, *Le Peuple*, appeared in 1891.[2]

Guadeloupe had hit a rough patch by 1899, and it seemed that nature and the global economy had it in for the small Caribbean island. As the island's deputy Gerville-Réache put it following an earthquake in 1897, "there are very few countries so cruelly afflicted in a half-century . . . : the earthquake of 8 February 1843, the hurricane and floods of 1865, the cholera epidemic that same year, the fire of 18 July 1871, several yellow fever epidemics, the sugar crises of 1883 and 1895, the financial crisis of 1896–1897, and now the earthquake of 29 April 1897. All these calamities . . . seem to have been conjured up to bring about the island's demise."[3] In this case, however, it wasn't darkest before the dawn. Though the earthquake killed few—only four died, with about forty wounded—it destroyed the infrastructure of Point-a-Pitre: the port's quay walls destroyed by the shaking and perturbed sea, homes in crumbles, and the island's commerce in shambles. Combined with numerous catastrophes in the long term, as well as a prolonged drought in the short term, the end of the nineteenth century was a bad row for Guadeloupe economically. As Senator Alexandre Isaac put it, "the earthquake had struck a most foul blow to [Guadeloupe's] general fortune."[4]

Such conditions provide context for two new types of disaster, both political in nature: incendiarism in Guadeloupe, which challenged the political status quo and eventually led to the destruction of the island's largest city, Pointe-à-Pitre, in 1899, and the general strike of 1900 in Martinique, which intentionally disrupted the island's sugar economy to raise standards of living for the island's black laboring class. Natural disasters and civil disorder share many parallels in emergency organization, preparedness, and authority response. From the authorities' viewpoint, both can be equally disruptive and unforeseen, and both foreground existing socioeconomic and political tensions. The social context within which people act is quite different, however, because an event of civil disorder intentionally challenges the status quo, whereas the impetus following a natural disaster is either to return to the status quo or to refashion the afflicted society in the authorities' image.

Incendiarism in Guadeloupe and workers' agitation in Martinique prompted a political disaster in 1900, when Antillean politics became embroiled in the culture and politics of a fin-de-siècle France riddled with labor unrest and a rising demand for social justice. The 1899 fire reached a prominence heretofore unseen because of its physical scale, and because it stoked the administration's and the sugar lobby's fears of criminal activity among Guadeloupe's Indian immigrant and black laboring population. The fire came at a pivotal and difficult time in Guadeloupe's history when the Antilleans' overlapping class and racial divisions erupted into outright conflict.[5] A hurricane in August 1899, which killed sixty-three individuals and destroyed the year's sugar harvest, made issues worse by, in the words of the finance minister, "augmenting the already large misery [from the fire] in our colony."[6] The sugar crisis compounded this misery, prompting the French Caribbean's first general strike the following year, which entangled

Antillean collective action in metropolitan debates about labor unrest and issues of social welfare, nearly toppling France's coalition government and precipitating the identification of socialists in the metropole with black laborers in the Caribbean. Incendiarism and the strike in 1900 forced the central government and the island's administration to cease talking about disaster relief and Antillean rights in coded language and instead address racial and class dynamics outright, not just in the Caribbean but in mainland France as well.

Key to this conflict was the rising prominence of Guadeloupean socialist Hégésippe Légitimus, who had begun to fight for the rights of the island's black population. Politics on the island had changed, much to the alarm of the government. As the governor of Guadeloupe—none other than Corsican-born Delphino Moracchini, who had led the relief efforts in Martinique in 1890 and acted as governor during the 1891 hurricane—put it, "Blacks had for a long time been docile, passive, and not taking part in politics except to vote for this or that candidate, white or of color."[7] What had changed, according to the governor, was how black politicians now pandered to a black electorate that excluded white people, while exciting the black masses to action with promises to help them rise above their station. For alarmists like the governor, race solidarity had trumped "true" republican beliefs, as the black electorate voted strictly for people "of their color." This had ushered in an age of political dissension, wherein blacks assumed local offices with "an exaggerated sense of dignity and independence" that engendered a "lack of respect for employers."[8] Such fears were not isolated to worrisome republicans. The rise of the island's black socialists concerned traditional leftists as well, because the Guadeloupean version of socialism revolved around racial identity and the right wing took the bad publicity as an opportunity to lambast the left's ultimate class-based goals. In 1899 Alexandre Isaac, the longtime left-wing senator from Guadeloupe who had himself run afoul of the socialists under Légitimus, proclaimed that "the socialists of France and the false socialists of Guadeloupe have nothing in common," to which right-winger Charles le Cour-Grandmaison responded that one "is the copy of the other!"[9] The black socialists in Guadeloupe had been fighting for their place among the socialists of France, proclaiming that "the blood of the black is as red as that of the 71 massacred individuals at Fourmis"—referring to the city of Fourmies in Le Nord, France, where police opened fire on labor demonstrators in 1891.[10] The socialist newspaper *Le Peuple*, which Légitimus himself edited, depicted racial hatred as inimical to real progress on the island and emblematic of historic regression, as those on the right "want the blacks to return to being simple beasts of burden." This attempt to roll back the clock and scale back blacks' rights yielded cries of "Down with the Black! Long live the Reaction!"[11] In a political climate marked by a socialist ascendancy, a liberal distrust, and a conservative backlash, incendiarism in Guadeloupe, as well as the general strike of 1900 in Martinique, represented a moment of both physical and political disaster in the colony as well as in the metropole.

Under Pressure: The Troubled Year of 1898

At the close of the nineteenth century, the island of Guadeloupe repeatedly erupted into flames—both literally and figuratively. Contemporary observers had begun to treat this as inevitable even before the largest urban fire to afflict the island of Guadeloupe in at least thirty years occurred in April 1899.[12] Guadeloupe, like much of the Caribbean, was not unfamiliar with fires. Several of the island's towns had at one time or another been set aflame: Grand-Bourg in 1838, Basse-Terre in 1844, Port-Louis in 1856 and again in 1890, Le Moule in 1873 as well as 1897, and Pointe-à-Pitre in 1871 and 1899. Fires restricted to small homes and isolated cane fields were a mainstay of life on the island.[13] In 1878, for instance, there were seventy-four fires in Pointe-à-Pitre alone, and in 1879 there were sixty-four, several of them fires set to harvests in the cane fields. Many of these were incendiarism aimed at political protest, but no further collective action occurred and the government believed that it had dealt with the protesters swiftly and firmly. Fire starters received punishments varying from eight to twenty years of hard labor, and the fires themselves typically caused little perturbation beyond the initial cleanup.[14] In the words of a captain in the French navy, "Pointe-à-Pitre was a tidy and animated city with important commercial functions despite repeated disasters."[15]

All this changed by the start of 1898, when tensions began to mount as a number of localized fires and "acts of marauding" menaced the region around Pointe-à-Pitre. According to the *béké*-dominated newspaper *Le Cour-*

rier de la Guadeloupe, protestors allegedly cried, "Down with the Whites and Mulattos! Long live the fire!" during a likely accidental fire in May.[16] Incidents within Pointe-à-Pitre in June 1898 prompted an investigation by the prosecutor general, who claimed to have found that vagabonds had ignited a fire in an under-construction home as well as a warehouse, and that indentured immigrants had burned down a church. No one was caught or tried in any of the cases, since, in the words of the prosecutor general, incendiarism "is a crime that most often escapes justice."[17] And yet the French and local government bemoaned that discontent among out-of-work and migrant workers sowed instability among Guadeloupe's population, particularly as fires spread to plantations on the northern end of the island by the month's end. In fact, enough fires had been set in and around Pointe-à-Pitre to prompt the French navy to send a warship to the island to calm a population stirred by the "malevolence" of "isolated miscreants and black conspirators," as well as by the Indian immigrants that planters had brought to the island as indentured servants to help with sugar cultivation.[18]

Between 1853 and 1889, roughly fifty thousand indentured servants had been brought to Guadeloupe from India, Africa, and China, of whom nearly sixteen thousand remained living in the colony.[19] The rest had been repatriated. Most of these immigrants in Guadeloupe (roughly 85 percent) were from India, as French authorities brought exclusively East Indians to Guadeloupe during the Third Republic to keep down labor costs by skirting planters' reliance on free black workers.[20] This action sowed discord between the island's black laboring class and the indentured servants, and in 1888, British authorities outlawed Indian immigration into the French Antilles due to civil strife. The final group of Indian indentured servants arriving in 1889 were facing repatriation after finishing their ten-year contracts by 1899, prompting them to acts of civil disobedience alongside the black laborers. Both groups felt disenfranchised: the former by their contracts and circumscribed legal status, and the latter by their economic situation.[21] In response, the prosecutor general urged the local government to prosecute the fire starters "with great diligence" and to catch their accomplices, lest the mounting "inquietude" continue as workers become increasingly "jealous of their neighbors."[22] Such increased military presence did little to enervate the islanders' spirit. If anything, it threw fuel on the fire and alienated potential allies among Guadeloupe's republicans, who voiced a firm opposition to the presence of "warships [that] have entered into our ports . . . [with] cannons pointed at our unfortunate land."[23] Many more would later sign a petition to the Ministry of the Colonies to cease military interventionism in July 1899.[24]

When a storefront burned down in December 1898 due to unknown causes, likely an employee who neglected to extinguish a candle upon closing the store, local merchants demanded police find someone responsible despite the lack of concrete evidence.[25] In response the governor wrote to the minister of the colonies to complain about the insufficient funding of the police force in Pointe-à-Pitre, arguing that the law of 5 April 1844 had hamstrung local law enforcement by placing its funding and direction on the shoulders of the communes themselves. The metropolitan law, which was specifically extended to Martinique and Guadeloupe, had been designed to standardize the organization of municipalities across France with a locally elected mayor and legislative council, and to ensure that each commune would be subjected to the same juridical regime. In effect, however, it meant that in colonial Martinique and Guadeloupe, central funding and direction for the police force had ceased. Enforcement thus fell to the local police departments, largely because the national public safety force, or gendarmerie, was virtually nonexistent in Guadeloupe—a military detachment of only 120 surveilled an island of 170,000.[26] The reliance on local police forces wrested control from the colonial governor's office—a conflict in play in the disasters of 1890 and 1891, when the governor stood at odds with Martinique's communal governments. In this instance, officials saw discord between public safety and the public itself—between the appointed and elected government—arguing that locally chosen juries consisting of *nègres* were not impartial and thus repeatedly acquitted, and perhaps sympathized with, known criminals.

This antagonism extended to the relationship between the gubernatorial office and the mayors themselves. For example, the governor believed that the mayor of Morne-à-l'Eau—a "black" in the words of Moracchini—had misrepresented the tranquility of his commune when asked point-blank about incendiarism there, allowing discontentment to fester rather than alerting the authorities.[27] The central government in Paris shared Moracchini's distrust of the local government. According to the minister of the colonies in Paris, dissatisfaction had multiplied because "certain weakness in the suppression of crimes reigns in all of Guadeloupe."[28] As was the case in the 1891 hurricane, the metropolitan government believed that locally elected officials—increasingly people of color—could not be trusted with the affairs of state, because local officials sympathized with their constituents who acted against labor practices. That the governor and the ministry had no direct authority to easily oust rightfully elected representatives by French citizens irritated them.

The political climate worsened in 1899 when alleged arsonists with "unclear motives," according to governmental officials, attempted to start three urban fires in late February, as well as several more fires in the cane fields outside town. Many on the left saw those arrested as scapegoats, sacrificed in the name of public order, while the rich white proprietors of the sugar plantations and factories in Guadeloupe were the real villains.[29] To put it bluntly, both leftist republicans and socialists held a strong distrust of "reactionary officials," like the prosecutor general, who were all too willing to cry foul at the left. Turning a blind eye to the social inequities the island's left-leaning political parties highlighted, some officials claimed not to understand why incendiarism seemed to be on the rise, leading the prosecutor general, P. Girard, to ask "[W]ere these attempts committed with the intention of benefiting from terror and panic to pillage . . . to sow desolation and ruin among the rich as well as the poor?"[30] For such officials the specter of riotous, illogical mob behavior, and not any deeper societal cause or inequity, loomed behind the rash of fires.

Others, however, were more astute. The governor of Guadeloupe, Delphino Moracchini, had extensive experience with disasters and conflict in both Antillean islands, having been Martinique's public official in charge of distributing relief supplies during the fire of 1890 and the governor who oversaw the relief effort after the 1891 hurricane. He became governor of Guadeloupe in 1895 and had already dealt with a number of smaller incidents of arson, as well as the 1897 earthquake that killed six, wounded forty-two, and caused roughly five million francs' worth of damage.[31] Though his prejudices at times led him to take a hard-nosed approach toward the Antillean population under his charge, his experience and republican convictions nevertheless gave him a sense of the pulse of the people, and in 1899 he noted how an inequitable exchange rate had sowed misery among the islands' poor by increasing the cost of food and consumer products.

Repeated natural disasters had already amplified Guadeloupeans' economic misery, such as when the 1891 hurricane doubled the price of islanders' principal food crop, manioc. By 1899 the Méline tariff had for years strained the working poor by increasing the cost of imported goods, and now it was accompanied by a debased Guadeloupean currency. Under the Third Republic, each colony in the French empire, Guadeloupe included, had its own wholly independent currency issued by private colonial banks tasked with providing credit to local agricultural and industrial endeavors. These colonial currencies were exchanged with the metropolitan franc according to market forces. When trade between metropole and colony was balanced, the two currencies traded at a one-to-one ratio. However, when trade dropped and the colony entered a deficit, its currency depreciated against the metropolitan franc.[32] Thus colonial banks fulfilled another vital function: negotiating currency exchange contracts with metropolitan financial institutions. In their negotiating, colonial banks could financially engineer the exchange rates to some degree to offset what they saw as detrimental market forces.

To this end, under pressure from factory owners facing declining profits and a mounting trade deficit, the Banque de la Guadeloupe made market prime adjustments in 1897 to favor the sugar industry. Their adjustments colluded with a market downturn to dramatically debase Guadeloupe's currency, which dropped by more than a quarter of its value as the exchange rate skyrocketed from just 2 percent in 1894 from to over 30 percent in 1897.[33] Given the political fallout and the divisions it underscored between the island's wealthy békés and working class, historian Christian Schnakenbourg has deemed the 1897 exchange rate hike to be the "detonator of the wider political crisis" of the decade to follow, because it grossly favored a wealthy minority while dispossessing the poor majority, and because it led to the first rupture between the island's white business elite and the metropolitan government's appointed administration—namely Governor Moracchini—since the abolition of slavery nearly forty years prior.[34]

The colonial bank's maneuvering aimed to create a favorable balance of trade and ensure financial liquidity, for the benefit of the bank's shareholders and customers but at the expense of the island's working population. As one French colonial journalist, Henri Desroches, explained, "In principle, the Bank should therefore push the exchange rate as high as possible, even if the interests of its constituents are absolutely contrary to those of the majority of the population."[35] A high exchange rate weakened the island's currency, which in turn increased both incomes and tax receipts by inflating the Guadeloupean franc. The weakened franc also increased exports, because Guadeloupean goods were now comparatively cheaper. Since debt balances remained flat as currency became easier to come by, inflation further privileged the sugar elite by making it easier for them to repay the debts they had accrued in expanding and retooling Guadeloupe's sugar production since 1870. In turn, the repayment of debts helped the colonial bank by securing cash flow and ensuring the opening of new credit accounts.[36]

On the other hand, the weakened Guadeloupean currency burdened sugar workers by decreasing the value of their labor, and it disadvantaged the poor by increasing the cost of food, which was largely imported. Consequently the islands' republican representatives, led by mulatto deputy Gaston Gerville-Réache, vehemently opposed the forced devaluation of the Guadeloupean franc, for, as Governor Moracchini estimated, by 1899 local merchants had marked up their products by as much as 50 percent to offset the increased costs of imported goods.[37] An exchange rate of 30 percent meant that a worker's daily pay of 1 franc 25 centimes was in reality worth only 88 centimes, because the weakened currency simply could not purchase as much nutrition as it once had.[38] Some agricultural workers in Guadeloupe earned as little as one franc per day, perhaps as high as one franc fifty centimes, depending on employment.[39] Underpaid workers turned away from imported goods and began consuming more locally obtained foodstuffs like manioc, which in turn drove their prices upward.[40] For instance, the price of a kilogram of cod increased to one franc sixty centimes—potentially over 150 percent of workers' daily wage.[41] While the bank maneuvered to increase the exchange rate in the hope of boosting Guadeloupean exports, which saw limited effect (figure 17), the price hike in foodstuffs deepened the desperation among workers and their families for whom the years-long downturn in the sugar economy had already translated into unemployment for some and fewer workdays for others.

FIG. 17. **Sugar production in Guadeloupe, 1880–1905**
With the ascendancy of beet sugar, Guadeloupe, like Martinique, witnessed a steep decline in its sugar production by the 1890s, so that by 1900 the island produced half the tonnage it had produced ten years earlier. Graph created in R statistical package with data from France, *Annuaire statistique* 15:734; Rolph, *Something about Sugar*, 242.

Despite the changes to the exchange rate and the colonial bank's attempts to mitigate the island's trade deficit, the sugar industry in Guadeloupe continued to falter. By 1890, Europe and to a lesser extent the entire world had shifted away from cane cultivation toward beet sugar, a more lucrative and efficient product than cane sugar. Though worldwide cane sugar production remained relatively stable between 1882 and 1897, beet sugar saw a meteoric rise, growing 280 percent over fifteen years (figure 18). This drove the worldwide price of sugar downward, a blow to Guadeloupe's sugar industry. Falling revenue led to a drop from fifty-seven million kilograms to just shy of forty million kilograms in sugar production in Guadeloupe between 1882 and 1899. Moreover, the island had seen four massive sugar shortfalls due to storms and hurricanes in 1885, 1891, 1894, and again in 1899. While

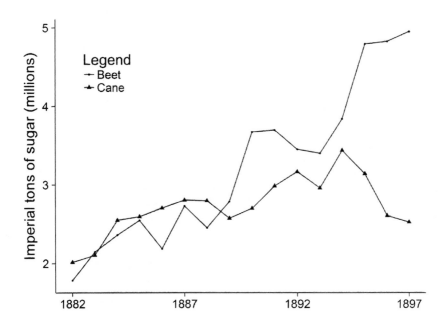

FIG. 18. **Worldwide sugar production, 1882–97**

By the close of the nineteenth century, beet sugar had far surpassed sugar cane production worldwide. Whereas production levels of beet and cane sugar had been roughly equal in 1882, the world produced twice as much beet sugar as cane sugar by 1897. Graph created in R statistical package with data from U.S. Department of State, *Commercial Relations*, 551–54.

all three of the island's largest sugar companies had seen a profit in 1899, they had struggled for nearly fifteen years. Worse, a poor harvest in 1900 due to incendiarism, drought, and the hurricane in August 1899, producing eleven million fewer kilograms than the prior year's harvest, wiped away the 1899 profits.[42] By 1900 the islands' three largest sugar producers had seen a net loss of nearly 1.8 million francs since 1882 and they owed about twice that figure (3.6 million francs) to creditors—again, reason for them to support increasing Guadeloupe's exchange rate. The largest central sugar factory, Usine d'Arboussier, had also seen a decline in profits; from 1876 to 1883, it received approximately 53.10 francs per thousand kilograms of sugar, while from 1894 to 1899 this figure dropped to 37.75 francs per thousand kilograms.[43] Guadeloupe's sugar industry was deeply under water.

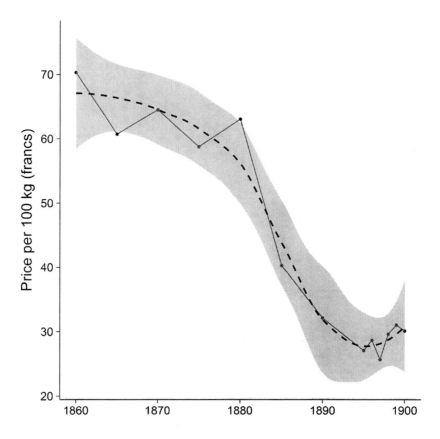

FIG. 19. **Price of unrefined sugar in France, 1860–1900**
With a worldwide surplus of sugar, the price of raw sugar in France dropped
dramatically over the second half of the nineteenth century, further distress-
ing the economies of Martinique and Guadeloupe, which relied heavily on
a sugar monoculture. Local regression trend line (LOESS). Graph created in
R statistical package with data from Hélot, *Le sucre de betterave*, 212.

Guadeloupe's representatives had brought the monetary crisis in the
Antilles to the Senate floor numerous times, most recently in March 1898
when Senator Alexandre Isaac—one of Guadeloupe's most prominent men
of color—asserted that France had created the islands' sugar crisis by cul-
tivating beets and by not adequately providing support following "public
disasters, earthquakes, [and] fires, that have exhausted its last resources...
[and] caused a monetary crisis more serious than all those preceding it."[44]

Despite his advocacy, little had changed one year later, and the colonies remained, in the words of Isaac, "totally forgotten and even more totally neglected." The government was torn between providing assistance as if the monetary crisis were itself a disaster, and telling individuals to pick themselves up by their own bootstraps—or, in the words of Governor Moracchini, "Help yourself, and heaven will help you!"[45] Consequently the people of Guadeloupe believed their voices had been unheard and that they had no recourse to ameliorate their situation. In a moment of clarity one week before the burning down of Pointe-à-Pitre in April 1899, Moracchini remarked that "this mode of vengeance [arson] . . . returns to us from the time when the torch was the only instrument of vengeance left to the slave."[46]

By 1900, Europe's turn to more economical means of producing sugar through beet cultivation, as well as a worldwide surplus of available sugar, had caused a steep decline in the production of the French islands' major crop: sugar cane. The price of sugar cane had fallen by about 25 francs per hundred kilograms, and Guadeloupe was, according to Senator Isaac, "the colony most mistreated by the crisis."[47] Consequently workers were receiving fewer days on the job, and they blamed the administration for the hardships they met at home. This was particularly true for the immigrants who had been brought to the Antilles after the abolition of slavery as indentured servants to harvest sugar cane; they had no rights beyond those outlined in their work contracts but nevertheless had a history of demanding fair work and pay. By 1880, for example, enough servants had deserted their posts in Martinique to prompt the minister of the interior to ramp up the surveillance efforts of the so-called labor police charged with enforcing the indentured servants' contracts. The minister encouraged police to search homes and places of work, and he ensured that the names of work deserters appeared in the official governmental newspaper.[48]

Consequently, by 1899 unrest among indentured servants as well as the island's black laboring class was a substantial issue—one the conservative party and political infighting in Pointe-à-Pitre made more pronounced. Just two weeks before the fire, Governor Moracchini insisted that Pointe-à-Pitre's conservative party, which had grown increasingly antagonistic since the application of universal suffrage on the islands, exaggerated the incidents to curry favor with their twenty-five hundred or so members and to drive wedges between the islands' republicans.[49] He voiced his anger with the press for throwing restraint to the wind and publishing passionate, biased commentaries that "excited spirits" on the island.[50] Guadeloupe's republicans also lamented this "reactionary spirit" among employers, which they felt foisted "inequities and horrors . . . [on] a naked proletariat, worn and absolutely disarmed" on the island "as in France."[51] In their eyes, the local conservative press used the island's colonial, slave history—as well as present-day racism—to lure the metropolitan government into blaming Guadeloupe's republicans and socialists for asserting their rights as French citizens, in turn causing grave injury to Guadeloupean democracy. Just as in the case of the cultural understanding of Martinique, which pitted republican people of color against an antiquated planter class, Guadeloupe was plagued by intransigent *békés* who sowed discord—allegedly to cries of "Down with the negro! Down with the Republic!"—in order to roll back the clock to the Ancient Regime—an era that lacked the ideals of "liberty, equality, and fraternity" and precluded emancipation and enfranchisement of the island's slaves.[52] Some went so far as to accuse whites of setting the fires in order to alienate the government from the black population.[53] In turn, seeing the recent incendiarism as emblematic of a race war that emancipation had initiated in 1848, the conservative press called the quintessential black laborer a "dirty Negro, sorcerer, thief of Indians, arsonist."[54] By accusing black laborers of recruiting disgruntled East Indians in their machinations against the *békés* as well as exaggerating the "pillaging of harvests" and the crimes against property, the conservative party hoped to convince the central government to rectify the unfair international and domestic competition that they saw crippling their industry, while at the same time curtailing the rights of people of color, socialists like Légitimus and left-leaning republicans like Gerville-Réache, who had been increasingly obtaining governmental positions since the onset of the Third Republic.

While it was clear that many of the fires were deliberate, it was unclear which exactly could be properly attributed to malfeasance, since in 1899 the island was experiencing such a severe drought that in the words of the prosecutor general to the governor of Guadeloupe, "a poorly extinguished match thrown by a passerby or by a *cultivateur* would be sufficient to enflame a plantation's straw."[55] Amplified by the uncertainty, fervor stirred in the colonies as conservatives sought to exploit the situation to roll back tariffs and workers used a slave's last resort—setting cane fires—to seek a voice in local and metropolitan politics. Many local and metropolitan officials picked up on this tension. Letters between the prosecutor general and the governor show that they were increasingly worried that the arsonists' motives were political in nature rather than personal vendettas or "jealousy," rhetoric used by *békés* to discredit slave resistance prior to emancipation. As evidence mounted that the fires might be—or might become—deliberate acts of political speech, officials now worried that the fires marked the coming of collective action. One letter from the owner of a sugar refinery put it starkly: if salaries did not increase for the workers, there would be no sugar harvest this year. At the close of one workday, he had found in the factory's scales an anonymous letter, in which one worker asserted, "No government exists that can prevent us from setting fire [to the fields]. Adieu harvest, adieu sugar cane, we cry for you."[56]

Despite the warnings, political and social discord continued to rise, and proprietors began to hire private guards to protect their property. At the close of March inhabitants near the Darboussier sugar factory assembled and threw rocks at the employees running the railway, while reports of the theft of sugar cane from large and small proprietors saturated the courts.[57] Guadeloupe's general secretary, Joseph François, endorsed repression, saying only the military "could produce the necessary moral effect" and more aggressive tactics "would intimidate the malefactors and prevent future attacks."[58] Increased repression did little more than stoke the flames of discontent among a population that felt it had a right to protest as much as any in France proper—in the words of the island's republicans, to safeguard "the republican ideals of justice and social emancipation."[59] By April 1899 things had come to a head.

Fire to the City: The Burning Down of Pointe-à-Pitre, Guadeloupe

Shortly after midnight on 18 April 1899, a recently fired employee of a local pharmacy broke in and caused a fire unintentionally, setting the largest town on the island, Pointe-à-Pitre, ablaze.[60] As in 1891, powerful Antillean winds fueled the fire, which consumed 313 homes and caused three million francs' worth of damage. The inferno destroyed roughly one-tenth of the city and left three thousand people without shelter.[61] Local Guadeloupean newspapers, as well as the office of the governor, readily pinned this on malfeasance, and the island's mounting labor unrest amplified the ensuing political fallout.

"The series of criminal fires continues . . . a great inquietude manifests itself," wrote a Guadeloupean businessman and local councilman in a letter to Alexandre Isaac, the island's senator who tried to mitigate between the workers and the *békés*, on the morning after the great fire of Pointe-à-Pitre.[62] To many observers, Senator Isaac foremost among them, the fire on the night of 17 April 1899 marked the expression of the mounting discontent among the wider working-class population, and represented the culmination of the island's growing civil unrest that threatened, in Isaac's words, "to ruin the city in one night, as had happened in [the fire of] 1871."[63] Landowners, businessmen, and planters demanded the French government protect them from such acts of criminality. They felt, along with Senator Isaac, "entitled as citizens of France to measures of protections."[64] Considering the double threat of civil unrest coupled with natural hazards, investors and creditors alike worried that going to the colonies presented a risk to capital and health perhaps too high for Frenchmen to take.[65]

Such a sentiment was what had infuriated the workers; that is, workers lamented that Guadeloupe continued to be a colonized space where the concerns of rich investors trumped those of the poor. Many of the island's poor population supported the seizure of cane from the harvest by workers—the so-called marauding acts—in the name of social justice, just as protesters in the bread riots of the eighteenth- and nineteenth-century in England had seized grain in the name of a "just price."[66] When three private watchmen of English descent stopped a creole man in the nearby town of Les Abymes from stealing some cane from the harvest, a crowd of six hundred—the "neighborhood's entire creole population," according to reports sent to the minister of the colonies—armed to the teeth with cutlasses and batons marched on the plantation in retaliation, screaming, "Help! To the Assassin!" The angry mob of "creole workers" attacked and vandalized the home of the planter who employed the security guards, chasing the guards indoors and seriously beating them.[67] They then proceeded to shatter all the windows, flip over all the furniture, and rip the doors and floorboards from the home and throw them into a nearby cane field. Eleven people were arrested for orchestrating the attacks, and the relationship between the authorities and the wider population had reached its breaking point. When the courts handed down a guilty verdict to four of the crowd, judges reputedly blamed it on "the prevailing unwholesome excitement, more or less fomented by a Socialist propaganda."[68] After the great fire, rumors spread that Pointe-à-Pitre's denizens were antagonistic toward the firefighters and rescue personnel, thwarting efforts to extinguish the fire in order to voice their dissatisfaction.[69] These rumors built on the narrative established by the government that the islanders were themselves the *incendiaires* who wished to burn the island's establishment to the ground.

The fact that the incendiarism did not cease on the night of 17 April supported the officials' accusation. While the rubble in Pointe-à-Pitre still fumed, a man disguised as a woman and armed with a cutlass—reminiscent of the *petroleuses* who set buildings aflame to protest the end of the Franco-Prussian War and voice their dissatisfaction with the founding of the Third Republic during the Paris Commune—attempted to burn down a store on 19 April.[70] More unidentified persons set fire to wealthy homes in the neighboring towns of Sainte-Rose, Port-Louis, and Grand-Bourg. At Sainte-Rose, roughly fifty soldiers and mariners from a steamship helped extinguish the fire, and then arrested about a dozen people—one of whom had a stick of dynamite. In the coming weeks, five additional sugar fields and six refineries went up in flames.[71] In one such instance near the town of Morne-à-L'Eau, local authorities sentenced three individuals—two Indian indentured servants and one black laborer—to ten years' hard labor.[72] The gendarmerie and Guadeloupe's leadership feared that continued civil unrest threatened to reduce the island's sugar economy to ashes, while Governor Moracchini attempted to project a veneer of calm on the island's population, promising that "tranquility reigns in all the towns he visited."[73] This did not assuage local anxieties over the civil unrest, and one Guadeloupean newspaper lampooned Moracchini by sarcastically claiming that "the arsonists are tranquilly continuing their work of destruction in Pointe-à-Pitre as well as in other towns."[74]

Behind closed doors, Moracchini had a more nuanced understanding of the root causes behind the recent outbreak of fires, and he argued that mere repression would not be sufficient to quell the unrest. Shortly after the 1899 fire, he wrote, "It is incontestable that fire has been here an instrument of vengeance of the workers against their employers from time immemorial.... We are experiencing an outbreak [of such activity.] . . . The cause? Political excitations say some; the misery caused by the exchange rate that has increased prices across the board to previously unknown heights, say the others."[75] Moracchini advocated the creation of small landholdings among the laboring black class to isolate them from the whims of the international market and inequitable customs duties, arguing that "the solution to the economic and social problem in Guadeloupe is the creation of small proprietorships" by "giving land to the proletarians to create . . . their own livelihood . . . as exists in France."[76] Such an idea had been prevalent in the mainland at this time as a solution to metropolitan labor unrest.[77] Republican Guadeloupeans—united in a common goal of "the moral aggrandizement of France"—demanded the rectification of the island's inequities, writing to the president of the Republic in January 1900 to express their support for the eight-hour workday, the superiority of civil diplomacy over military might, and the continuation of the 1884 law that allowed for the organization of labor unions.[78] All of these demands resonated with the islands' metropolitan brethren, mostly coal miners and smelters, who continuously launched strikes throughout the first two decades of the twentieth century—including a general strike in 1906 for the support of the eight-hour workday.[79]

Therefore, while Moracchini attributed the recent wave of incendiarism to local political excitations and the exchange rate, he also saw workers' discontent as part of larger "social problems" plaguing France and the rest of Europe where "a similar state of things has produced terrible strikes," leading him to ask, "Why is criminality on the rise in France [as in Guadeloupe]?"[80] According to the Guadeloupean left, who referred to themselves as "citizen-electors," metropolitan workers' agitation—what Moracchini called criminality—had inspired the island's proletarians with their own struggle for rights and social justice, and vice versa. The struggle for equality in the face of inequity in the Caribbean as in Europe was mutually reinforcing. Workers demanded the ear of the state, claiming that "universal suffrage must be respected in Guadeloupe as in France."[81] To Moracchini and many others, it seemed that through incendiarism Guadeloupeans were participating in a widespread phenomenon in France at the turn of the century, as anarchists turned arsonists and used fire to voice their discontent with the French government—and indeed all governments everywhere. For instance, August Valliant lobbed a nail bomb at the French Chamber of Deputies in December 1893, shouting, "Death to the Bourgeoisie! Long live Anarchy!," at his hanging.[82] His infamous attack inspired Émile Henry to detonate, three months later, a bomb that killed one and wounded twenty in a café at the Gare Saint-Lazarre train station in northwestern Paris, largely to protest the division of Paris into two cities: one inhabited by the "haves" and the other by the "have-nots."[83] That same year another French anarchist, Martial Bourdin, carried out a suicide bombing outside the Greenwich Observatory in the United Kingdom, and an Italian anarchist assassinated French president Marie François Sadi Carnot. Drawing on a history of anarchism dating back to Proudhon's famous declaration that "property is theft" in 1840, the wave of prominent anarchist attacks in fin-de-siècle Paris, where nearly one in ten people were jobless and many worked eighteen-hour days, led Senator Isaac to claim, "It's the époque where great attacks take place in France, and it seems in this moment that some people feel disposed, in Guadeloupe, to imitate the authors of such attacks."[84] Indeed one Parisian bank observed, "The inhabitants show themselves more and more frightened by the progress [in Guadeloupe] of anarchist propaganda."[85] For better or worse, physical distance had not isolated Guadeloupe from the ideological strife that characterized France at the end of the century. Moracchini was thankful that strike activity had not yet manifested itself in Guadeloupe, though, unbeknownst to him, such a strike was just over the horizon on Guadeloupe's sister island of Martinique.

Fire and Water Yield Steam: The Hurricane of 7 August 1899

At 11 a.m. on 7 August 1899, a category four hurricane struck Guadeloupe— the worst storm to affect the island in eight decades. When the waters from the storm hit the broiling frustration of the islands' working class, discontentment skyrocketed in the French Caribbean. Contemporaries saw natural disasters and civil disorder as inherently linked—one mutually reinforcing the other. As the left-wing-coalition republican journal *La Cravache* stated,

"To the natural scourges that strike it [Guadeloupe] and cut into its material prosperity each day, we must add the plagues of order and different natures which ruin its moral prosperity."[86] Since the proclamation of the Republic in 1870, the colony had received no respite from earthquakes, fire, and cholera outbreaks, which had fueled the discord between the "different natures" of Guadeloupe: reactionary whites, mulatto liberals, and socialist blacks. Some on the island sought a rapprochement between republicans and socialists, since disastrous events had allowed divisions to grow between the three main political groups and opened the door to a reactionism that relied on the old adage "divide and conquer."

Despite the terrible strength of the storm, which had wind speeds of upwards of 150 miles per hour, the overall physical damage on the islands was limited, because the storm had grazed the island on its northern side.[87] Officials were grateful that the economic damage was far less than Martinique had suffered in 1891, which had set back sugar production by roughly five years. From a humanitarian standpoint, however, sixty-three people died during the tempest in August 1899, and damage was concentrated in six towns: Le Moule, Anse Bertrand, Port-Louis, Petit Canal, Morne-à-l'Eau, and the outlying island La Désirade—all, with the exception of La Désirade, sugar-growing sites of civil discontent and incendiarism in the preceding months.[88] In other words, the area that had just burned was the hardest hit, virtually destroying Pointe-à-Pitre and its environs, with buildings tossed one over the other and entire livelihoods lost in a matter of hours. In Le Moule, where fire had ravaged the town in 1897, the storm surge completely submerged the oldest part of the city and the wind had, in the words of one observer, displaced houses as far as an entire block."[89] Likewise, water completely enveloped Port-Louis, and nothing was left of Anse-Bertrand.

The impact of the storm on the coffee and cacao harvest, as well as on the morale of the people, was substantial. The drought that worsened the fires had severely constrained the sugar crop, leaving it so small that the storm had little impact. But the light damage—in places the cane stalks' roots had been ripped up, which meant potentially decreased harvest in future years—further distressed workers concerned that the already small harvest would now be infinitesimal, which would further decrease their paid days of work.[90] Powerful winds had overturned nearly all the homes of the islands' agricultural workers and small *cultivateurs*—largely because these homes were little more than hovels pieced together with nearby materials, which could not withstand the strong gusts. In other words, the storm had left destitute the island's small-time farmers and agricultural workers, whom Moracchini claimed were the most affected and had little in savings. Moreover, the manioc crop, Guadeloupeans' primary food, had been lost, which further exacerbated the rising food prices on the islands.[91] The very workers who had grown so dissatisfied with their government bore the brunt of the destruction, leaving them with few resources and little motivation to continue the civil unrest that had marked the year prior. The storm sapped their incendiary spirit.

Moracchini opened up a provisionary credit of thirty thousand francs to purchase necessary foodstuffs to alleviate suffering across the island, particularly in the north, while the metropolitan government opened a line of credit for the colony in the amount of three hundred thousand francs, of which sixty thousand had been earmarked for the purchase and transport of food and other necessities.[92] The metropolitan government charged the colony's line of credit sixty thousand francs for several shipments of flour, biscuits, rice, red beans, cod, and salted beef, leaving the local government with 240,000 francs to provide assistance and offset budgetary losses.[93] Moracchini also offered a small "salary" to help the afflicted purchase necessities, and he began distributing food and clothing to the worst-hit areas, distributing the supplies as he saw fit. For instance, Port-Louis's and Le Moule's inhabitants received monetary aid to purchase clothing, since "in these two communes very little of the population lived off products destroyed by the hurricane."[94] Moracchini admitted, however, that no matter how much care was taken in distributing the aid, "some abuses are inevitable."[95] As in the 1890 fire, many saw the distribution of aid as inequitable and, in the words of the socialist press, slanted toward the friends of local officials and those workers who fell in line with the sugar industry's wishes. In other words, the socialist press saw the distribution of aid as a form of social control by the sugar industry, whom the press described as "pimps" who "exploit once again the 'naiveté' and misery" of the victims following disaster.[96] Colonial societies and the planter lobby echoed such negativity, blaming Moracchini for his "strange and culpable apathy" and calling for him to be removed from office, partly because of the hurricane and partly because they considered his response to the fire to be at best insufficient and at worst "an odious revolutionary campaign."[97] The historic record does not establish whether food distributors committed malfeasance, as workers accused, nor is it the real issue; rather, the utterance of the rumor highlighted the social discord and distrust between the populace and the government.

As was the case of the 1891 hurricane and would be the case of the 1902 eruption of Mount Pelée, the storm did not affect everyone equally. Whereas workers and poor *cultivateurs* had been hit the hardest, their sole recourse for compensation lay in the public dole: the foodstuffs, supplies, and money that Moracchini distributed to help the poor rebuild. He set aside some of the money for helping to turn homes upright and return the poor to some sort of shelter, which might be the hovel in which they lived before the storm. Whereas Guadeloupe's proletarians had nothing to indemnify with lucrative insurance policies—they had nothing to their name aside from their ability to perform labor—the more well-to-do, particularly plantation owners and property managers, had recourse to insurance indemnities that helped them rebuild.[98] As is common following disasters, the poor bore the brunt of the physical costs of the disaster and the rich the financial, and reconstruction efforts therefore privileged the rich. The island's republicans therefore complained that "in rich neighborhoods . . . homes are insured for 5 to 6 times their value."[99]

Guadeloupe's local government requested a loan of three million francs "destined to go to proprietors ruined by the cyclone . . . to rebuild their devastated properties." The interest-free loan was to be drawn on metropolitan accounts, and individual borrowers, who were expected to repay the loan over the course of twenty annuity payments, received the funds.[100] Victims of the fire in April received nothing, much to the chagrin of Deputy Gerville-Réache, and only those who could demonstrate concrete material losses from the hurricane and guarantee the loan's repayment would have had access to funds. Gerville-Réache deemed the ploy a "very weak alleviation for the incalculable suffering" on the island, though he nevertheless advocated it as a stopgap measure to the minister of the colonies.[101] The metropolitan government rejected even this "very weak alleviation," deeming it unnecessary to the "reconstruction of the colony."[102] Having left the island with too little resources—to the extent that the U.S. Department of State deemed the French government's aid "utterly insufficient, considering the widespread character of the disaster"—the hurricane had magnified the societal inequity that plagued the island prior to its arrival.[103]

While the hurricane had amplified the suffering of the islands' working class, it had dampened the workers' incendiary spirit. Though workers' activities had undermined the legitimacy of Moracchini in the eyes of colonial societies like that of Le Havre and financial interests like the Chamber of Commerce of Bordeaux, who saw the governor as a colonial shill with neither the power nor the courage to quell local resistance and secure their financial interests, workers' frustrations never coalesced into an organized strike that would capture the metropolitan imagination.[104] This is not to say that there were no work stoppages connected to the unrest of 1899—to the contrary, four hundred workers at the Darboussier factory as well as two hundred workers in Lamentin and Pointe-à-Pitre ceased work in protest during March of the following year—but the sporadic and isolated workers' agitation never blossomed into an island-wide strike.[105] The hurricane aside, the lack of island-wide organization had several causes. Guadeloupe's unions and mutual aid societies had been reluctant to push for strikes, as they strained the relationship between union leadership, elected representatives, and the metropolitan government.[106] Moreover, scholar Philippe Cherdieu has deemed Guadeloupe over this period to be "the failure of colonial socialism" in light of what he saw as Guadeloupe's weak union leadership and its lack of a true urban proletariat.[107] Although the workers' movement in Guadeloupe predated that in Martinique by over a decade, the island's socialist leaders failed to mobilize workers along class-conscious lines, and instead formed a movement around *nègrisme* that was antagonistic toward whites and mulattos alike.[108] Fearful of a Haitian-style revolution, planters and governmental officials in turn did not hesitate to employ military force to keep workers in check. Consequently, Guadeloupe would not see its own large-scale, economy-stopping general strike for another decade, when demonstrating workers brought the island's sugar production to a standstill in 1910.

The hurricane had not quenched the incendiary spirit on Guadeloupe's sister island of Martinique, which had been experiencing similar economic hardships at the hands of the sugar crisis. Not only was Martinique spared the brunt of the passing storm, but it was also where workers' frustrations coalesced into a widespread strike in which nearly the entire working population participated. On an island closely connected to metropolitan politics via an interstitial and politically engaged mulatto class, a direct confrontation between the Caribbean's working and ruling classes was at hand. While incendiarism in Guadeloupe had strained the island's relationship with the metropole and eroded administrators' trust in black Guadeloupeans' citizenship, the strike in Martinique would become embroiled in metropolitan politics, consequently threaten the stability of the Parisian administration, and further socialists' coidentification between labor troubles in mainland France and those on the island.

Fire to the Fields: The General Strike in Martinique

Although Guadeloupe's sister island of Martinique had been spared the storm of 7 August 1899, it had not been spared the civil discontent that preceded it. Laborers' frustrations continued to mount over the following months, and on 5 February 1900, agricultural workers on the sugar plantations of Saint-Jacques, Pain-de-Sucre, and Charpentier in the northeastern communes of Marigot and Trinité on Martinique threw down their tools and refused to work. A day later, workers on the other side of the island in Le Lamentin went on strike as well. Within a few days, workers were marching throughout the island asking that their compatriots cease their work in solidarity. What began as a highly localized demand for a wage increase extended to the sugar refineries along the coast, and as sugar production came to a grinding halt, the alarmed governor dispatched the colonial militia. Around four hundred workers congregated at the refinery near Le François on 8 February to voice their complaints, and a military detachment met them.[109] When told to disperse, the strikers responded with Mirabeau's revolutionary phrase, "We are here by the will of the people and we shall yield only to bayonets."[110] The soldiers opened fire and killed eight agricultural workers and wounded fourteen others. Over the next two weeks, the strike spread across the island, and as homes and plantations were set ablaze, rumors of insurrection erupted in the sensationalist U.S. press and stoked the fears of French conservatives.

Although the escalation of the strike prompted the French government to reinforce the garrison at Fort-de-France and to send several French cruisers to the island, the mainstream French press did not initially give the strike prominence.[111] Newspapers in the nearby United States reported it in sensationalist fashion, in keeping with their reputation for yellow journalism established in the "Remember the Maine!" incident two years earlier that supported an imperialist U.S. agenda in the Caribbean. What the United States characterized as open rebellion akin to the Haitian Revolution that might open opportunities to obtain the strategically located Martinique for U.S. interests, the French papers covered as labor troubles incited by French socialists, American provocateurs, or gubernatorial incompetence. Though the shooting at Le François sparked outrage in the metropolitan socialist paper *L'Aurore*, which deemed it a "massacre" and declared the paper's "sorrowful sympathy with the workers in Martinique" who were the "unfortunate victims of bourgeois capitalism and militarism [under the Marquis de Gallifet]," the general strike often emerged in the Parisian dailies under the rather bland heading: "The Troubles in Martinique."[112] But U.S. coverage threw fuel on the fire of downtrodden French workers staging their own strikes in the metropole, leading to a heated parliamentary debate over labor unrest in Martinique and the efficacy of the French government that lasted long after the strike ended in late February. Throughout the parliamentary sessions in 1900, "Martinique" became a buzzword those on the left and right mobilized as they fought for control of the French Chamber of Deputies.

While natural disasters and civil disorders share much with regard to emergency organization, preparedness, and authority response, the willfulness of civil disobedience creates a different social context that frames the event as an expression of the public's volition rather than the results of an unforeseen eventuality. Throughout the event, French officials readily mapped their preexisting political tensions onto the events in Martinique, as they debated whether the individuals involved were to be treated as citizens who needed protection or criminals to be prosecuted—or, in the case of Le François, executed. The delineation between illegal civil disorder and legitimate civil disobedience was grounded in the same political and social prejudices of the left, right, and center that were applied to labor movements within metropolitan France.

Employing a French Precedent

On 7 February, delegates the striking workers at Sainte-Marie had chosen sent a letter articulating demands for an increase in salary and pay rate to the justice of the peace of Trinité. Though technically wage rates in Martinique were higher by 1900 than they had been in previous decades, workers were paid "by the piece." As in Guadeloupe, the growth of beet sugar in Europe and the resulting worldwide overabundance of sugar subjected Martinique's plantation economy to fluctuations that burdened workers with an unreliable pay rate based on production amounts. Though tariffs on beet and cane sugar set in 1892 and equalized in 1897 helped to mitigate the downturn in the Antillean economy, they also forced the Antilles into direct competition with mainland beet sugar and prevented trade with the United States. As agricultural workers suffered a worldwide crisis of overproduction, which resulted in the collapsing price of sugar in France, Martinique lost a quarter of its sugar factories by the close of the century, and real wages were a fraction of what they had been prior to 1884.[113]

Drawing on metropolitan legal precedents, Martiniquais workers demanded their salary increase in accordance with the Labor Law of 1892, which provided legal means for workers to arbitrate demands with their employers. This law, developed for mainland France, contained a caveat in article 16 that extended its application to the old colonies of Martinique, Guadeloupe, and Réunion.[114] Though the explicit statement underlined the colonial status of these colonies, the extension of this metropolitan law nonetheless reflected their special status within the French empire in comparison with newer colonies. Asking for a salary increase in light of what the workers identified as a recovering sugar economy between 1897 and 1900, their letter directly invoked the civil rights outlined in the law of 1892, demanding "equality of treatment for all workers."[115]

The workers' letter marks the first invocation of the 1892 law in Martinique, and it couched the workers' demands in markedly French terms. With the takeoff of the industrial sector in the latter half of the nineteenth century and beginning of the twentieth, strikes and labor unrest came to characterize France and French politics. Between 1893 and 1903, nearly six thousand strikes and lockouts plagued metropolitan France, and about 10 percent were successfully resolved according to the provisions of the 1892 law.[116] The Martiniquais workers were participating in a widespread French phenomenon: labor unrest and arbitration, both successful and unsuccessful.

Most of the plantations made a deal with the strikers on 13 February at Sainte-Marie: workers would receive a pay increase of 25 percent.[117] Some workers found this compromise satisfactory; others saw it as a copout or even treason. On 14 February, a second arbitration at Rivière-Salée granted a wage increase of 50 percent, effectively bringing an end to the first general strike in Martinique. By 21 February, most of Martinique's agricultural laborers had returned to work, and though bands of forty or fifty "agitators," as the U.S. press described them, continued to harass workers on the island, most of the sugar refineries and plantations had returned to full operation.[118] Although there were several more fires and demonstrations at the end of February around Trinité and in the southern plantations, events had calmed by early March.[119]

Debating the Strike of 1900

Although the general strike had ended, the controversy had not. Given that the workers themselves were drawing on precedents that were rather controversial in French politics, it is unsurprising that the February strike in Martinique quickly became bound up in contentious metropolitan politics. The socialists began to term the shooting at Le François the "Colonial Fourmies," recalling the massacre of French workers in Nord in May 1891, which is widely regarded as a foundational moment of French socialism.[120] Both the political left and the colonial ministry argued that Martinique's deputies had failed to make good on promises to raise their constituents' wages.[121] The center-right, arguing that the strike was emblematic of electoral fraud, an issue plaguing metropolitan politics throughout the Third Republic, implicated the socialists. Approaching the issue as an administrative problem, the right took the occasion to discredit Waldeck-Rousseau's coalition government and tried to retake the chamber. In other words, the strike fed mounting tensions between left, right, and center in French politics, and the only thing all sides agreed on was that the problems it represented—

whether attributable to Waldeck-Rousseau's ministry, Martinique's governor, members of the chamber, or the electoral process—were an extension of those in metropolitan France.

As the issue entered the realm of French politics, disagreements over the cause and impact of the strike were legion. According to Guadeloupe's socialists, the Martiniquais workers were unsatisfied with their deputies, Osman Duquesnay and Denis Guibert, because once taking office they had, in a reversal, sided with the more conservative elements of the French legislature. Likewise, colonial minister Albert Decrais and others in the chamber accused Deputy Guibert of having unwarrantedly promised wage increases as part of his electoral platform. Duquesnay and Guibert blamed Governor Gabrié for calling out the troops to achieve his own political motives.[122] Guibert went so far as to accuse the governor of organizing an uprising designed to influence the local election, claiming that Gabrié delayed two days before responding to the situation in an attempt to strong-arm voters. He refused to call the strike a strike, claiming the government invented it as an excuse to cover up gubernatorial disorder and corruption.[123]

Similarly, having witnessed the peaceable negotiation of a wage increase in January by agricultural workers in the north, Duquesnay claimed that he saw the February strike coming and that he had tried to warn the colonial minister, M. Decrais, but no one heeded his warnings.[124] Like Guibert, he argued that the workers were provoked into a riot, and as a result of the government's mishandling of the situation, "French blood was spilled on French soil."[125] By 1900 Duquesnay sought more autonomy for Martinique and vociferously opposed assimilation into the metropole. Despite having been one of assimilation's most vocal supporters just sixteen years earlier, he reached a rapprochement with the island's powerful békés later in his political career. Consequently he appealed to conservatives' "blood and soil" understanding of French identity when discussing the events at Le François, and his appeal to local autonomy and French identity resembled—in language as well as content—those made by traditionalists who championed the distinctiveness of the local pays within the metropole.

The constant allegations shrouded the strike in controversy, leading Guibert to publicly assert that the U.S. press was better informed than the French.[126] Though the record does not support this assertion, he rightly identified scant and conflicted information in the French press. Operating on the official information wired to Paris by the governor, the French press initially reported that the troops at Le François had been attacked and thus implied that the use of force was warranted.[127] The commander of the military detachment, Lieutenant Kahn, had claimed that since the "rioters" had attacked his troops, he was left with no option but to fire. However, it soon became clear that evidence did not support this story: the police chief present at Le François claimed the soldiers fired on the strikers without warning or provocation, three men died from bullets to the back, and most of the wounded and killed were found at least thirty meters from the soldiers.[128] To address the conflicting reports from colonial officials, Waldeck-Rousseau announced that the state should conduct a formal investigation into the events at Le François, and that Édouard Picanon, inspector general of the colonies and lieutenant governor of French Cochin China, would conduct the investigation under the direction of the colonial ministry.

The heatedness of the debate precluded Decrais's Colonial Ministry from having full discretion in handling the problem as a purely colonial matter. On 21 February, citing "the emotion produced in the hearts of Parliament by the current events in Martinique," "the accusations leveled against the republican population of the island by its own representatives," and "the maneuvers employed by a political party to deny the purely economic and social character of the agricultural strike," the General Council of Martinique resolved to conduct its own examination into the social and economic situation which gave rise to the strike.[129] By this resolution, local officials in the Council named the unrest a legitimate strike, declared the island's inhabitants to be inherently republican, and expressed disapproval for the character attacks leveled against the workers. Martinique's General Council was not willing to cede full authority to Decrais's Colonial Ministry.

Likewise, the Chamber of Deputies followed Decrais' every move, holding standard sessions in February and March, as well as a special session in December, to discuss Martinique's general strike. During the March session when it was decided that the Colonial Ministry would investigate the strike, the socialists sent their own investigator, Guadeloupean deputy Hégésippe Jean Légitimus—whom many accused of having incited the unrest in Guadeloupe during the previous year—to Martinique to investigate the shooting at Le François.[130] The special session in December was convened to evaluate the ministry's handling of its investigation. Not only were many in the chamber dissatisfied with the ministry's handling of the report, but some of the more radical members even claimed Decrais had falsified information.

From the outset, the ministry's investigation was contentious and laden with political baggage from metropolitan struggles in the chamber. When Waldeck-Rousseau announced the investigation, he declared the need—to the boisterous applause of the left and protestations from the right—to give "to the population of our colony the impression that, there like elsewhere, we mean to enforce, at the same time, order and liberty." In response, Deputy Lasies from the right exclaimed, "What a nice phrase! You treat us worse than the negroes!"[131] As labor, politics, and race were superimposed on one another, French legislators fell into distinct camps: those who viewed the workers' actions as part of a riotous uprising and those who saw them as part of an organized struggle for economic equality. Despite the blatant racism exhibited by deputies like Lasies, the problems brought to light were, in many ways, endemic to metropolitan France: as the push for social justice gained ground at the close of the nineteenth century, many on the left condemned the right for the plight of all workers, and many on the right considered all collective action to be unwarranted, riotous behavior. As a moderate coalition, Waldeck-Rousseau's ministry was stuck between a rock and a hard place.

REMEMBER MARTINIQUE, REMEMBER CHALON!

During the meeting of 14 February, the Socialist Party of France proclaimed, "The Committee general of the French Socialist Party affirms the sympathy which links it with the workers of everywhere without distinction of sex, race and color. It declares itself to be in solidarity with the working victims of Martinique and denounces with public indignation the new crimes of the capitalist middle-class and militarism."[132] In stark contrast to the claims from the right, socialists held that the agricultural workers had been calm and moderate in their demonstrations during the strike. Despite the factory and plantation owners' attempts to incite the workers and thereby justify the type of repressive action witnessed at Le François, the workers by and large maintained a cool and collected demeanor.[133] Parliamentary debates reflected this sentiment: socialists opened their ears to Gerville-Réache, who did not believe that strikers set the fires, accusing "criminals"—that is, the plantation owners—of setting the fires to attract military intervention.[134] His accusations resonated with those made against the *békés* during Guadeloupe's unrest, and consequently his politics earned him no fans among the "order and liberty" crowd; during his years as deputy, the Parisian police maintained an extensive dossier on him.

On the twenty-ninth anniversary of the "Bloody Week" in May 1871 that brutally repressed the Paris Commune, demonstrations were held across Paris. According to newspaper reports, somewhere between twelve thousand and twenty-five thousand people took to the streets and marched through the Père-Lachaise cemetery. As the socialists marched shouting "Long live the Commune," they waved red banners that read "To the victims of Galliffet! To the victims in Martinique!"[135] Gaston de Galliffet was one of the generals who had led the attack against the communards, and he was the minister of war under Waldeck-Rousseau until his resignation two days after this demonstration. In remembering the communards, therefore, protesters drew a straight line from the bloody foundational moment of the Third Republic to the repression of the strikers at Le François—evidencing the integration of Martinique into the socialists' narrative of French history.

Socialists therefore conjoined metropolitan labor troubles with those in Martinique. Shortly after the general strike in Martinique, a strike broke out in early June at an ironworks in Chalon-sur-Saône. Police confronted over one thousand workers, and after a heated exchange the police opened fire on the crowd, killing one striker and seriously wounding twenty others.[136] Throughout the socialist congress held from the twenty-eighth to the twenty-ninth of September, party members cursed the bourgeois class for exploiting the French proletariat in incidences of strike repression, repeatedly uttering "Martinique" and "Chalon" in the same breath. For instance, as one citizen was criticizing the Waldeck-Rousseau cabinet as overtly bourgeois during the second day of the meeting, those in attendance took up the cry "Les massacres de Chalon et de la Martinique! Massacreurs!"[137]

The socialist congress met in Lyon the following year. Faced with what they called the greatest crime against the working class since the Paris Commune, members present at the Third Socialist Congress in May 1901 issued a manifesto to the workers of Martinique in which they proclaimed, "Your enemies are our enemies. . . . Count on us as we count on you. Long live socialist Martinique! Long live the social Republic!"[138] The socialist journal *Le mouvement socialiste* also highlighted the bond of common class struggle: "What happened here shows that the proletariat of the Antilles—with its strikes and organizational tendencies (unfortunately blocked by exterior causes thus far)—already entered into the conscious phase of class struggle. It disciplines itself more and more in this form of activity that makes the working class the great factor of transformations to come."[139] For French socialists, the strike marked Martinique's rite of passage into full working-class consciousness.

Fears of the Right

Although the more liberal republicans and socialists were willing to treat the strike in Martinique inherently as a labor issue, the conservative press treated the strike as a matter of "the black question" and foreign interference. As was evident during the Pointe-à-Pitre fire in 1899, officials in France worried about a rising anarchosocialism among the island's black population, while the sensationalist U.S. press issued a warning against allowing "rioting blacks" to go unchecked.[140] Witnessing the political agitation of a predominantly black population, the conservative press was quick to label the worker action as riotous at best and rebellious at worst. For instance, the bimonthly review *Questions diplomatiques et coloniales* readily viewed the strike as a black insurrection: "In the course of a strike with as of yet undetermined causes and importance, a part of the indigenous population, those employed in agricultural work, entered into insurrection."[141] The conservative interpretation of the event—evident in the Chamber of Deputies and particularly prevalent in the U.S. press—asserted that the labor unrest was the result of granting black citizens the right to vote in 1848.[142]

A conservative article for the magazine *L'Illustration* focused on the "black question" in a similar fashion, insisting that the strikers were indeed rioters who forced hardworking men to stop their work on the threat of death; plantation owners in Guadeloupe had made similar accusations against black laborers with regard to indentured servants. Seeking to validate the actions of Lieutenant Kahn, the author claimed that the riotous black workers menaced the white population the day after the incident at Le François, burning plantations and crying out "Down with the whites! Long live the negroes! Vengeance!"[143] Le Figaro echoed this fear of the black masses.[144] Overall, the conservative press treated the shooting at Le François as a hard lesson to brigands and rioters.[145]

Though much of the rhetoric surrounding the strike was overtly racist in nature—and intricately tied to a history of chattel slavery—it also represented the right's growing fears of internal contaminates in French society, typified by the political struggle between the dreyfusards and anti-dreyfusards.[146] When Lieutenant Kahn was pulled from active duty following the Picanon investigation, the monarchist newspaper Le Gaulois reported that "the disgrace of M. Kahn—a new victim of the dreyfusards, and a Jewish victim, this time—is a token paid to the socialists who had threatened to vote against the current cabinet in mass until the return of the investigation into the affair of Martinique."[147] The fear was not merely that colonial subjects were revolting against their colonial government, a situation that military strength would rectify, but that members of French society who, like Dreyfus and his advocates, simply did not belong, or who, like the socialists, would undermine French society. With regard to the "old colonies," where nonwhites held the legal status of citizens and not subjects, the "black question" resonated with the right's fears over foreign "contagions" within France's civil society that threatened their mythic "blood and soil" image of France.

The right's fears also had an international dimension. The U.S. press unambiguously sided with Lieutenant Kahn, consistently reporting that his troops had been attacked and were merely defending themselves.[148] U.S. journalists warned that Martinique would follow in Haiti's footsteps by constantly proving that it could not handle the freedom slaves had won.[149] Frustrated by what it saw as the French downplaying the situation, the New York Times asserted that while "nothing short of a rebellion is in progress there, due to maladministration, . . . the official reports attribute the trouble entirely to labor agitation, and take the most hopeful view of prospects for an early settlement of the trouble."[150] The French press seized on this sensationalism and accused the United States of jealously eyeing Martinique, attempting to use racial unrest to foment a rebellion in order to seize it.[151] In fact the

United States had been actively asserting its own dominance in Caribbean affairs since the Monroe Doctrine eighty years earlier, and had recently seized Cuba and Puerto Rico during the 1898 Spanish-American War.

The French political right therefore bound the events to growing concerns over international competition and interference in the French West Indies. According to a letter from the public prosecutor, a rumor that the English queen had ordered the French government to pay its workers two francs each and that she had sent two million francs to the proprietors to be distributed among the workers had caused the strike. As the rumor went, the proprietors refused to distribute the francs, so the workers went on strike.[152] Throughout the strike, plantation owners and managers claimed to have heard shouts about the "queen" and her guaranteed "price" from the strikers. In one such instance, the plantation manager of Le Lamentin claimed that one striker shouted, "The queen has granted this price. Give it to us!"[153] That these rumors existed seems likely, given their use in the French Caribbean to motivate revolutionaries and transmit vital information during the Age of Revolutions. The myth that a "liberating monarch" from a faraway metropole would enact emancipation or squash planters' malevolence had long served as an animating factor behind slave revolts in the Caribbean, dating back to the slaves of El Cobre in the seventeenth century.[154] Always accompanied by the notion that local authorities were standing in the way of the far-off decree, similar rumors led to revolts in Barbados in 1816 and Jamaica in 1831, and they played a vital part in Guadeloupe's pro-republican insurrection in the 1790s as well as Martinique's antislavery uprising in 1848.[155] In this case, the traditional rumor behind slave revolts had transformed into one about labor arbitration and economic fairness, motivated in part by the 1892 arbitration law that had come from the metropolitan government and purported to guarantee an equitable approach to wage disputes. What had united slaves against local authorities earlier in the century now animated workers against factory owners at the century's close.

While the rumor had united the workers, it struck fear into the hearts of the right. Certainly the rumor of the "queen's price" terrified planters and financiers whose social position had been threatened in the past by such tales of royal benevolence, but also conservatives and nationalists who were simultaneously opposed to collective worker action and international intervention. At the turn of the century, France's relationship with England was severely strained, and conservatives feared aggressive action against France's holdings in light of the Boer War. In early May 1900, the French government appropriated nine million francs to strengthen Fort-de-France's fortifications, and conservatives generally agreed that this would stave off English or American imperial aggression.[156]

Coming to Blows in the Chamber

On 26 March, the ongoing investigation of the events at Le François was discussed in the Chamber of Deputies, and a deep-seated disagreement between the political left and right in metropolitan France rapidly manifested in the aftermath. The *Journal des débats* denounced the chamber's "nondiscussion" of Martinique as one of a series of debate made sterile by this conflict: "Most of the serious incidences that arise in the colonies as in the metropole—from without as well as within—belong to politics in general, participating in its incoherent, contradictory, anarchistic, and brutal nature. It is impossible for it to be otherwise."[157] Rising labor unrest within France prompted conflict as to whether the factory owners or Martiniquais deputies had promised salary increases to the workers; the socialists accused the deputies from Martinique of standing by during the exploitation of the Martiniquais proletariat.[158] As emotions escalated over the course of the hearing, tensions between the left and right reached their boiling point. The disagreements over Martinique—truly disagreements over labor politics in mainland France—became physical, as a socialist deputy punched a nationalist deputy while returning to his seat, an event that rapidly overshadowed the issue at hand.[159] Paul Deschanel, a member of the French Academy and a reporter on legislative events, criticized the chamber for the episode:

> As for the inhabitants in Martinique, they are a wise and tranquil people; the factory managers, if one believes MM. Duquesnay and Denis Guibert, are the model patrons; the workers, if one believes M. Gerville-Réache, are the sheep one leads where one wants, and who let themselves be sheared nearly without protest. There is the good governor. But M. Decrais does not want to believe that it was he who enraged this docile flock. There is Lieutenant Kahn who commanded the firing on these innocent victims.

But, M. Decrais continues to say all the military witnesses of the affair affirm that he behaved with prudence and composure.

In Martinique, there are thus no elements of trouble; all goes well or nearly well. But at the Palais-Bourbon! It's there where the spirits are excited and overheated; it's there where one yells, where one throws punches; struggles and games flourish more than eloquence. The orators transform themselves suddenly into boxers, and the political battles take infinitely various and unexpected sides which delight amateurs.[160]

Striking in Martinique had not only fueled tensions between left and right but also brought about a serious challenge to the current government. Lumping together the strike in Martinique and those in the mainland, conservative republican deputy Alexandre Ribot claimed that a weak government that cannot deal with the increasing number of strikes within France could not remain in power for long. He condemned the Waldeck-Rousseau government as dependent on the socialists.[161] Several other deputies on the right echoed his sentiments, and the chamber held a vote of confidence that could have overturned the Waldeck-Rousseau government. In a speech that played a crucial role in preserving Waldeck-Rousseau, socialist Maximilien Carnaud addressed other deputies in his party, proclaiming, "My friends and I do not want to mingle our votes with those men who always fought with a rough energy the claims of workers, nor to provide to some ambitious men the occasion to collect a portfolio from the blood of the workmen of Martinique." The support of Carnaud and other socialists was uneasy, but the vote split 285 to 239 in favor of preserving the ministry, and the deputies cried, "Long live the Republic!"[162] The Waldeck-Rousseau ministry's narrow victory suggested the mounting labor tensions that had polarized members in the chamber and resulted in numerous changes of government throughout the 1890s.

The Bonapartist newspaper *La Presse*, which was highly critical of Waldeck-Rousseau's government, repeatedly criticized the ministry on the basis of the events in Martinique. For instance, when the match makers went on a general strike in mainland France in October, Louis Resse of *La Presse* blamed the ministry, citing the right of workers to seek conciliatory measures from their employers and events in Martinique and Chalon as

A la Martinique

PAR HERMANN-PAUL

— Les députés ont télégraphié que le ministère Ribot serait de notre couleur.....

FIG. 20. Caricature of a Martiniquais sugar worker, 1900
The caption reads, "The deputies telegraphed that the Ribot ministry would be of our color [of our opinion]." "À la Martinique," *Le Figaro*, 29 March 1900. Courtesy of the Bibliothèque Nationale de France.

proof the government was mishandling the mounting labor dissatisfaction within France. Sardonically, he asked, "What can shock us after Martinique and Chalon?"[163] The rising labor frustration, as well as the violent repression of collective action, led many to lose faith in the current government.

Immediately following the parliamentary session of March 26, a political cartoon appeared in the conservative newspaper *Le Figaro* satirizing the attempted overthrow of the ministry in the chamber. In the rather desolate-looking drawing, a black agricultural laborer stands before a cane field and looks calmly at the onlooker, stating that "the deputies have telegraphed that the Ribot ministry would be of our color." Here, the phrase "of our color" simultaneously refers to the cane worker's skin color and means "of the same opinion." On the surface, this image conveys the workers' disappointment with the current ministry's handling of the strike. However, this cartoon possesses a rather multivalent meaning. Though the colloquial phrase "of our color" hints at the racial difference between mainland France and Martinique—that Ribot is of the workers' skin color is simply not true—it also opens the possibility that a white member of the chamber could be identified with the workers in Martinique. Both shared a disdain for the Waldeck-Rousseau ministry's handling of the strike in Martinique and the subsequent shooting at Le François. The extent to which the event resonated in Paris suggested that the strike had indeed struck a nerve with regard to metropolitan labor unrest.

Since Ribot was not known as an advocate for workers' rights but was in fact a staunch critic of the socialists, the cartoonist also seems to be sarcastically emphasizing that the real issue for the Chamber of Deputies was not the well-being of the worker, or even the nature of the strike, but disagreements between the Waldeck-Rousseau ministry and its opposition over metropolitan concerns. Ribot was a vocal opponent of secularization, an opponent of the socialists, and an ardent supporter of the Catholic Church. Upon coming to power, the Waldeck-Rousseau ministry further attempted to secularize the Republic, much to the acclaim of Antillean republicans and socialists who believed he "would neither permit reactionism in general nor clericism in particular to put the republic in peril."[164] As a result Ribot and Waldeck-Rousseau had a highly public conflict. In a bit of racially charged humor, therefore, the cartoonist's caption points to the irony of Ribot and the black workers being on the same side, as it were, against the Waldeck-Rousseau's ministry.

There is yet another layer to this cartoon: the deputies. That they have telegraphed what seems to be misleading information—Ribot was not a champion of racial equality or workers' rights—recalled the charges leveled against them by the socialists and other Martiniquais politicians, that is, that they falsely promised wage increases as part of their campaign platforms. Though this image can be read in a variety of ways, it nevertheless suggests that colonial politics and metropolitan politics overlapped. Though the political use of the event in Paris may suggest that the strike served an instrumental purpose in metropolitan politics, the fact that it carried so much weight in the chamber suggested a resonance that goes beyond colonial concerns. The problems the strike in Martinique brought to light rhymed with those plaguing the metropole at the turn of the century.

On 25 July, a fire broke out among casks of rum and straw crates in the basement of the Martinique pavilion at the 1900 Universal Exposition. It took over an hour to extinguish, though it did not destroy the integrity of the exhibit. Primed by the previous years' incendiarism in Guadeloupe, police suspected malfeasance and began an investigation. Firefighters found two distinct points where the fire started, each in adjoining straw crates.[165] They had even found evidence that a tightly bound bundle of rods had been used as a fire starter. The Martiniquais strike had come home, and the specter of the labor unrest had been cast over one of the largest World's Fairs. Event organizers had made a marked—yet ineffective—attempt to make the exhibit exotic and alluring, but the unfolding political drama in the Chamber of Deputies made Martinique seem more germane to metropolitan politics than exotic and exciting. Contemporary observers remarked that the old colonies and their political intrigues too closely resembled those of metropolitan France to be of any interest to passersby. As one observer put it, the French Antilles, where "the indigenous peoples acquired a certain degree of civilization [and] the administration is nearly the same as that of the metropole ... [,] have presented strikes and social conflicts which have nothing to envy from those of France: here we are quite far from Soudan or the coast of Somalia!"[166]

The Special Session of the Chamber

By early June, Picanon had compiled his report on the causes of the general strike and on the actions of Lieutenant Kahn at Le François. To defend the actions of the government and the current ministry against further "votes of no confidence," M. Decrais tried to coerce Picanon to alter his report to be in accordance with the testimony already provided in the chamber in March: that aggression had led Kahn to fire on the crowd, and that the events in Martinique were not a general strike, but rather a politically motivated revolt organized to influence local elections. Picanon refused to comply, and

Decrais promptly sent him back to Indochina, denying him the opportunity he had been offered to be governor-general of East Africa. He also blocked the publication of Picanon's official report in the *Journal officiel de la Republique,* presenting a censored summary of the results to the chamber.[167] On 19 June, M. Decrais announced that Picanon's investigation showed that Lieutenant Kahn had acted hastily in firing on the crowd and therefore he would be withdrawn from service, but not prosecuted.[168] Though the investigation revealed that the strike's cause was economic, Decrais shifted the focus by declaring that the local police would be better recruited, the gendarmerie reinforced, and public functionaries forbidden from intervening in electoral campaigns.[169]

Politicians on both sides would condemn the report and Decrais's maneuvering. While conservatives believed the report's focus on economics showed that Picanon had caved to socialist pressure, socialists saw the report as indicative of an exploitive, bourgeois bias in Waldeck-Rousseau's ministry.[170] For instance, on 19 October, organizers of the Universal Exposition held a grand banquet to honor those who had helped create and run such a successful international fair. However, with the government's handling of the Martinique strike still vivid, hard-line socialists did not want to invite Alexandre Millerand, the minister of commerce, to the gala. Since Millerand was a socialist whom hard-liners believed was working in collusion with a corrupt "bourgeois" government, they blamed him—rather than the colonial ministry—for the mishandling of Le François and Decrais's subsequent attempt to alter the Picanon report.[171] The slippage here is quite interesting: the socialists held responsible the minister of commerce rather than the colonial minister, suggesting that for them the strike in Martinique was a French labor issue rather than a colonial concern.

Deputy Guibert continued to push for the chamber to discuss Picanon's report, to examine how the government handled the situation and to clear his own name with regard to the accusations of political misconduct. It was not until December, in a special session of the chamber, that the issue was finally heard.[172] Decrais claimed the unrest had died down and the elections went off without a hitch (that is, they mostly went to the republicans) and that therefore it was unnecessary to publish the report, which might reignite unrest. He argued that Martinique's government needed no change except to strengthen the governor, because Martinique's politics "are those politics that inspire the government in the metropole and which receive so often the blessing of the Parliament."[173] The socialists did not contradict Decrais's underlying assumption that Martinique occupied the same political sphere as the metropole. Indeed, in demanding that M. Decrais help bring justice to the colonies of Martinique and Guadeloupe, leftist deputy Gerville-Réache claimed they had submitted fully and devotedly to the ideals of the Republic.[174]

Ultimately, the special session decided to treat Martiniquais labor issues in the same fashion as those of metropolitan France. On 21 December, the chamber resolved by a vote of 273 to 202 to prevent troops from interfering in strikes and to maintain the enforcement of French labor laws in Martinique.[175] The Picanon investigation and the debates in the chamber settled, albeit uneasily, around the idea that the strike had begun for economic reasons, rather than being a colonial uprising, and thus it was included and analyzed in the following year's publication of the *Statistiques des grèves* by the Ministry of Commerce and Industry. In fact, out of a total of 902 strikes in France in 1900, the Martiniquais strike was listed as one of the 580 strikes in France that a demand for wage increases had sparked.[176] Moreover, in 1900 and 1901 the victims and families of the victims at Le François received indemnities from the General Council and the Ministry of the Interior. The General Council of Martinique had resolved to provide indemnities as early as 10 February, just days after the shooting at Le François, and consequently long before the results of the Picanon investigation.[177] After the special session in December, the Chamber of Deputies concurred with Martinique's General Council. Of the total seventeen thousand francs made available, 2,574 francs were split among those whose wounds prevented them from working, which meant they received twice the daily wage throughout the term of their disability. The remainder was split into twenty-nine parts and went to the families of those killed by the gendarmes.[178]

Conclusion

What began as incendiarism in Guadeloupe turned into a general strike in Martinique and ended a political disaster in Paris that nearly fractured Waldeck-Rousseau's coalition government. At the close of the nineteenth century, workers' discontent rose as the national economy and international competition increasingly imposed hardships on those on the lowest social rung. As Guadeloupeans sought to be heard in the French legislature, they put their vexations to the flame, as they had done during the age of slavery when all legal means of their political engagement were prohibited. In this case, the means of legal engagement were not banned but exhausted, as the metropolitan government had repeatedly overlooked the economic needs of its Antillean citizenry in favor of European beet sugar, higher tariffs, and unfavorable exchange rates. While the 1890s had seen the ascendancy of blacks into its political sphere and the early 1900s witnessed several spontaneous work stoppages in Guadeloupe , which had alarmed metropolitan officials, the island would not see a full-scale general strike for another decade, when, as one contemporary socialist described it, workers' collective action in "February 1910 marked the awakening of the Guadeloupean people."[179] Although the 1899 hurricane had in part extinguished Guadeloupean frustrations by occupying them with the more pressing matters of surviving and then rebuilding, at least for the time being, the storm had spared the sister island of Martinique, where grievances were at an all-time high. Erupting into the French Caribbean's first general strike, protestations from Martinique invoked French precedents set in the 1892 Law of Arbitration and prompted a reevaluation of workers' place in the French Republic.

Conservatives and socialists alike in the Chamber of Deputies struck a strident chord in a polarizing debate throughout 1900, and the newly created Ministry of the Colonies had very little role in addressing the worker strike. The socialists and more left-leaning republicans sided, at least rhetorically, with the workers in Martinique, while the nationalists and more right-leaning republicans condemned the events as a riot. Where socialists saw a legitimate demand for a wage increase based on the Arbitration Law of 1892, their political opponents saw a black insurrection that called to mind colonial resistance and a slave past. That is, socialists saw the events of 1900 as an inherently French issue, while nationalists saw it as strictly a colonial problem.

Socialists used the events in Martinique as leverage in their struggle to oust bourgeois elements from the government; moderates and reformists used the event to highlight issues of electoral fraud and administrative misconduct within the metropole; and the right took the occasion to question the social ideals of the Republic, using the events of 1900 as an opportunity—an excuse, really—to discredit the Waldeck-Rousseau government. While the strike, or riot, was clearly merely an instrument in larger political battles, a question nevertheless arises: why was something that happened on a distant island in the Caribbean nearly sufficient to topple a government at home, and why did the debates over unrest in Martinique so readily turn toward labor unrest within the metropole itself?

Though the Caribbean's events were not unequivocally treated as a metropolitan problem—a colonial investigator was indeed sent to the island and racism lurked in the background—civil strife in the Antilles could not be neatly classified or reasoned away as a remote colonial concern. At stake was whether to view Antillean agricultural workers, who were invoking the French Arbitration Law of 1892, as French workers, unruly colonials, or some third element—neither citizens nor subjects but something in an unsettling middle. French Antilleans had made clear demands as citizens for quality pay for quality work, as did many of their counterparts within France. In this they invoked for Parisians the "black question" of untraditional or unruly French citizens *within France's borders*, a question that haunted the Dreyfus Affair and metropolitan discussions of labor unrest and social justice alike. The Picanon report and the subsequent restitution paid to the workers at Le François revealed that nonwhites in the Caribbean were, at least by the letter of the law, French citizens, and as such entitled to invoke the laws and rights granted to all citizens of France. But increasingly, within France as within the Antilles, the question as to what those rights were with regard to laborers was open, and the struggle intensified as socialists and conservatives weighed in throughout 1900.

Many in Paris viewed the French Caribbean as not exotic enough to be strictly colonial—both those advocating civil disobedience as well as those championing law and order. Whereas incendiarism in Guadeloupe called to mind the escalating crisis of European anarchism and the ascendancy of the socialist left, the shooting at Le François in Martinique seemed uncannily familiar in relation to unrest in places like Chalon. This discord stuck in the French imagination. Two years later, with the eruption of Mount Pelée in 1902, French socialists were still using the events in Martinique and at

Chalon as evidence of the bourgeois excess of a "republican regime that is republican only in name."[180] The extent to which the strike in Martinique influenced French politics and resonated with metropolitan concerns at the turn the century clearly illustrates the need for historians to attend to the colonies in discussing historical developments within metropolitan France. Metropolitan events—the struggle between socialists and conservatives, as well as labor unrest and the crisis of French identity—were not simply influenced by the colonies; rather, the colonies were themselves part and parcel of them.

5

Marianne Decapitated

The 1902 Eruption of Mount Pelée

As one of the world's deadliest natural disasters, the eruption of Mount Pelée has its place today among the best-known volcanic eruptions, with Vesuvius, Mount St. Helens, Tambora, and Krakatoa. At the time, contemporaries took the event to mean that the French colonial project in the Antillean islands had invoked the wrath of nature. In the French imagination, it was part of a long history of natural hazards and unnatural dangers—from the Martinican pit viper to incendiary civil unrest, from hurricanes to urban fires. In reality an ill-prepared and ill-informed government put a population of thirty thousand people in harm's way. In misunderstanding this fact, France would solidify the association of risk with the French Caribbean and crystallize the ideological division between the Frenchness of Antilleans and the tropical space in which they lived. The press coverage of the disaster as well as the governmental relief campaign mapped political divisions within the metropole onto this colonial disaster, as officials in Paris and in Martinique understood the event through the double optic of colonial liability and governmental responsibility.

The present chapter will first explain the events leading up to and including the eruption on 8 May 1902. Desensitized to the perpetual dangers that presented themselves in the Caribbean, governmental officials failed to take the threat of Mount Pelée seriously. Relying heavily on misinformed colonial scientists who concerned themselves with the wrong threat, they encouraged rather than discouraged people to stay in Saint-Pierre even as the volcano polluted the air and emitted rumblings. The chapter will follow this discussion with an examination of how the eruption of Mount Pelée was cast as a national emergency as well as a colonial tragedy. Though it evoked "solidarity" and a "great emotion" from metropolitan France, this national emergency was cast in the molds of imperial economics, political infighting, and racial prejudice. Finally, the chapter will explore the ramifications of this event for the place of Martinique, and the Antilles generally, within the French imagination. As colonies of citizens, Martinique and Guadeloupe had liminal status in the French legal framework, but the guiding ideological framework drew a distinction between the islands as a tropical space and their people as members of the French race. On the one hand, Martinique itself was seen as a space that was by its very nature excluded from the republican definition of the French nation. On the other hand, the island's population was included within the definition of French nationality and the three races of its population mapped, albeit problematically, onto political divisions within the French metropole.

The Eruption

On 23 April 1902, the deadliest volcanic eruption of the twentieth century began, as Mount Pelée polluted the air with cinders and ash, wracked the ground with violent temblors, and obscured the sky above Saint-Pierre, the cultural capital of Martinique, known as "the Paris of the Antilles." Over the next two weeks, the volcano's rumbling and the stench of sulfur menaced the island. However, thinking of the loud yet unproductive rumblings of Pelée's anticlimactic eruption in 1851, the populace of Saint-Pierre initially stood by and watched the volcano's peak with more curiosity than alarm. Such nonchalance was due to the French Antillean islands' inactive volcanoes having been known to fume but not to erupt. In addition to Pelée's fruitless grumbles of 1851, La Soufrière's numerous fumaroles had spewed sulfuric gas on Guadeloupe for decades but had not erupted in recent memory. In fact, nearly a hundred years prior, Eugène Édouard Boyer de Peyreleau had predicted that La Soufrière "will soon extinguish itself altogether" as it is "on the border between activity and inactivity" already.[1] The threat from the volcano seemed so remote, therefore, that the republican newspaper *Les Colonies* had announced a picnic organized by the local Gymnastic and Hunting Society on its slopes for 4 May, just four days before the violent eruption that destroyed the entire city of Saint-Pierre. Although the picnic was ultimately postponed following an increase in volcanic activity, on 2 May *Les Colonies* still expected it to go ahead, and the newspaper reminded its readership that the picnic would be a "fine opportunity" to see "the yawning hole from which, in the last few days, thick clouds of smoke have escaped."[2] When the society cancelled the picnic on 3 May, the paper lamented the decision, arguing that time would prove the precaution to be unnecessary.

Convinced that the volcano posed little danger to those within the city limits and dedicated to maintaining public order, the governor of Martinique, Louis Mouttet, encouraged people to stay in Saint-Pierre. He was operating on intelligence from a team of colonial scientists, among them chemists, engineers, and professors of the natural sciences, who believed Saint-Pierre to be in little to no danger. Mouttet, who had served in Senegal, Indochina, Guadeloupe, French Guiana, and the Ivory Coast and who no doubt felt confident of his ability to function in varying climates, even stationed the local garrison along the forty-kilometer-long route between Saint-Pierre and Fort-de-France to turn people back to Saint-Pierre. He temporarily reassigned some of the gendarmerie in Fort-de-France to Saint-Pierre to help keep the peace, and personally refused any requests for leaves of absence from the increasingly anxious military and civil personnel in Saint-Pierre. Mouttet himself stayed in Saint-Pierre rather than returning to the governor's mansion twenty miles away in Fort-de-France, although he did request direct command over the naval cruiser *Le Suchet*, in port at Fort-de-France, suggesting he wanted to be able to make a quick retreat if the volcano erupted.[3] The decision cost him his life, but given the recent memory of the general strike in 1900 and the subsequent shooting at Le François that resulted from the mobilization of the militia, Mouttet's critics saw his use of the garrison as an attempt to mollify by force the increasingly panicked population. Conservative critics long after the eruption continued to levy accusations against Mouttet, using the police presence to accuse him of forcing the population to stay and creating a false sense of security to keep the population calm, portray governmental competence, and win his party the election slated for 11 May.[4]

Though people left the countryside in droves, it seems likely that few people actually tried to evacuate from the northern half of the island altogether. Articles downplaying the impending danger from the volcano abounded in the republican newspaper *Les Colonies*, and Saint-Pierre's mayor assured the population that Mount Pelée posed no immediate danger and that damage "would be localized in those places that have already suffered"—meaning the agricultural farms and villages directly surrounding the base of the volcano.[5] Though the *Journal officiel de la Martinique* described a "dreadful fear" gaining ground after a column of mud killed roughly 150 people on 5 May at the Guérin sugar estate just two miles north near the coastal town of Le Prêcheur, Saint-Pierre's population continued to swell.[6] To those seeking shelter in Saint-Pierre, it seemed that the eruption was a dangerous rural phenomenon from which civilization would offer sanctuary.

To quell the population's mounting fears, the mayor of Saint-Pierre, Roldolphe Fouché, addressed the population via posters placed throughout the city in the days leading up to the eruption: "We are confident that we can assure you that, in view of the immense valleys that separate us from the craters, no immediate danger is to be feared, and that the lava will not reach the city." He pointed out that the scientific community was asserting the safety of Saint-Pierre, and recalled the island's successful recovery from disasters past to embolden the population: "Do not, therefore, yield to groundless panic. Do not be discouraged. Please let us urge you to redouble your efforts, as you did in 1890 and 1891. Resume your normal occupations in order to give the courage and strength necessary to the impressionable people in and around Saint-Pierre in this hour of public calamity."[7] With the mayor promising safety and the governor policing the exit routes, the press suggested that Saint-Pierre's residents go on with their lives as normal while Mount Pelée stirred on the horizon.[8]

In response to the accumulating damage in and around Saint-Pierre, the governor had brought in six metric tons of disaster relief provisions and had begun distributing them in Le Prêcheur, where volcanic activity was the greatest and most deadly. As Mouttet approached Le Prêcheur on a chartered boat on 6 May—just two days before the fateful eruption—a crowd of panicked citizens overwhelmed his ship, most of them small landowners and agricultural workers who were fearful of the mudflows—deadly slurries of volcanic ash, rock, and water—that had poured from Pelée's caldera, Étang Sec. Their homes and livelihoods had been destroyed, and many feared for their lives. Mouttet took the refugees back to Saint-Pierre, assuring them that they would be safe there. Saint-Pierre's population ballooned to nearly thirty thousand as refugees from the mountainside sought shelter. For many in the rural countryside, the urban landscape of Saint-Pierre, with its stone structures and military presence, seemed a safe respite from the threats of the now awakened volcano. Nevertheless, an air of concern persisted in Saint-Pierre, and in response, Mouttet requested an additional detachment of thirty soldiers to patrol the streets. The detachment was scheduled to arrive on the morning of 8 May.[9]

After two weeks of waxing and waning disquietude, as moderate damage accumulated in the environs of Saint-Pierre and among the plantations at the base of Mount Pelée, everything changed for Saint-Pierre. While the mayor's assertions that Saint-Pierre was safe from Pelée's lava flows proved accurate, lava was never the real danger. As bystanders convened to watch a fireworks display commemorating the abolition of slavery and the unveiling of a new statue to the French abolitionist Victor Schoelcher on Ascension Day, 8 May, the volcano awakened, spewing hot gas and rock onto Martinique's cultural capital of Saint-Pierre. The final telegram from Saint-Pierre read "Allez"—a signal to the telegraph operator in Fort-de-France to begin the day's transmissions at just before eight in the morning. The hands of the clock atop Saint-Pierre's hospital froze in time at 7:50. Pyroclastic flows of searing rock and gas blasted from the mountain's side, sweeping down the slopes at speeds exceeding 160 kilometers per hour to drape the city and its environs in hot volcanic dust. This *nuée ardente*—a mixture of water vapor and superheated rock—reached temperatures up to 250 degrees Celsius, and as it blanketed the city, those who were not instantly killed by the high temperature died from suffocation.[10] The event was so quick and the destruction so vast that only one person from within the primary city limits survived: a prisoner in a subterranean cell in the city jail, who would later tour the United States as a sideshow in the Barnum and Bailey circus.[11] Thirty thousand people, Governor Mouttet and his wife among them, perished in the span of a few minutes.

The eruption of Mount Pelée was the deadliest eruption of the twentieth century and the third deadliest eruption on earth since 1500, and it wrought an unprecedented amount of havoc and destruction on the northern portion of the island of Martinique.[12] The eruption continued throughout the remainder of the year, with lava and mudflows pouring through small towns well into August.[13] With the destruction of Saint-Pierre and its environs, approximately twenty thousand people from thirty-five hundred families became refugees, displaced to the southern part of Martinique, to the administrative capital of Fort-de-France, and to the neighboring islands of Guadeloupe and Saint Lucia.[14] Others fled as far as Trinidad or moved to Paris. Homes, plantations, and subsistence farms—even entire villages— were left completely abandoned. Animals and livestock were left behind as people fled in search of safety.

Over the next several months, the volcano remained active, with a secondary eruption on 20 May and another on 28 May. This kept the population ill at ease and in refuge in the south, while the north of the island remained a desolate, smoldering wasteland. Most sought refuge in Fort-de-France, where the city's central park, the Savane, swelled with a populace looking for food and shelter. It was even reported that an English reporter could not find a room to rent for upwards of two thousand pounds per night—an outrageous and likely exaggerated figure roughly equivalent to the combined yearly salaries of fifty French workers that underscored the rampant price gouging after the disaster.[15] As people began to return home at the request of the new governor, Philema Lemaire, Mount Pelée erupted once more. In Le Morne-Rouge and other communes around Pelée's base, an additional one thousand people died in the tertiary eruption on 30 August.[16] While the eruption in late August marked the last significant activity, the flows of lava, smoke, and volcanic lightning emanating from Mount Pelée forced yet another evacuation by the mayor of Fonds-Saint-Denis in September 1902.[17] All told, the damage caused by Mount Pelée continued long after the dreadful morning of 8 May 1902.

A National Emergency

Both French officials and the international community saw the eruption of Mount Pelée as a national emergency, as a terrible event that struck the entire nation of France. In part, this reflected the unprecedented devastation that shocked France and the world, as well as the number of *békés* and white functionaries—family members of people living in the metropole—who had perished in Saint-Pierre. But the casting of this event as a national emergency also spoke to the relationship between Martinique and the metropole, one that often made people forget that the island was a colony and not an official part of France.

The ambiguity of Martinique's position caused problems for disaster relief. Much as in the period following the 1891 hurricane, the metropolitan government was at a loss for how to legally provide assistance to Martinique, since it was a colony but seemed so much like an integral part of France. On 4 May, just four days before the fatal eruption, Governor Mouttet had requested a nominal credit of five thousand francs from the central government's reserve fund, titled "Aid for Agriculturalists for Agricultural Calamities," to help those around the base of Mount Pelée, as well as the agricultural workers and proprietors at Le Prêcheur. The minister of the colonies forwarded this request along with his good graces to the minister of agriculture, who promptly denied the request, because those credits were reserved for agriculturalists in the metropole, and "neither the inhabitants of our colonies nor those of our Algerian departments can be recipients of this aid."[18] Moreover, the agricultural minister remarked that even if Martinique were a metropolitan department, it would only be able to receive assistance after a proper evaluation of damages, and even then the credit could only amount to a total of 5 percent of those damages.

What the denial of this modest credit shows is that while some, notably the governor and the minister of the colonies, believed that Martinique should be entitled to the national governmental assistance, the legal structures in France precluded colonies from receiving funds set aside for metropolitan interests. This was largely the same battle Secretary Étienne and Senator Allègre had fought following the 1891 hurricane, when they requested assistance analogous to that provided to Alpes-Maritime following the 1887 earthquake, as if Martinique were a department. This is not to say that the French legislature was not prepared to set aside money for the victims in Martinique after the magnitude of the disaster became apparent and thirty thousand people died, but that prior to the eruption, the French government was willing to lend money earmarked for metropolitan concerns neither for the smaller-scale catastrophes nor for preparatory efforts. It would take a catastrophe proper to prompt them to action.

The vast devastation that came shortly after the governor's initial and modest request overwhelmed officials' initial qualms. Following the eruption of 8 May, the French legislature opened a credit in the amount of seven million francs, which was used to settle public accounts, relocate refugees and displaced agricultural workers, and carry out public works. In addition to official budgetary line items and legislative allocations, the French government also organized two relief committees to raise funds from the French populace. The local committee was situated in Fort-de-France and staffed by members of Martinique's General Council, governor's office, and diocese, while the national committee was headquartered in Paris and run by the Ministry of the Colonies. The national relief committee was directly modeled on the fund-raising campaign from the 1891 hurricane, and it was tasked with raising support—both money and in-kind goods—from prefectures, departments, communes, and individuals in the metropole. The committee was made up of members from the colonial bureaucracy, and Jules Godin, the center-right republican deputy who represented French India in the national legislature, presided. The local committee in Martinique was charged with distributing the aid received by the national committee, and the national committee set the general guidelines for that distribution.

The disaster relief campaigns cast the eruption of Mount Pelée simultaneously as a national disaster and a colonial misfortune. People in France mourned actual blood relatives as well as figurative members of the French family. The Ministry of the Colonies initiated a national donation campaign to benefit the victims of the disaster similar to the one it had launched after the Great Fire of Fort-de-France in 1890, asserting in newspapers and broadsides that all of "France is in mourning . . . [as] an immense cry of pain was raised in the entire world."[19] Employing patriotic language, the call for aid framed the disaster as a national catastrophe with victims in Martinique as well as in metropolitan France. Accordingly described as a "mission of patriotic solidarity" that was "addressed to the heart of France," the national campaign called on the rich and the poor in the metropole to "cooperate in this work of social assistance, reparation, and salvation." Mayors, prefects, colonial governors, and foreign diplomats repeatedly wrote to offer their condolences, invoking Martinique's status as an old colony.[20] Throughout greater France, fundraising galas, public collections, and newspaper campaigns raised money. One such benefit gala by the Literary and Musical Association of Bouches-de-Rhône in Marseille raised five thousand francs in a single evening.[21]

President Theodore Roosevelt asked Congress to give $500,000—it ultimately provided $200,000 in food and medical aid—to the national French relief effort, and he created a national committee to raise private donations.[22] France warily accepted the assistance. As it had after the 1900 strike, the French readily saw the United States' involvement as characteristic of its "hegemonic spirit . . . with respect to all dependences in the New World"— the same spirit that would coalesce into the Roosevelt Corollary in 1904 that forbade European intervention in the Western Hemisphere.[23] French officials were disdainful of American involvement, because they saw it as a challenge to their own national pride that would justify the United States' belief in the "powerlessness of Europe with respect to its American colonies."[24] Aid took on the weight of international competition, and American sailors and journalists were not averse to mocking the French for taking U.S aid. French officials expressed concern about accepting aid from the United States especially after its seizure of Puerto Rico and its journalists' suggesting that Martinique would fare better under American control.

Anglophone criticism of the French also came from the British Empire, which had a history of aggression against French possessions in the Caribbean as well. Great Britain had occupied both Martinique and Guadeloupe early in the nineteenth century during the Napoleonic Wars. In June, while the volcano continued to spew noxious fumes and lava continued to pour down the mountain's slopes, it was reported in the French press that two Americans were hospitalized in Fort-de-France after being burned by hot gases in an ancillary eruption while on a nearby ocean cruiser: Clara King, a mulatto governess, and her charge, Rita Stokes, the orphaned child of a wealthy white family. In fact they were British subjects who resided on the island of Barbados. After they were discharged from the hospital, the governess and child found lodging in a first-class cabin on the cruiser *L'Eden*. Clara King told a group of shocked passengers that she had to pay 350 francs in hospital fees, crying, "And in Fort-de-France, this is the way you pay for the timely generosity of the United States? What better can we expect from these two new Haitis that you've let develop in Martinique and Guadeloupe. . . . And there it is, the Negro blunder!"[25] The French were scandalized by reports of the accusation, and quite concerned that they had lost standing on the world stage. To save face with the United States and to calm growing frustration in American papers, the mayor of Fort-de-France, Victor Sevère, wrote a letter to the American consulate expressing his regret for the charges to Clara King and Rita Stokes, rightly identifying them as English and not American, as well as refunding their hospital fees, which had ballooned due to overcrowding.[26] Warning that the anglophone press was already saturated with criticisms of the French government, a scandalized reporter for *L'Illustration* asked, "Did the *mulâttress* speak the truth?" Had the French underinvested in Martinique? The reporter declared that his faith in the French paternal stewardship of Martinique had been shaken. The local aid commission declared it unwarranted criticism, however.

After several months of fund-raising, the Comité renewed its call to the French populace in October, requesting more donations in the service of "human solidarity" to help alleviate suffering both in Martinique and in Paris.[27] This second call came after the deaths of nearly one thousand Martiniquais who had returned to the disaster zone and subsequently fell victim to a renewed eruption of Mount Pelée on 30 August. Spurred on by competition with the United States and repeated invocations of national pride and patriotic duty, the fund-raising campaign was highly successful. By the end of December 1904—nearly two and a half years after the fateful eruption began—the relief committee had raised about 9.4 million francs for the benefit of victims in Martinique, far outstripping both fund-raising campaigns for the 1890 fire and the 1891 hurricane.[28] The French state itself had contributed 1.5 million francs to Martinique.[29]

While raising money seemed to proceed flawlessly, distributing that money to the Martiniquais in need was another story. It was reported that over half of the $200,000 apportioned by the U.S. government, as well as a large portion of the private relief funds raised by a national committee in the United States, remained unspent in U.S. coffers. Likewise funds were slow to arrive from mainland France. That money had been raised but not distributed rankled many. In September, a note delivered by left-wing senator Auguste Delpech called out the delay in distribution: "It seems that the needs of the Martiniquais should be pressing enough, their miseries large enough, for them to count on efficacious and prompt aid from the *mère-patrie*, and for them not to learn without amazement that the millions raised sleep tranquilly in the coffers of the metropole."[30] Nevertheless, the U.S. press reported that the French government had the situation well under control.[31] Feeling that the situation in Martinique had stabilized,

Roosevelt's administration decided in late 1904 to divert the bulk of the remaining money to the Philippines, and to return the remainder to the individual donors.[32]

Overall the national relief committee had the best of intentions, but it was split between conservatives focused on financial interests and the island's bleak economic outlook, and republicans dedicated to colonial assimilation. Made up of financiers, representatives from the colonial banks, and political conservatives, as well as dedicated assimilationists and social republicans, the committee included people who believed it should help Martinique as if it were an integral part of France and others who sought to restrict aid to the *békés* and white families.

The intermingling of racial understandings with republican ideology was evident for conservatives and republicans alike. In response to the government's "patriotic call of solidarity," the metropolitan press abounded with imagery of a distressed Martinique calling to its motherland. As with previous disasters, press reports relied heavily on the familial metaphor that characterized Martinique—and the Antilles more generally—as among the dearest "children of the *mère-patrie*." Underscoring that "the *mère-patrie* never forgets its children," the metropolitan press seemed to highlight the outpouring of aid—both international and national—as an example to all the children of the motherland.[33]

Moreover, the committee declared its intention to distribute the assistance equally among the thirty thousand victims who "came from all categories of the population . . . Factory owners, laborers, proprietors or merchants, rich or poor, they were all reduced to the same level of deprivation. It is to this refugee population that it was necessary to distribute assistance."[34] The committee made its explicit aim to return things to the status quo, helping people get back what they had lost financially on 8 May. To this end, the state estimated the losses of those affected, generating countless tables that tracked the health, location, and needs of victims as they moved throughout the Caribbean and settled in France, determining the amount to grant them based on their alleged need.[35] Assistance was given in the short term as "definitive" awards or in the long term as "perpetual" aid. As can be expected, the state awarded far more "definitive" awards than perpetual ones, since they cost the taxpayers less in the long run and fit within an ideology that privileged getting victims "back on track." For instance, in 1903, the government granted 59,910 francs in permanent aid but 2,126,900 francs in definitive aid.[36]

The committee sought to help what it saw as two types of refugees: those who had fled before the disaster, predominantly to the south of the island or to Guadeloupe, Saint Lucia, or Trinidad, and those left destitute by the disaster. Using roughly half its funds (about 5.4 million francs), the committee focused on finding employment for the able-bodied, and used much of the remaining money (about 2.7 million francs) to provide direct relief to orphans, the elderly, widows, and the infirm. To the former, mainly working-age males, the state distributed aid in the short term that was tracked cumulatively and weighed against the total losses the individual or family suffered.[37] Direct aid roughly amounted to 75 centimes per person per day, with those on the necessary registers eligible to receive a daily food ration that would supply roughly twenty-five hundred calories: 300 grams of bread, 300 grams of rice, 10 grams of salt, and either 150 grams of salted meat or 200 grams of cod with 6 centiliters of oil.[38] To the latter, predominantly widows, orphans, and the infirm, the state awarded perpetual state aid distributed on an annual basis—though this assistance was far from equally distributed. Some received as little as thirty francs per year, while others received as much as thirty-six hundred francs per year.[39]

For those on perpetual aid, state assistance was insufficient to maintain a decent standard of living without some form of supplemental income. The state awarded the average perpetual aid recipient approximately 150 francs per year, which was about a tenth of an average Frenchman's yearly wage and less than a quarter of that of an Antillean sugar laborer.[40] One fifty-two-year-old blind man from Fort-de-France, known only as le petit Hypolite, received 180 francs annually from the colonial dole, for instance.[41] This amount was about equivalent to the yearly salary of an indentured servant who received his food and clothing as a matter of contract.[42] Hypolite, by contrast, had to provide for himself, and almost all of his funds would have gone toward maintaining his base caloric intake. At the end of the nineteenth century, one of the island's principal staples, manioc, could cost as much as fifty centimes per liter.[43] As it takes nearly two liters of manioc per day to sustain a two-thousand-calorie diet for an adult, Hypolite's yearly food cost would have equated to twice that of his allowance, excluding supplemental costs like shelter, medical care, and other essentials. Orphans—some as young as a year and as old as eighteen—received much less than poor Hypolite, being awarded an average of about seventy-five francs per year between 1903 and 1919.[44] Presuming that orphans would be taken in by other family members, and believing that these children would one day become self-sufficient, the commission designed orphans' awards to taper off as the children aged. For example, a twelve-year-old boy from Schoelcher was awarded 200 francs his first year as an orphan, 150 for years two and three, and then 75 francs per year for the next five years.[45] His financial aid expired on his twentieth birthday.

The state was discerning in how it distributed the funds, and many applicants were refused state help. In 1903, for instance, roughly 34 percent of all applicants for perpetual state aid were refused.[46] Of the 214 individuals denied perpetual state assistance by October 1903, most were individuals categorized as "diverse" applicants—that is not orphans, widows, the elderly, or the infirm.[47] Typically those who were refused aid were deemed of working age, and most were in their twenties, thirties, and forties. In one instance, however, the state refused aid to a ninety-one-year-old woman from St. Esprit.[48] In determining who received aid and who was denied, the French government granted individual victims and their families a hearing to ascertain whether perpetual state aid was warranted, and in those cases, it was incumbent on the victims to demonstrate real losses that had resulted in their perpetual indigence.

To this end, the local government of Martinique tasked a special commission with collecting official "declarations of losses" from the disaster victims and their relatives.[49] The main task was sorting out inheritance and governmental assistance for the deceased's relatives, as well as updating civil registers. The official questionnaire asked for the demographic information of the victim's relatives: their name, age, familial relationship, and place of residence. It then asked for a detailed enumeration, with supporting documentation, of all property losses to the family: homes, possessions, outstanding debts, cash, land, mortgages, and so on. A bureaucratic nightmare ensued, requiring a level of accounting that strained the already taxed local resources and required a disheveled citizenry to take a detailed account of its familial worth. Initially, the official assistance campaign set a three-month time frame to process families' claims for assistance and share decisions with the local townships via the Comité situated in Fort-de-France.[50] In reality it took several years. In the two years from June 1902 to June 1904, the national relief committee had examined and processed at least 8,146 dossiers of loss claims.[51] In the official report, the commission reported that their work to allay the "perturbation and incertitude" in this "unfortunate colony" had taken far longer than they had originally hoped, and that it was not complete. The process took longer than was anticipated, because many people fled the island of Martinique following the eruption, only to file claims much later.[52] Governmental assistance for the displaced families from northern Martinique continued for decades.

For some the process was much smoother. By August 1902, the French government had begun actively supporting students resident in France but originating from Martinique whose families were affected by the eruption of Mount Pelée in order to "assure them a future and a career."[53] Of the 9.4 million francs raised by the relief commission for the families of the thirty thousand dead and twenty thousand left displaced and destitute, over 1.4 million francs went to a mere 529 students—fewer than 1 percent of those affected by the catastrophe—who had begun their studies in Paris, reflecting a strong bias toward the plantocracy and the wealthiest of the mulatto middle class.

Most of these students were the children of colonial functionaries or came from landed interests in Martinique. The majority had lost their familial wealth, if not their entire family. For instance, one medical student studying at the University of Paris had lost twelve sisters; another student, at an *école polytechnique*, whose mother had financial interests in Saint-Pierre, was left completely destitute. The French government provided each student with an educational grant ranging from one thousand to ten thousand francs to help offset educational and living costs. As a result, this group of students received a staggering proportion (nearly 15 percent) of all funds raised by the relief commission, which was equivalent to about twenty-seven hundred francs per student living in the metropole. By contrast, the approximately 155,000 people left in Martinique, many of whom faced far steeper losses, each received, on average, less than 53 francs. Even if we restrict those eligible

TABLE 9. *Use of funds raised by public subscription campaign, 1902–4*

HOW THE FUNDS WERE SPENT	AMOUNT (MILLION FRANCS)	PERCENTAGE OF MONEY RAISED
Assistance for the able-bodied to find employment	5.5	57
Educational grants for students living in metropolitan France	1.4	15
Direct assistance for the old and infirm (i.e., life annuities)	2.7	28
Total	9.6	100

Note: The allocation of all funds received by the National Relief Committee, as reported in 1905.
Source: FM SG MAR 58, d.479, ANOM.

to the twenty thousand deemed destitute by the state, that figure rises only to the average of about 250 francs per victim.

Among these students were the two daughters of Senator Amédée Knight, the left-leaning republican representative who lost not his life but his familial fortune in the eruption of 1902. Others included the children of wealthy proprietors and governmental functionaries. One child in law school received a stipend even though his family was unharmed and relatively financially secure, because his father had lost his second home in Saint-Pierre. Another law student had his education covered because his mother, the widow of a brigadier in the French navy, had suffered a steep decline in her commercial enterprises in Fort-de-France.[54] Neither Allègre's children nor the two law students had suffered the loss of their parents.

The emphasis on the wealthy emerged early. In the first week after the eruption, the Parisian press focused on news of metropolitans' family members, many of whom were either members of the wealthy plantation class with strong ties to Bordeaux and the financial sector of Paris or were members of the burgeoning colonial bureaucracy. A quantitative textual analysis of all reports in the Parisian paper *Le Temps* reflects this emphasis. "Family" was the thirteenth most frequently used word in reports on the disaster, and the first such word not directly related to a narrative description of the events (*martinique, saint-pierre, catastrophe, ville, colonies, volcan, president, fort-de-france, montagne, cendres*) or the governmental agents reporting on the event (*ministre, president*). Moreover, those words collocated most closely with *famille* were the notable, wealthy members of Martiniquais society: functionaries, bankers, planters, senators, and so on. The metropolitan press focused, therefore, on how the French government could help the afflicted upper crust of Martinique, particularly those with strong ties to the metropole. Some went so far as to suggest that the true victims were those metropolitans who had lost family overseas. A member of the relief committee asserted just five days after the eruption that the government's primary aim should be to help the victims left in France, for "those in Martinique have perished, whereas in Paris and in France, they find themselves in a precarious position and it is necessary to help without any delay."[55] The victims in France were the families of metropolitan functionaries, wealthy mulatto politicians, or *békés*. While there were also some from Martinique who had moved to the metropole to find employment, as young Creole women often moved to Paris to work in the service sector, others from more well-to-do families had moved to the metropole to continue their education.[56]

The masses who perished in the eruption remained nameless in French newspapers, while the familial names of elite victims appeared in the paper. One such family was the Plissonneau family, the most frequently discussed in the week following the eruption. The Plissonneau family owned one of the largest mercantile firms on the island and had been wealthy and lucky enough to charter a steamer to leave Saint-Pierre prior to the eruption.[57] The family had lost its fortune and sought refuge in Castries, Saint Lucia. Ultimately, the family requested assistance from the local Martiniquais aid commission presided over by Victor Sevère and was awarded the same rate (seventy-five centimes per day) of assistance as other refugee families.[58] But the Plissonneaus had recourse to making loss claims that helped the family recuperate its lost wealth, and Georges Plissonneau had access to a much wider base of capital investment. For instance, in July 1903, Georges Plissonneau posted his family's claim to three shares of a Martiniquais shipping company worth 375,000 francs, as well as three shares of a sugar factory at Le Lamentin that was worth two million francs.[59] The difference between an average laborer and the privileged in their means of recuperating losses was substantial, and financial security remained the realm of the island's white plantocracy.

Members of the white plantocracy repeated this emphasis, such as when one member of a family that owned two plantations and belonged to the upper crust of Guadeloupe's white society estimated that only seven thousand perished in the catastrophe, acknowledging that the number might be much higher "if you include the coloured people."[60] In fact Saint-Pierre was considered a predominantly white space, and not coincidentally was termed the Antillean "Paris" in part for its culture and in part for its racial composition. This dynamic can even be seen in the fears of the right, which often imagined persecution of white victims. In late June the Bonapartist paper *La Patrie* published an article titled "Scandal in the Antilles" that outlined a conspiracy in which the government knowingly gave more assistance to the island's black population based on political imperatives:

> Because the Negroes are radicalized and the whites are republicans, the former are favored over the latter. Before handing out aid, the functionaries of the French government busied themselves not with a victim's actual situation, but with his political leaning. . . . The districts containing a radical and revolutionary black majority received the most funds to the detriment of those districts where whites are the majority. The committee of Fort-de-France is responsible for these iniquities.[61]

Despite the paranoia of the reactionary right that the government was actively placating the unruly with food assistance, the mulatto population was far more republican than the intransigent white planter class, the vast majority of the island (95 percent) was nonwhite, and the relief system was set up to privilege those from the upper echelons of Martiniquais society. While direct assistance to refugees in the immediate aftermath roughly amounted to seventy-five centimes per day, or a few hundred francs per year for those eligible for perpetual assistance, insurance claims and capital reinvestment restored the losses of the wealthy. Nevertheless, the rumors of conspiracy elucidated the mounting tension between the socialist left and the nationalist right, and it highlighted the racialization of aid distribution.

A mounting mutual distrust between the administration and the populace arose in this context. The shooting at Le François two years before had planted the seeds of this distrust, and the populace was frustrated with the delay in distributing the aid in Martinique itself, which was at least partly due to the relief committee doling out funds to those marginally affected in the metropole. Resentment mounted among those who believed that the French government had mishandled the distribution of aid, and as the newspaper *L'Opinion* put it in September 1902, "our valiant brothers sigh in vain . . . when, finally, a new disaster has been added to the horror of our situation."[62] This new disaster was the ongoing suffering of a refugee population of over twenty thousand and the inequitable distribution of aid. Knowing much of the relief fund remained unspent in French coffers, while the poor continued to suffer and the wealthy seemed to benefit, further strained the relationship between authorities and the population.

The local administration looked down on the poor, convinced that the refugees sheltered in Fort-de-France were prone to criminal behavior and were apt to abuse the provided material relief. Such fears of large populations assembled in urban spaces had characterized officials' responses following the 1890 as well as 1899 fires and the 1891 hurricane. Provisional governor Georges Lhuerre telegraphed Paris to inform the Ministry of the Colonies that the ruins of Saint-Pierre have become the "theater of pillaging marauders," and thus he has instructed the military garrison to maintain surveillance and ensure "the security of all other communes."[63] A number of arrests had been made. A news correspondent further reported that the land around "Saint-Pierre is not policed, and bands of Negro robbers are terrorizing the natives, burning and pillaging. All persons are going armed to protect themselves from the robbers, who have committed numerous assaults and have no fear of legal punishment. Men have been killed in several places."[64] The French Press repeated the assertion that pillaging "marauders" were menacing the remains of Saint-Pierre's urban landscape, and that the colonial infantry had been dispatched to put a stop to the criminal activity.[65]

Memories of the strike fueled the fear of looting, making it even stronger than it had been after the 1890 fire and the 1891 hurricane, in spite of a lack of evidence of chaos. Just as officials had debated whether the demonstrating laborers were proper strikers or mere looters and brigands, the administration under Lhuerre and later Philema Lemaire conflicted over whether the suffering people were refugees or troublemakers. On 15 August, food distributions ceased in Fort-de-France and Governor Lemaire ordered the refugees back to their homes at the base of Mount Pelée even though signs of an additional eruption were apparent, because he believed that urban refugees were necessarily troublemakers.[66] A second eruption that destroyed what remained of Le Morne Rouge killed over one thousand people because of this forced return.

Such disregard for the well-being of the island's workers is astonishing, but officials' fears were not out of step with approaches to labor and urban malcontents in the metropole. Strikes there ended quickly as the government wasted little time stepping in to put down collective action, sometimes violently due to officials' concern that workers were always on the edge of rioting—such was the case in Le Fourmies in 1891 and in Chalon in 1900.[67] In particular, French officials worried that waves of proletarian riots in Saint-Étienne would hamper production in the coal-mining region around it, which was prone to mining disasters and occupied a similar rung on France's economic ladder.[68] During the mine collapse in 1899, for instance, angry workers, whom the government accused of imprudence and the press racialized as black, waved the red flags of socialist revolution during the state-sponsored funeral for the victims.[69] Local authorities had dispatched police forces to watch over the cemetery. In fact, the French government frequently dispatched the military to Saint-Étienne to stop what officials saw as "workers' riots." In 1869, for instance, the military killed eleven demonstrating workers and then subsequently put down the city's Commune in March 1871.[70] Moreover, given the rebellious reputation of coal miners, companies and local officials pushed workers back to work in the interest of tranquility and economic production, and consequently mining disasters often followed in quick succession, as in Saint-Étienne, where a mining disaster struck every year between 1889 and 1891. Often this was met with resistance. For example, after the Courrières mine disaster in 1906—which had killed eleven hundred—nearly forty thousand striking miners faced off against twenty thousand troops.[71] Such was the relationship of the state to "colonial metropolitans." Following disastrous events, state interest privileged law, order, and a return to work in metropole and colony alike.

In Martinique, the left pushed back against the right's fears of dispossessed laborers, and Lhuerre's initial assessment of the situation stood in direct contrast with the appraisal of Senator Amédée Knight, the leftist Martiniquais republican who moderated the strike of 1900 and would later work on a republican entente with socialist leader Joseph Lagrosillière. "Energetically protest[ing] the tendentious news against the attitude of the population" that was prevalent in the metropolitan press, which he said smacked of conservatives' treatment of strikers in France, Knight reported to the ministry that the population was "calm and dignified in the regions that suffered the most."[72] In his estimation, the laborers of Martinique, whom he typically characterized as "good republicans," wanted to resume work and were waiting on the grand proprietors to get their acts together. This situation had not been resolved by the following year, and the tension persisted between republican representatives and the appointed executive. In June 1903, Martinique's General Council even put forth a motion to protest the emergency military measures Governor Lemaire had taken to quell what amounted to little more than dissatisfied grumbling.[73] The military had continued to surveil and police the island for weeks after the eruption.

Modern environmental scientists have found that natural disasters disproportionately affect the rural poor, with strong contrasts between urban and rural as well as between wealthy and indigent. While the wealthy shoulder the bulk of the financial costs, the physical and human costs primarily fall on the poor, who find it much more difficult to recuperate their losses than wealthy individuals who can find solace in insurance claims or the overall diversity of their investments.[74] In the case of the eruption of Mount Pelée, the claims process privileged those grand proprietors whose families could use financial valuations from the colonial banks to petition for compensation of their financial losses. Conservative French officials saw people like the Plissonneau family, who were able to reestablish their mercantile fortunes, and the well-to-do students in Paris, as vital to securing the economic future of the island. Consequently, these Martiniquais were given access to subsidies, insurance claims, and grants, even though they had their own liquid assets.

Granted, laborers who have little in the way of financial capital or landed estates lose fewer assets in absolute terms than the economically privileged and propertied.[75] But of the thirty thousand who perished in the eruption, 53 percent (sixteen thousand) were black, 33 percent (ten thousand) mulatto, and 13 percent (four thousand) white.[76] Much of the direct assistance the working class in Martinique received went toward paying transportation and educational expenses with the express goal of finding employment for the under- or unemployed. While some of the funds were used to set them up with available land, or to help find them housing, the ultimate aim was, in the words of the committee, to "allocate aid in order to permit them to create for themselves a new existence."[77]

Though the committee strove to jump-start the Martiniquais economy by equitably distributing aid, it did so in a way that would privilege those with bright economic prospects. The special subcommittee created to evaluate Martinique's losses and process the individual claims unanimously agreed that "the allocation of [funds] to victims should have for its goal the reparation of damage and not the realization of a gain," further resolving to toss out any requests coming from people for whom the loss of family members would not have affected them in "the normal order of circumstances."[78] The committee felt that discerning between these claims was part of its mission to ensure the equitable distribution of aid and to prevent abuse. In fact, the committee claimed in its final report it had fulfilled its mission to bring equal aid to all who needed it, and had employed a discerning eye for those claims that it felt had overstepped their bounds. But casting the relief as an effort in restoration had funneled a disproportionate amount of the aid to those who least needed it.

The pattern established in the 1891 hurricane, when colonial investigators had claimed that many of the island's ramshackle homes and unkempt buildings were "valueless," and consequently the government needed only to repair those buildings that were valuable—and even then only to a quality of construction that reflected the island's overall lack of maintenance— repeated. Unfortunately for the island's laboring and lower middle classes, the eruption did not simply alter figures on a balance sheet; it had killed whole families, ruined an entire way of life, and left many destitute. The relief committee deemed the laborers had not lost anything but their own labor, and therefore it must actively help them "find the work that they had lost" rather than providing any substantial amount of direct aid. Proprietors, merchants, and industry leaders received the means to "reconstitute their lost position," not least because they would re-create the lost jobs so essential to the Martiniquais economy.[79]

These actions reflect a clear divide between the republican ideology and its application to governmental relief. Drawing on patriotic language and mobilizing national support to raise over 9.6 million francs for the victims, the committee asserted the equal impact of the catastrophe on all and the need to equitably assist those who were made equal in indigence. Claiming that this was an issue of national pride and "human solidarity," the committee directly compared the 1902 eruption and the subsequent charity to the national response of the French public to the flooding in Toulouse in 1875 and the earthquake in Nice in 1887, and the international response to the flooding in Murcia, Spain, in 1879. The relief committee further asserted that it was the state's role to "do its part in effort and assistance" and "take as its charge works of general interest."[80] The state felt a stronger obligation to the movers and shakers of the Caribbean sugar economy, however, and ultimately the bulk of the financial assistance went toward returning each segment of Martiniquais society to its rightful social status.

Economic and Cultural Consequences of the Eruption

The eruption brought Martinique to an economic standstill that made the consequences dire even for those unrelated to the thirty thousand dead and twenty thousand or more displaced. It caused between two hundred million and three hundred million francs' worth of damage—fourfold that of the 1891 hurricane—and it destroyed the commercial hub of Saint-Pierre. Much of that year's harvests were lost, and even those harvests that were not destroyed were still affected. Even though the sugar plantations on the rest of the island, as well as the industrial hubs of Le François and Le Lamentin, were not in the immediate path of the eruption, ashfall had killed many of the crops all across Martinique. Since the laboring population was displaced throughout the island and the Caribbean more broadly, getting people back to work was an uphill battle. It took years to get the Martiniquais sugar economy back on track, and it was not until 1906 that sugar production levels met their pre-1902 levels.

The eruption of Mount Pelée also had far-reaching consequences for politics on Martinique, as well as for the colony within the French national sphere. The eruption came in the midst of a hotly contested election scheduled for 11 May. Socialists had marched through the streets singing the Inter-

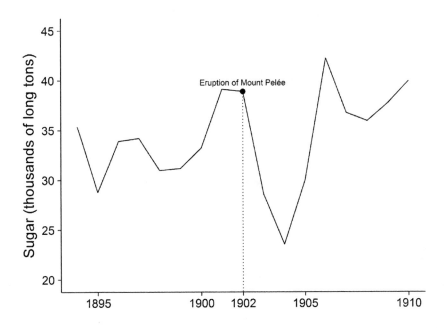

FIG. 21. Sugar production in Martinique, 1894–1910
Notice the drop in production between the years 1902 and 1906. Graph made
in R statistical package using data from Rolph, *Something about sugar*, 242.

nationale, stoking conservatives' fears of a repeat of the 1900 strike.[81] While
many lauded Martinique's governor, Mouttet, as a martyr who steadfastly
upheld the values of good government and republican benevolence, his
political detractors, most of whom were from the far conservative right,
argued that with the election of 11 May on the horizon, he stayed in Saint-
Pierre to assuage voters at the behest of minister of the colonies, Albert
Decrais.[82] Although the elections were never held, Caribbean historian
Franklin Knight has observed that the death of many of the Antillean whites
who had graspingly held on to strategic administrative and professional posts
accelerated the rise of Martinique's colored population.[83] Nearly 13 percent
of all those who died in Saint-Pierre were white, while only roughly 5 to 7
percent of the island as a whole—or between ten and fifteen thousand—
were white. On that fateful day in May, therefore, between one-third and
one-half of the island's white population died.[84]

The eruption had crystalized the political tensions between the republican center and both conservatives and socialists that came to the fore during the strike of 1900. In this environment, the literal decapitation of Mount Pelée resulted in the decapitation of the government as well. While previous disasters had largely left the administration intact, the death of the governor, as well as so many civilian and military personnel, had left the administration in disarray, and many in France now believed that Martinique was headless, even though Fort-de-France was the administrative capital. For French officials, the island's insolvency was clear, and the strain on the French currency unacceptable.[85] Following hurricanes, fires, and a two-decades-long sugar crisis, the eruption left Martinique unable to stand on its own and consequently worthless to France. Without the sugar crisis, such an outlook would not have gained as much traction, to be sure, but coupled with the Antilles' already declining economic importance at the hands of globalization, it seemed that Pelée had put the final nail in the proverbial coffin. The point of view of the Parisian daily *La Petit Journal* that the entire Antilles might be "destined to disappear in the next disaster," represented the idea that sending aid might be throwing good money after bad to save a colony that could not and should not be saved.[86]

If disaster had previously characterized how the French understood Martinique, and the tropics more generally, the eruption of Mount Pelée solidified that association. Since Martinique had been imagined as a colony of French settlement and nearly an integral part of France—almost a department in many ways, or at the very least an Algeria—the eruption of Mount Pelée had a significant impact on how the French viewed themselves. The dangers of the tropical environment, which ethnographers and journalists had feared for decades, became all too real. The sword of Damocles had finally fallen, and for some this event shook their belief in French progress and their very faith in republican civilization. Shortly after the disaster, a journalist for the Parisian periodical *L'Illustration* described the disaster's impact on the republican faith in progress in the following way:

> This office boy is an old republican. Like many men of his generation, he has an absolute faith in the progress of the human race; as proof of his convictions, he climbed the barricades and received a bullet in his thigh.

He does not regret this wound that mars his walk. Instead, it reminds him of his collaboration in the work of liberty. He dreams with pride of the day when the meek will receive more justice, and he hopes that the time will come when fraternity and equality reign as absolute masters over the world.... He ardently loves humans; every day he discovers new characteristics in them; he sees their strength grow and doesn't doubt that they'll become gods.... This catastrophe has profoundly touched him; he weeps for the thousands of beings who were snuffed out by the flaming materials launched by the volcano; but he also feels his faith stagger: *our race, is it as grand as we had imagined it?* Hasn't this disaster belied all these grand ideas? He moans, "In the 20th century! Is this even possible?" We all secretly have the same thought.[87]

The catastrophe shook the French belief in man's triumph over nature and the Third Republic's ultimate victory over inequity. Previous disasters had had a huge impact on the built environment, but this catastrophe had utterly destroyed an entire city and its population. For those who had truly begun to believe that Saint-Pierre was the Paris of the Antilles—a French settlement where the French race had been transplanted into tropical soil, producing what contemporary scientists saw as a mélange of European and African "bloodlines" particularly suited to the hazards of the Atlantic world—the eruption of Mount Pelée left them bitterly disillusioned, questioning whether the French race—which contemporaries used synonymously with civilization, and to which Antilleans of color had laid claim—could triumph over tropical space, or whether civilization could triumph over nature more broadly.

Since thousands had flocked to Saint-Pierre for safety, only to die, the eruption had shaken people's faith in the safety of civilization. The press printed and reprinted numerous articles detailing historic eruptions like Vesuvius and more recent ones like Krakatoa, along with depositions on the world's so-called dangerous zones for seismic activity. With the nearly simultaneous eruption of Soufrière in Saint Vincent, the eruption of Mount Pelée had stoked French interest in the volcanic regions of the world, from California to the Mediterranean to Southeast Asia to the Pacific Islands. With the earthquake in 1887 in the Alps, as well as an increase in seismic activity that same year in Europe, it seemed that such an event could happen anywhere. But the French began to convince themselves that with proper planning and science, they could restore their faith in civilization, blaming the incompetence of the local government for the loss of life.[88]

As one of the most destructive and deadly natural events, as well as the only significant volcanic disaster in French history, the eruption of Mount Pelée became the prevailing leitmotif for Martinique in the French imaginary, dwarfing all other associations. As figure 22 demonstrates, one in every four books published worldwide in French that mentioned Martinique also mentioned Mount Pelée in the year or so following the eruption, up from one in twenty the year prior to the eruption. As the graph shows, it became vogue to mention Mount Pelée in the same breath as the island of Martinique, and even today no tourist guidebook worth its salt fails to mention the dramatic eruption in 1902.

The association of Martinique with the eruption of Mount Pelée was in part merited, for the devastation was hitherto unfathomable. In fact, modern earth scientists have designated a class of volcanic eruptions named after the 1902 event: among the most violent and lethal kinds of eruptions, a "Peléan eruption" is characterized by pressurized gases blasting suddenly and forcefully from the side of a volcano to travel at high speeds close to the ground.[89] The damage was so extensive and long-lasting that the French government was still fielding requests for public assistance and building shelters for the victims in northern Martinique well into the 1930s, particularly after another eruption in 1929.[90] Saint-Pierre and its environs never really recovered. Though some of the surrounding townships were rebuilt, the once bustling city of Saint-Pierre is even today a fraction of its size in 1900.

As it had done in covering other disasters in Antilles, the press focused primarily on the loss of Saint-Pierre as a commercial hub rather than on the extensive suffering and loss of life, and as was the case with the 1890 fire and the 1891 hurricane, journalists were preoccupied with the disaster's effects on the port city's docks and shipping infrastructure.[91] On behalf of the affected plantation owners and merchants of Martinique, the president of the Chamber of Merchants, an organization representing Parisian financial interests, asked the minister of the colonies for an indemnity to cover the costs of the damages to property and commerce.[92] Once declarations from

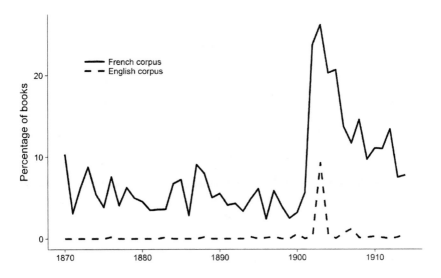

FIG. 22. Percentage of French and English books
mentioning Mount Pelée, 1870–1914
The graph, with a smoothing of 0 and normalization
against books that mention Martinique, was created
in the R statistical package with data from Google
N-Gram viewer. Michel et al., "Quantitative Analysis
of Culture Using Millions of Digitized Books."

the "disaster victims living in the metropole" as well as those "in the colony"
had been collected, financial assistance was provided by the minister of the
colonies in conjunction with the local government of Martinique.

But, at the same time, the language of compatriotism and citizenship
with regard to Martinique resurged among republican officials and within
the daily press. French as well as foreign representatives characterized the
eruption as a "grand misfortune [that] had struck France."[93] As they had
done after the 1890 fire and the 1891 hurricane, the French underscored their
shared citizenship with the afflicted in Martinique, and while this emotional
bond must be understood against the backdrop of financial concerns and
colonial inequities, it is nevertheless significant that many treated the aftermath of the eruption of Mount Pelée as an issue of national emergency. In
fact, the exact phrases "citizens of Martinique" and "citizens of the Antilles"

spiked in all French texts contained within the Google corpus following natural disasters in the years 1891, 1896, and 1902, and the spike following the eruption of Mount Pelée was the largest. Despite the limitations of the Google corpus, the three spikes show an association between natural disasters in Martinique and the idea of citizenship, as well as a profound association between Martinique and victimhood.

Moreover, syndicates within the metropole took interest in providing relief to northern Martinique, mobilizing benefits for the victims across metropolitan France and calling for demonstrations of solidarity.[94] Although socialists generally seized the opportunity to poke their political opponents, taking strong umbrage with the *fêtes de charité* the bourgeoisie had run that they deemed as full of opulence, characterized by self-congratulation, and deficient in terms of real aid, they nevertheless underscored the very real need to help their compatriots in Martinique and couched their call to aid in strongly assimilationist and republican terms. As Ernest Vaughan—the founder and editor of the leading socialist newspaper, *L'Aurore*, and editor of Zola's famed article in support of Dreyfus, "J'accuse"—stated, "The survivors of the catastrophe that has destroyed the most flourishing part of Martinique from top to bottom are our compatriots, in the same title as the inhabitants of any of our provinces. It's not alms, no matter how rich, that we owe them; it is full compensation for what they have lost. Republican France has an urgent debt to repay."[95] Vaughn thus reaffirmed the right of the Martiniquais to French citizenship, and thus the debt owed to them,

FIG. 23. (*opposite*) **Percentage of French books discussing compatriotism and victimhood, 1880–1910**
This graph shows the prevalence of the n-grams "citoyens de la Martinique" and "citoyens des Antilles" in French texts. Notice the jump following the 1890 fire, the 1891 hurricane, and the 1902 eruption of Mount Pelée. The spike in 1896 may have been connected to the very strong tropical depression in early December 1895, while the jump in 1886 is possibly related to the split between Hurard and Deproge in 1885. Although there is an increase in patriotic language following each disaster, the notion of victimhood dwarfs this increase, particularly after 1902. Graph created in R statistical package with data from Google N-Gram Viewer: Michel et al., "Quantitative Analysis of Culture Using Millions of Digitized Books."

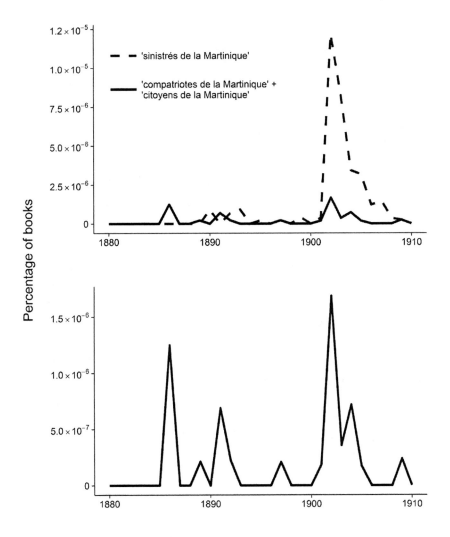

not just because of their participation in a vision of the social republic but also because of the colonial legacy and suffering under slavery that had not yet begun to be repaid.

Outside the socialist press, however, assertions of Martiniquais citizenship and compatriotism often ran alongside reaffirmations of Martinique's colonial status. Official correspondence, as well as both the centrist and the conservative press, frequently referred to Martinique as "one of the oldest and most dear of the French colonies" and affirmed shared citizenship and compatriotism. At the same time the national relief campaign underscored Antilleans' belongingness to the French nation, when all of France was draped in sorrow and journalists bemoaned the consequences of such a horrific disaster for the French nation, the phrase emphasized Martinique's status as a colony, just as it had following the 1890 fire and the 1891 hurricane, repeatedly underscoring Martinique's status as a colony in the same breath that it stressed compassion.

Other colonial disasters had tested the limits of French compatriotism, and the amount of public support for the victims in Saint-Pierre following the 1902 eruption set a precedent for French support of other colonies. When the Pacific hurricane known as the Froc Cyclone made landfall in French Polynesia in December 1902, Charles Depince, a delegate from the Chamber of Commerce for Tahiti, asked for more governmental support for both the "French and indigenous populations" in the French South Pacific. Invoking the precedent of the "generosity that was so largely exercised for the benefit of our Antillean colony," he argued that there was an "evident analogy of situations between these two colonies which, within several months of each other, were ravaged: one by fire, the other by water."[96] In fact, he even asked that some of the money raised by the national campaign for Martinique be diverted to French Polynesia, though this request was denied on the grounds that people had donated those sums under the assumption that they were destined for Martinique.

In spite of these hopeful signs of French regard for Martiniquais as equals, however, racist, stereotypical renditions of the people, especially women, living in Martinique resembled those that had followed the 1890 fire: engravings of the *mulâtresse créole* and the *négresse* stood side by side with drawings and photographs of a destroyed Saint-Pierre. In June 1902, the *Journal des voyages*—a colonial periodical that purported to bring information about all of "overseas France" into bourgeois metropolitan homes—reported on this catastrophe that wracked one of the *"plus anciennes colonies françaises"* by juxtaposing idyllic and stereotypical depictions of the island's nonwhite population with the flames, lava, and ash covering Saint-Pierre. Highlighting both the island's long history with France and its racial mixture, the *Journal* explained,

And what a population! What charming grace is drawn on the face of this creole (in the accompanying image), the result of the crossing of white and black. . . . The *métis* are today the guiding class in Martinique. The *négresses*, as our photograph shows, are not lacking in a certain appeal. Blacks or Negroes constitute what is called over there the third class of the population. As a result of contact with our civilization, they have lost little by little their apathy and inveterate indolence. The women seem completely transformed.[97]

The article continues by recounting a story by Louis Garaud in which a twelve-year-old black girl buys bread and a bouquet like a "real Parisian," leading the paper to conclude that as "one of the colonies most devoted to the *mère-patrie*," the island of Martinique "occupies an honorable place in our colonial domain."[98] As this article demonstrates, the French Antilles were simultaneously seen as French and colonial, tropical yet familiar. Mulattos were nearly—and quite condescendingly—French, as were the island's "third-class" black population who had become less "apathetic" and "indolent." The French considered Martinique's environment dramatically and volatilely foreign and therefore un-French. The juxtaposition of a hostile environment and French civilization as it was embodied in the island's population resembled that which had followed earlier disasters.

By contrast to their fears of disorder in urban spaces during moments of catastrophe, the French idealized the Martiniquais of the countryside, who embodied for them a form of old-world France where traditional values carried the day and the pace of life was calmer and more moderate. Such stereotypes persisted, even though the strike of 1900, which demonstrated a rising demand for social equality among the islands' black laborers, who increasingly turned to the socialist party, belied them. Officials had privileged small cultivators in the countryside as French peasants in the 1891 and 1899 hurricanes, and in the months leading up to the 1902 eruption, the vicar-general of Martinique, Monseigneur Gabriel Parel, claimed to prefer the company of the island's rural population, whom American tourists deemed the "true Martiniquians."[99]

Racist depictions of the disaster in the press were often laced with sexism, as a preoccupation with Afro-Caribbean women—whom the islands' visitors described as "imperiously attractive" with a voice "qualified to charm"—dated to the times of plantation slavery. Few European women migrated to the West Indies, supporting the sexualized image of the slave woman among the islands' white male plantocracy. The image persisted after emancipation, becoming a projection of the French republic, of the successes of the civilizing mission and the establishment of "French civilization" in the most inhospitable of places.[100] As the image of Marianne came to embody the French Republic in the metropole, the image of the *mulâtresse*—as in figure 24—came to embody the "true Martinique" that had been acculturated to French values, styles, and beliefs. The stock image that covered the front page of *L'Illustration*'s edition about the eruption of Mount Pelée often accompanied news stories about Martinique, and was commonly reprinted on postcards and in travelogues about the islands.

This image of the Martiniquais woman—whose skin is light as a byproduct of racial intermixing—was prominent in the press, and it had deep roots in the colonial relationship between Martinique and the metropole. In an extensive report on the eruption in *L'Illustration*, one journalist made sure to remind his readers of the Martinique Pavilion at the Exposition of 1900, the World's Fair in Paris that had run contemporaneously with heated parliamentary debates over the 1900 strike in Martinique. Painting a sexualized and idealistic picture of Martinique as home to the beautiful mixture of the races, he remembered the exhibition sentimentally: "the visitors of the Exposition of 1900 certainly can't forget the beautiful Martiniquaises who were, if it can be said, the lively jewels of our colonial section. They wonderfully represented, for the pleasure of the eyes, one of the most exquisite types created by the fusion of two races: the quadroon [an individual one-quarter black]. . . . This female figure symbolized in a particularly characteristic way the collective humanity that had animated the life of the now vanished city." For him, Martinique was an idyllic and fanciful world, where the legacy of slavery had been mystically sublimated into the peaceful and carefree blending of African and European heritages, and the eruption cruelly disrupted the process. He lamented, "Charming Martiniquaises, carefree, a little frivolous, as it willfully is in the lands under the sun. How many of them perished in this dreadful massacre? How many passed instantly from smiling content to the torments of terror and death?"[101]

Ce numéro est accompagné d'un supplément musical.

L'ILLUSTRATION

Prix du Numéro : 75 centimes.　　　　SAMEDI 17 MAI 1902　　　　60ᵉ Année. — Nᵒ 3096.

LE CATACLYSME DE LA MARTINIQUE

UNE MARTINIQUAISE

FIG. 24. The Mulâtresse, 1902
    Stock image used as the cover piece for a magazine article about the erup-
    tion of Pelée. "Le cataclysme de la Martinique," *L'Illustration*, 17 May 1902.

FIG. 25. Poster for a disaster-relief benefit, 1902

A poster for a benefit held at the Hippodrome for the victims of Martinique. *Représentation de bienfaisance au bénéfice des sinistrés de la Martinique*, Affiche en couleurs illustrée. Femme et ses enfants devant l'éruption de volcan de la montagne Pelée, 1902, FR CAOM 9Fi474. © Archives nationales d'outre-mer (ANOM France).

Le Petit Journal

Le Petit Journal
CHAQUE JOUR 5 CENTIMES

Le Supplément illustré
CHAQUE SEMAINE 5 CENTIMES

SUPPLÉMENT ILLUSTRÉ

Huit pages : CINQ centimes

ABONNEMENTS

Treizième année | DIMANCHE 1ᵉʳ JUIN 1902 | Numéro 602

LA FRANCE VIENT AU SECOURS DE LA MARTINIQUE

FIG. 26. Illustration of France coming to Martinique's aid

An article in the Parisian periodical *Le Petit Journal* depicts the republican Marianne coming to the aid of Martinique, embodied as a mulatto Marianne. The two are locked arm in arm in solidarity. "La France vient au secours de la Martinique," *Le Petit Journal*, 1 June 1902.

The preoccupation with Martiniquais women went further than ethnographic essentialism. For many French republicans, the Martiniquais woman—most notably, the *mulâtresse* mother—represented the embodiment of Martiniquais culture as well as the very colonial relationship of the island to the metropole. As the images in figures 25 and 26 suggest, Martinique was a type of mulatto Marianne. The first image, taken from posters for a benefit in Paris to raise money for the disaster victims, displays the typified image of the mulatto mother, distressed by the eruption and the prayers of those suffering men clambering to the safety of the beach and the children clinging to her breast. The *mulâtresse* covers her mouth in disbelief as a classical blond embodiment of the French Republic reaches out from the hippodrome to bring her relief. Such images prevailed following Caribbean disasters at the close of the nineteenth century, typifying a subservient relationship grounded in republican values. In fact, an 1890 poster by Lefevre for a disaster banquet, which may have been the inspiration for the 1902 poster, depicted a similar scene following the fires of Fort-de-France and Port-Louis.[102] The poster, hung around town and printed in the *Le Courrier français* to stir donations for a banquet on the Champ-de-Mars in August 1890, showed a similarly blond, female representation of the French Republic embracing her kneeling mulatto counterpart from the French Antilles, with children in tow. In the illustration from *Le Petit Journal*, we see a somewhat different version of the mulatto Marianne and instead witness the embodiment of the French republic rooted more in French revolutionary traditions. Now without children, the mulatto Marianne wears a creolized garb reminiscent of the flowing garments donned by the republican icon, complete with a Caribbean stand-in for the Phrygian cap covering flowing black hair. Instead of being cradled, as she had been in the 1890 image, she clasps arms with the metropolitan Marianne in solidarity as the mulatto Marianne points to the destruction of her "Paris of the Antilles." While the mulatto Marianne looks to her metropolitan counterpart for help, the metropolitan Marianne looks in pain and disbelief at the destruction of Saint-Pierre. As in the other images, the disaster has brought this mulatto Marianne to her knees, and overall suggests that only support from metropolitan France and the graciousness of the Republic can save her from her woes.

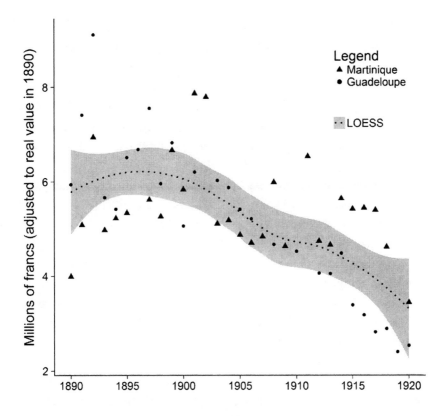

FIG. 27. **Yearly budget for the French Antilles, 1890–1920**
Adjusted for inflation, this graph shows a local regression trend line
(LOESS) on the average budgets of Martinique and Guadeloupe. Created
in R statistical package. The inflation index for 1890 to 1920 is based on
Pierre Villa's 1994 index cited in Thomas Piketty, *Les hauts revenus*, 689.
Data gathered from *Budget des recettes* for the years 1901–18; *Bulletin officiel
de la Martinique*, 1871–1908; *Guadeloupe et dépendances: Budget*, 1885–1918;
Martin et al., *Statesman's Year-Book*, 1880–1920.

Along with the association between the Caribbean and calamity came
reduced governmental funding for the Antillean colonies, which saw a budgetary downturn following the eruption of Mount Pelée (figure 27). After
Pelée, Martinique and Guadeloupe combined had about half the purchasing
power, adjusted for inflation, of that during the decade before the eruption.
With budgets normalized to the value of francs in 1890, the Antilles' annual

budgets were approximately six million francs from 1892 to 1902 but were well under four million francs by 1920. The eruption of Mount Pelée alone was not sufficient to prompt the French government to decrease funding to the two colonies, but it solidified a trend developed during the fires, hurricanes, and strikes of the previous decade. The decline in the sugar economy and a decade of disasters, topped by the environment rearing its head in the ugliest of ways, had persuaded the metropole to divest itself financially from Martinique and Guadeloupe.

Even with the surge in funding immediately following the eruption, the islands' budgets dropped steadily in the ensuing years, though Martinique's fiscal problems were much less pronounced than those on the island of Guadeloupe, where, as Elizabeth Heath has shown, advocates for sugar subsidies had failed to obtain financial assistance similar to that provided wine growers in southern France despite Antilleans' demands being predicated on shared citizenship.[103] Pelée's wrath had in part mitigated that failure in Martinique, where the metropole provided financial assistance to individuals and annuities to the colony as a whole to help it rebuild. In some ways, Republican Marianne had come to the aid of her mulatto sister. And yet, even with this assistance, Martinique's average budget still declined when adjusted for inflation: in the decade prior to the eruption, it stood at over six million francs; in the decade afterward, when the budget was that much more important to the colony's well-being, it dropped to an average of five million francs. By 1920 it had dipped below four million francs. Contemporaries had complained about underinvestment in the years prior to 1902, seeing the 950,000 francs per year put toward Martinique's public works as wasted capital.[104] After 1902 budgetary shortfalls became more pronounced as funds proved insufficient to rebuild what had been destroyed. In response, the French government liquidated Saint-Pierre's financial assets rather than rebuilding it, attaching the once great city to the nearby Le Carbet.[105] The once bustling city of Saint-Pierre was no more.

Conclusion

Contemporaries would describe the Paris of the Antilles after 8 May 1902 as a modern-day Pompeii, ignoring the stark difference that most people evacuated Pompeii prior to the eruption, whereas in Saint-Pierre the majority had not.[106] While only about a thousand people remained in Pompeii when Vesuvius erupted, Mount Pelée almost instantaneously killed approximately thirty thousand people who had thought, only moments before, that they were relatively safe within the confines of Martinique's cultural capital—a bulwark of French construction in the perilous tropics. Martinique's acting governor following the death of Mouttet, Georges Lhuerre, later reported that "even early on the fatal morning, no fresh catastrophe seemed to be impending, as cablegrams received at Fort-de-France described the situation as stationary."[107]

Having killed up to half of the island's white population, this tragic event wiped out a large portion of the white planter class, and was treated as a matter of national emergency. Colonial assumptions and racial prejudices strongly shaped what that meant. For some, the eruption of Mount Pelée was the epitome of the dangers of the tropical environment to French civilization—the capstone to a long history of fires, hurricanes, and earthquakes. For them the true victims were the approximately four thousand to seven thousand white people who died on the morning of 8 May, and despite a systemic privileging of the wealthy over the poor, they cried foul at the republican government's attempts to distribute national aid to nonwhites as well as whites. Those in the metropole who had lost family members—or indeed, their entire families—saw the eruption as the decimation of a member of the figurative French family as well as of their own literal families. Others saw the figurative suffering of the mulatto Marianne and the French response to it as emblematic of French solidarity regardless of the color line. As one contemporary observed in the days following the disaster, "Martinique . . . is eminently French. It has exemplified [Frenchness]. It has fought for, suffered for France. . . . Does it have negroes? Yes, Martinique has negroes. *Good negroes.* . . . All the negroes there are civilized French citizens!"[108] Ultimately, the eruption cemented the idea that the Martiniquais people were a bastion of French civilization in a hostile environment, while at the same time the loss of the most salient representation of Paris overseas furthered the idea that Martinique would forever be dependent on the metropole for security and solvency.

After the eruption, many became wards of the state, receiving nominal stipends because Mount Pelée had left them indigent.[109] Not everyone who asked for assistance received it, however, as the governmental committee in charge of distributing aid weighed a victim's indigence against other possible avenues of support, including family members, friends, pensions, and so on. In one instance, an elderly man was initially denied state assistance only to be granted help after his two sons refused to take him in.[110] On the one hand, the state's willingness to provide support for victims is a testament to the language of civic inclusion that demanded a spontaneous outpouring of support from France and its colonies. On the other hand, such stipends taxed the state's goodwill, playing into the calculus of disaster that would delay the Antilles' incorporation into the country until 1946.

By receiving public assistance, victims of Mount Pelée inadvertently confirmed the financial sector's worst fears that the Antillean economy was no longer worth their sustained effort, and that Antilleans were more than the bastion of French civilization in the tropics; they were a fiscal liability. Not only did the governor of Martinique report regularly to the minister of the colonies about distributions from what was known as the catastrophe fund, but receiving state aid was a matter of public record, as the aid commission published the names of those on public welfare in the government's *Journal officiel* for all to see, along with their age, place of residence, and the amount they had been awarded.[111] Caught between the two poles of civic-mindedness on the one hand and financial frugalness on the other, the victims of Mount Pelée suffered a second calamity. Though they would receive nominal aid from the state to allay their indigence caused by Pelée's fury, they would retain their second-class status as colonial citizens until after the Second World War.

By 1922, eight thousand inhabitants had returned to the ruins of what used to be Saint-Pierre. As a contemporary journalist put it, echoing Henri Monet's observations following the 1890 fire, such inhabitants "moved there despite the sword of Damocles that perpetually weigh[ed] on their heads." In turn, he asked whether the French had truly learned the lesson of 1902.[112] But the French had learned Pelée's lesson. When the volcano awoke again in 1929, officials did not delay in evacuating the northern half of the island and avoided the massive loss of life witnessed in 1902.[113] In fact, the state evacuated approximately ten thousand people from the affected areas.[114] Yet they had learned a second lesson—one much less positive. Just as Henri

Monet has observed thirty years prior, the French government considered the Caribbean islands as always perched on the precipice of disaster, sitting, as it were, at the banquet of French civilization with inevitable death and destruction looming over their heads. As one contemporary in 1922 observed, "Why have we allowed the reoccupation of a presumably off-limits area?"[115]

The lesson of 1902, therefore, was twofold: officials had learned to take nature's threats seriously, which was particularly relevant when the entire island of Guadeloupe was evacuated in 1976 as La Grand Soufrière began to fume, but they had also reconsidered the place of the Antilles in the French national sphere, heeding the warning Bordeaux's Chamber of Commerce made decades earlier that "it would be a mistake if we considered Martinique to be a French department ahead of planned assimilation, ignoring the profound divergences created by its geographical, physical, and agricultural situation."[116] In essence, ignoring Damocles' sword would spell catastrophe, and instead of assimilating the colonies, as Antilleans had demanded since the onset of the Third Republic, officials reevaluated the financial benefits of holding onto such volatile islands. Weeks after the fires that had wracked the two French islands in 1890, the governor of Guadeloupe had opined, "What neglected riches; what unexploited treasures!"[117] Now, after a decade of environmental destruction, civil discord, and the deadliest volcanic eruption in the Western Hemisphere, such riches had been overshadowed by Damocles' sword.

Epilogue

National Identity and Integration after the First World War

As the remnants of France's old empire dating back to the seventeenth century, the colonial citizens of Martinique and Guadeloupe had long participated in the French nation. During the eighteenth century, the military police in the Caribbean had recruited free black persons, charging them with defending the islands against numerous aggressive campaigns by the English. An ordinance in 1702, for example, declared that "all black inhabitants with a renowned loyalty" would be recruited to "serve for the defense of this island of Martinique." Over the rest of the century, this trend continued and soldiers of color played a vital role in the Atlantic Revolutions, participating in the American War of Independence as well as in the French Revolutionary Wars.[1] For example, Louis Delgrès, a mulatto military officer from Martinique who had been exiled by royalists, fought for the Republic against the British during the Revolutionary Wars, and later struggled against Napoleon for Guadeloupean emancipation, seeing the restoration of slavery as a betrayal of the Republic and its ideals. Black Antilleans fought for emancipation again in 1848, and even raised arms to support the Republic in southern Martinique in 1870. Eventually France granted Antilleans citizenship rights with the constitution of the Third Republic, ushering in a new era of political participation. As France enlarged its empire to its greatest extent and made subjects of countless peoples in Africa and Indochina, the oldest of France's colonial populations put forth a vision of a "tropical Frenchness" predicated on racial intermixing and environmental adaptability, but nevertheless rooted in French political and cultural traditions.

Over the course of the Third Republic, colonial bureaucrats actively reframed the French Antilles as a settler colony where French civilization had taken root, rather than an exploitive colony where Africans and their descendants had been mistreated for economic profit, thus yielding credence to the belief that French civilization and universal rights were one and the same. Yet officials met a troubling paradox, because the myth of settlement required a legacy of white settlers that did not exist. The "settler population" of the French Caribbean—if we can call it that—were in fact Africans who had been forcibly brought there as slaves and then acculturated over generations to the very French values that ultimately toppled slavery. Thus the population of Martinique and Guadeloupe that participated in the process of national integration as citizens of France, giving a unified national culture to the political entity known as France, was not white. This process dates to the French Revolution itself, when black Jacobins from Saint-Domingue participated in the National Assembly in the wake of the French Revolution and forced the new government to enact the ideals the revolution had purported to support: liberty, equality, and fraternity. Antilleans' tropical Frenchness challenged a competing vision of France rooted in a blood-and-soil narrative that traced French heritage back to the Gauls, helping to redefine, oftentimes by directly contesting, the national values and mores of a Third Republic forever stained by its brutal suppression of the democratic values of the Paris Commune.

Environmental disasters in the French Caribbean brought to the fore the existing racial and social tensions that tested the Republic's ideological convictions of assimilation and citizenship. As the republican project of empire came in contact with the environment of the Caribbean, the rhythms of Antillean life became a perceived threat to French civilization. The impact of hurricanes, earthquakes, fires, and volcanic eruptions, as well as the population's collective action and civil unrest, on the colonial economy and sugar extraction foregrounded societal issues that challenged the French state to safeguard its colonial citizenry. By intervening in the islands' economy, the French state put the French Caribbean's relationship to the metropole on display for all to see, particularly as representatives from the islands began demanding the economic and civil rights that belonged to citizens of French departments.

On the one hand, the tropical environment of the Caribbean separated it from the French nation, underscoring the creole distinctness of the islands and marking them as a dangerous, colonial locale. Yet, while the environmental climate distinguished the Caribbean as a world apart, the political climate coincided with that of the metropole, and the government's efforts at humanitarian aid reflected the Republic's faith in shared citizenship and a civic conceptualization of the French state that saw the French race in terms not of black and white but of cultural mores, political participation, and a unifying faith in liberty, equality, and brotherhood. The Republic's relationship to Martinique and Guadeloupe, therefore, demonstrates most clearly what Gary Wilder has described as the "imperial nation-state," for France articulated imperialism in the framework of a parliamentary republic struggling to accommodate a citizenry's demands for social equality and governmental protection through disaster relief within the metropole and within the colony. In other words, the same political formation—a semi-representative French bureaucracy—expressed both the parliamentary republic and the imperial administration with regard to the French Caribbean's representation in the French legislature. In response to this political co-identification and in light of what Josh Cole has described as the development of the "statistical state," the French government exhibited a form of bureaucratic humanitarianism that provided assistance to the suffering population in the form of economic engineering—an attempt to reconcile liberal, free-market economics and humanitarian intervention.

Therefore, at the same time that a language of citizenship that underscored compatriotism with the colonial citizens of Guadeloupe and Martinique marked French response to disasters, environmental disasters threatened the republican fantasy that placed mulattos at the heart of the civilizing mission and reinforced republicans' fear of the black laboring class, who, as socialists as well as a colonial population, were cast as agitators threatening the very fabric of the French nation. The response to the devastation of the island's sugar economy by the hurricane of 1891, which foregrounded the framing of human suffering as a statistical and economic problem ceded to the 1900 debate over the legitimacy of colonial citizens' right to strike, and then to the privileging of the white minority over the nonwhite majority in receiving governmental assistance and sympathy in the press after Mount Pelée erupted. Yet these disasters also forced the French state to publicly deal with issues of social welfare and social justice at a time when liberal economic theory stood against governmental intervention, and in turn the disasters helped define the relationship of the French state to its citizenry, not just in the colonies but more broadly in France as well. The general strike of 1900, which cast light on labor unrest within the metropole as well as the mounting dissatisfaction with the colonial economy in the Caribbean, in particular reflects this dynamic.

Through environmental disasters and civil unrest in the late nineteenth-century French Caribbean, this book has addressed two central questions: How did modern France reconcile its liberal convictions with its imperial ambitions? And how did a colonial citizenry transform the Republic and its concomitant definition of citizenship? Looking at the legacy of old imperialism at the close of the nineteenth century reveals that the colonial periphery helped guide France's national integration. The environment played a key role in the race-making identity formation and class-based politics that defined this nation, and the Caribbean ecology—both as it relates to sugar production and its rhythm of catastrophe—affected countless lives and shaped both colonial and national politics. Citizenship rights came into the public eye in the face of cataclysmic events, as the French nation wrestled with issues of national as well as colonial identity, race, class, and the very nature of French civilization.

*

When Europe plunged into war in 1914, tropical Frenchness came home to roost as the French government called on Antilleans to pay a "blood debt" to France as their motherland. While it may have seemed that the islands had little blood left to let due to the perpetual violence inflicted on them by nature's wrath, they nevertheless heeded the call. In general, Antilleans supported the enactment of conscription in the French Caribbean as essential to their integration into the French nation, just as small towns and villages within metropolitan France had integrated through military service by 1900.[2] Employing a colonial census taken in 1913 in preparation to draft young Antillean men into the looming war, the governor of Martinique, Georges Poulet, called on the colonial population to defend the *mère-patrie*. Confident of their courage, dedication, patriotic sentiment, and spirit of sacrifice, Poulet had little doubt that the old colonies would, in light of the "links that tie us all to the *mère-patrie*," rise to the call.[3]

And rise to the call they did. Upwards of twenty-five thousand young Antilleans of color boarded ships bound for Europe. Over half would be sent to the front lines, and more than three thousand would breathe their final breath in service to France on the battlefield. These numbers were unprecedented, and the number of French Antilleans sent to war was roughly equivalent to those lost during the eruption of Mount Pelée in 1902. Scholarship has thoroughly documented the importance of the First World War for the Antilles' assimilation into the metropole, typically focusing on the blood debt and Antilleans' sacrifice, which France would pay with interest upon the conclusion of the war.[4] The First World War not only cemented the French identity of Antilleans, which has been the underlying theme of this book, but also flipped the motherland-child relationship to some extent. Antillean soldiers would witness firsthand the brutality of France at war, exchanging the barbarity of the Caribbean climate for the barbarism of the European battlefield, which challenged the very idea of French civilization. On their return they would come to defend French civilization from itself as they solidified their demands to become part of the French nation.

En route to Turkey in May 1915, a young Martiniquais soldier traveling in a regiment made up of West Indians, Senegalese, Algerians, and Alsatians declared his "happiness to contribute to the defense of civilization" and his willingness to show himself to be "a worthy son of Martinique and his race."[5] Such a sentiment was common among the Martiniquais *poilus*—the French term for young soldiers, much like doughboys in the United States—who had been cast as irrefutably republican and treated as the bastion of French civilization against hostile external forces for the past four decades. As one enlisted man from French Guiana observed when discussing the colonial enthusiasm and patriotism for the Great War, "The remoteness of the Mère-Patrie does not diminish the sentiments of the children of France, no matter their origin or the latitude at which they see the day. There are not two ways to love France, as there are not two ways to be a Frenchman: one either is or is not."[6] While French Antilleans knew themselves to be French beyond a shadow of a doubt, they nevertheless felt the need to repeatedly prove their Frenchness to their comrades, who were by and large ignorant of just how French the French West Indies were.

Many Antillean politicians who had been struggling to integrate the islands into France proper saw the outbreak of war as an opportunity to prove once and for all the islands' indefatigable patriotism and thereby secure eventual departmentalization. Antillean soldiers saw themselves as embodying the wishes of the great Victor Schoelcher, the champion of emancipation and civic inclusion for black Antilleans, singing as they marched to battle, "Schoelcher, may your spirit quake, your dearest wish accomplished, whether your skin is light or dark, for all there is only one flag."[7] Since the end of slavery in 1848, and particularly since the codification of the Third Republic's constitution in 1875, the French Caribbean's elected representatives in the Chamber of Deputies and in the Senate had been pushing for integration into the French military service as part of their mission to make real the benefits of citizenship for the French Caribbean's former slaves. With the integration of the military on the eve of war in 1913, enthusiasm was high from Guadeloupe to Martinique to French Guiana, as individuals volunteered for service and were attached to infantry regiments in Rochefort, Marseille, and Perpignan.[8]

The white planter population, never supporters of republicanism or national integration, did not share the enthusiasm of Antilleans of color for the involvement of Antillean soldiers in the war effort. Viewing it as a republican conspiracy to harm the Antillean economy that the *békés* had controlled for centuries, they rejected republicans' oft-championed language of civic inclusion in favor of an economic calculus focused on the bottom line. Not only would they be losing their labor force, but also Antilleans' integration into French society threatened planters politically. The treatment of Antilleans as French citizens, obliged to join, belied the *békés'* belief that the Caribbean colonies had the sole purpose of increasing France's power and wealth.[9] As a token of their commitment to this belief, they had lobbied the French government to create a general colonial government for the Antilles and Guiana as had been done for Indochina and West Africa. This move would have consolidated their power and more firmly defined as colonial the relationship of the Antilles to the metropole.

The white planters were no more successful in blocking the participation of Antilleans of color in the military than they had been in creating a general colonial government. Over their objections the French state incorporated French Antilleans into the metropolitan French military, unlike those colonial troops assigned to colonial battalions. The planters had little opportunity to find willing ears in the French legislature. Although French officials defined political classes as racial categories vis-à-vis natural disasters and civil unrest, they understood the *békés* as the landed aristocracy of the Old Regime, the utter antithesis to the republican project. Meanwhile, the islands' mixed-race population, by virtue of their politics and their economic status as a local middle class, came to represent the republican project in the New World, while the black laboring population draped itself in the values of socialists' mounting challenge to the Republic's dilettantish parliamentarianism. Social divisions over economic rights and social welfare that resonated with similar class tensions within the metropole set the stage for the political impotence of the planters in this manner.

Antilleans' longtime role in the metropolitan military likewise doomed planters' objections. Antilleans of color had served in the colonial administration for decades and were at times renowned. In fact, a Caribbean mulatto named Thomas-Alexandre Dumas rose to become the general-in-chief of the army of the Alps during the Revolutionary Wars. Born of a white French noble and an enslaved African, Dumas was known for his military acumen during campaigns in Italy and later Egypt, and consequently the Austrians nicknamed him the "black devil" and Napoleon referred to him as a Roman hero who had come to protect France and its revolution.[10] Dumas's success in the French military, as well as his aristocratic upbringing, brought his family notoriety and wealth, which in turn helped his son Alexandre, author of *The Three Musketeers* and *The Count of Monte Cristo*, become one of France's most renowned authors and playwrights.

Such examples of nonwhite citizens using the military to climb France's social ladder were sobering to a white planter class who saw the mounting strike activity, civil unrest, and political fallout from natural disasters at the end of the nineteenth century as reflecting hatred of white people as well as an economic problem. As one prominent planter, Roland Pichevin, wrote in a report to the French legislature in 1906, all the islands' troubles began with the emancipation of the slaves, which "caused troubles to rise: assassination and fire were the savage response to this beautiful gesture from the metropole."[11] The natural disasters and civil unrest of 1870–1902 had hardened antagonism of the white elite toward black citizenship, when sugar production was paramount and civic inclusion was pushed to the sidelines. Participation in the Great War further threatened white control over black laborers, so vital to *békés'* economic dominance of the islands, while furthering the incorporation of people of color as French citizens. Planters' anxiety over losing control of their workforce grew now that financial valuations showed the Caribbean—and indeed all of France's colonies—to be vital for the war effort. As Guadeloupe's commissary described at the National Colonial Exposition in 1922, the islands' rum kept the soldiers warm and permitted "our poilus to stay in the trenches during the winter."[12] Meanwhile, the scarcity in Europe of sugar, coffee, and cacao—the staple cash crops of the islands for centuries—made the French Caribbean's produce that much more important and financially viable, exacerbating planters' unease.

The white planters' fear that the war would further the assimilation of the West Indies came to pass, however. Unlike West Africans and Arabs in the French service, who were infantilized as "little brothers" who had to be kept in line by paternal white captains, the military treated French Antilleans as comrades and equals. Soldiers from the Caribbean were not subjects but citizens of the empire. White officers, who had been told so many times by parliamentarians and fund-raisers of the dedication of the French Caribbean to French ideals, did not feel the need to use the firm grip it held on North and West African soldiers whose loyalty might be unstable.[13] Whereas Great Britain's army segregated its West Indian battalions from the general army, France placed the Martiniquais and Guadeloupians into mixed regiments where they served alongside white troops from the metropole, and they often held important posts. For instance, Commander Camille Mortenol, the son of a slave from Guadeloupe and the first black graduate of the École Polytechnique, received the Legion of Honor for his anti-air defense of Paris and long-time service at Brest.

Evidence of tension between white and black soldiers along the front nonetheless exists. One Martiniquais man, simply identified in his letter as "X," who had given up his government job as an accountant and volunteered for service, lamented the poor treatment of people of color by white Europeans on the Western Front. As a sergeant major in the artillery, he complained in a letter home in December 1915 that his comrades in the trenches from Brittany and Picardy watched the Martiniquais out of the corners of their eye, identifying "base prejudices in the Aurelle and Marseille barracks," and saying that soldiers "continue to offend, humiliate, and mistreat our black compatriots." However, in his eyes, not everyone in France believed that Antilleans were different or aberrant and untrustworthy. Many other soldiers he had met "unanimously said that we [Antilleans] show more patriotic spirit than those living in many French towns." He ended with a provoking question: "On the battlefield, as in the weapons depots, we [French Caribbeans] are none the less ready to sacrifice ourselves for our Patrie, and isn't that one of the best qualities of a good Frenchman?"[14]

Another contemporary soldier recruited from Martinique in July 1915 noted before his departure to France that what "distinguishes our sergeants [of color] from some of their white peers is that they neither despise nor disdain the colored race . . . [, but] interact with them as men and not as animals."[15] But he goes on to state that experienced recruits had warned him that "all this would change in France, where our compatriots find neither urbanity nor goodwill."[16] He hoped this prediction, that the congeniality among the white command and black soldiers would break down along the front lines, would not actually happen "for the benefit of us all."[17]

While some of the racial goodwill did dissolve in crossing the Atlantic, the military treated French Antilleans differently than they did the rest of the colonial troops, and this attitude influenced the civilian population. In many ways, French Antillean soldiers had to serve as a sort of cultural ambassadors who proved the islands' Frenchness to France. One creole Martiniquais soldier who had fought in Europe, Pierre Dalmas, explained in October 1915 that metropolitan France received him and his fellow countrymen more amicably than those from the newer colonies such as Senegal, in spite of the civilian population's ignorance of the West Indies. His account of his time in France, however, included French citizens often misplacing him on the racial hierarchy: "creoles suffer from the fact that they were relatively unknown in France," he wrote, angry at being confused for a West African, and experiencing prejudice as a member of the newer colony. But he also complained, "People imagined that the mere fact of being from Martinique, Guadeloupe, or Guyana necessarily implied the complete absence of culture. . . . Everywhere we go, we are questioned by people somewhat amazed to hear us express ourselves in French and curious to know how we came to possess our modest French culture." At times he had to explain to his fellow countrymen that his homeland of Martinique had belonged to France for three centuries, that the educational system there mirrored that of the metropole, and therefore that there "is nothing extraordinary about [creoles] resembling [the French] with regard to civilization." Yet he felt that as an ambassador for the French West Indies among the military population, he could explain to civilians that he was not from a "barbarous" population, and "old prejudices disappeared."[18]

The experience of war, on the other hand, was barbarous. Whereas natural disasters in the Caribbean amounted to Damocles' sword suspended over the heads of the Antilleans, fighting for France meant a gun pointed at their backs. As another Martiniquais soldier, Corporal Banaré, stated after a raid on his trench in September 1916, his life was now one of "horrible carnage" and he expressed fear and frustration at being perpetually surrounded by mortal dangers. Of the nine fellow Martiniquais who had recently been assigned to his regiment, two days after deployment, only three remained alive.[19] Facing the horrors of war and the true meaning of the blood debt, many Antilleans deserted, as did others in the French military. Antilleans' belief that French civilization was glorious, however, may have been more fragile than that of their compatriots born and raised in metropolitan France.

The barbarity of French war and the pride of valiant service combined to enable Antilleans like Pierre Dalmas to see themselves as the protectors rather than the recipients of French civilization. The ideology of the "civilizing mission" that had privileged Europeans over colonial populations by putting the latter in the tutelage of the former broke down. Citing the valor and bravery the colonial troops with whom he had served displayed, Dalmas rejected outright the idea of superior and inferior races and tacitly jettisoned the civilizing mission as whole, as did many of his contemporaries who had faced the barbarity of European warfare and claimed a definition of resilience and honor forged in the tropics rather than Europe, yet considering it French in character.

The First World War and its horrors provided a foundational experience for the integration of the Antilles into the French nation. As the Guadeloupean newspaper *La Démocratie colonial* expressed at the end of the war,

Antilleans' "secret thought, while we asked to be allowed the honor of serving France during this time of war, was to be in return for our modest sacrifices fully assimilated as French."[20] The process that had begun under the barbarity of the Caribbean climate had finished under the barbarism of war. Reflecting on the old colonies' participation in the war, General Émile Ruillier, a white creole from Guadeloupe, wrote, "Mixed with soldiers from France, the Antilleans of all colors showed themselves dignified by their discipline, their dedication, and their courage, meriting once again the title of Frenchmen."[21] The occasion, his visit to Pointe-à-Pitre for the Antilles' ter-centennial of Guadeloupe coming under French control in 1635, gave weight to these words.[22] As in metropolitan France, war monuments inscribed with names appeared in communes throughout the French Caribbean as early as the 1920s to commemorate those "heroic" children "who died for France" and for the "fatherland."

In the years following the Great War, the metropolitan government con-curred that Antilleans had proven themselves French. The French Republic held up Antilleans' participation in the war as emblematic of the islands' spe-cial relationship with France, and recognized the brave defenders of French civilization who "died for France during the war 1914–1918" by inscribing their names in a book marking colonial heroism, a *Livre d'or* that would be stored in the Pantheon alongside the greats of French history.[23] The book underscored the heavy price paid by Caribbean combatants throughout the war for Antilleans' participation in French nationalism. Each commune in the Caribbean received a copy of the *Livre d'or* with condolences and a list of inhabitants from that commune who had perished in the war to safeguard the French Republic. Those who received the distinction "*mort pour la France*" were eligible to be buried in France's state military ceme-teries. Enshrined in the Pantheon and entombed on French soil, Antillean soldiers were integrated into the French nation.

As historian Veronique Hélénon has shown, Caribbean participation during the First World War played a vital role in the assimilation of the old colonies into the metropole, and Antilleans continued to see enlistment in the national French army as an act of ultimate patriotism long after the final shots were fired in 1918. In what historian Jacques Dumont calls "a quest for integration," Antilleans amplified their demands for integration after the war, particularly as a way to further distinguish Antillean citizens from colonial subjects. This sentiment became that much stronger as Antillean, as well as other colonial, intellectuals flocked to Paris throughout the 1920s and 1930s. As one such intellectual, Jules Monnerot—founder of Martinique's communist party—stated in 1935, Antilleans "are the descendants of ancient settlers, serfs, slaves, all imported, mostly mixed of two races intimately connected—racial prejudices notwithstanding—and who feel and live as Frenchmen."[24] The war had helped cement this view. In 1919, for example, former soldiers formed a veterans' association in Martinique that repeatedly lobbied the governor and the metropolitan government for colonial equality, using the theme of the blood debt to substantiate their demands; France now owed them, rather than the other way around.[25] The dedication of the Antillean soldiers who gave their hearts and souls in the conflict proved, beyond doubt, the French Caribbean's devotion to France. In 1921 the Colonial Institute in Paris paid its respects to the unknown colonial soldiers who died during the Great War, proposing, "Perhaps overseas France has nurtured this obscure soldier, dead to save the Homeland and the world from barbarism."[26] In reality, however, France's colonial aspirations and national pride had created the barbarism from which the colonies had spared it, just as it had in the rest of Europe. French civilization owed Antilleans a debt of gratitude dating back nearly three centuries, as Antilleans not only had safeguarded French civilization from physical destruction in the tropics but also protected the Republic since 1871 from the vestiges of the *ancien régime* as embodied by the *béké* planter class.

The service of Antilleans in World War I made the incorporation of Martinique and Guadeloupe as departments of France in 1946 possible, although the language of citizenship that went with France's civilizing mission in all its colonies had set the stage for the eventual integration of the French Antilles into metropolitan France. Racism did not dissipate overnight, however, and the old Caribbean colonies remained stuck between integration and segregation. To this day the Overseas Ministry administers the *départements d'outre-mer* of Martinique and Guadeloupe, simultaneously making them integrated parts of the metropole and cordoning them off as different and distinct—a tropical France linked to the *mère-patrie* by a postcolonial relationship marked by income inequity and economic dependence. The natural and political disasters this book has described, occurring when the Caribbean sugar economy was in its twilight years, cemented the view that despite the cultural affiliation of metropolitan France with the Antilles, the islands were a distinctly different and dangerous locale. The Great War had done little to overturn this association, and one hundred years later Antilleans continue to be French and not French.

Through the cycle of Caribbean catastrophe at the close of the nineteenth century, this book has described a shift from extracting capital from the island in the form of sugar to the injecting of capital in the form of disaster relief. The age of new imperialism left investors and many zealots of free-market economics in the governmental bureaucracy dissatisfied with the old colonies. They had hoped that the strategic injection of capital would reinvigorate the sugar economy. But as that economy waned and began to die in the 1890s when the cost of rebuilding seemed to wax, many questioned why France held onto a colony as costly as Martinique or as unruly as Guadeloupe. Such detractors and their critics came to the same answer: cultural affiliation and tradition. Therefore, as the French state injected capital into the islands, they simultaneously began to extract a new resource: the dedication of a citizenry devoted to the ideals of the Republic, the very citizens who would bolster the military's ranks during the First World War. At a time when bureaucrats began to believe that the Antilles had lost their utility to the French nation and become a drain on national resources, the First World War not only rekindled sugar production on the islands, largely transforming it into the production of rum for French *poilus* during the war and the Prohibition-era United States afterward, it also reinvigorated the close association between France and its oldest colonies in the Caribbean.[27]

The cycle of environmental catastrophe had at last transformed the republican ideology of the civilizing mission by redefining French citizenship rights to include an entitlement to governmental assistance. The First World War catalyzed this trajectory vis-à-vis a blood debt that cut both ways; just as Antilleans owed the *mère-patrie* their allegiance in time of war, so too did the state owe Antilleans for their sacrifice. The wartime experience, like the countless disasters before it, helped put forth an alternative image of the French citizen with a tropical rather than Salic or Gallic heritage.

Servicemen solidified this compatriotism in the trenches of Europe, and the so-called civilizing mission had reached its endpoint by the middle of the twentieth century. Nevertheless, the specter of geographic, racial, and climatic difference continues to haunt French Antilleans who still fight, as they have since 1789, for social, civic, and economic parity in a Republic that purports to champion liberty, equality, and fraternity.

NOTES

Citations to documents from the French archives I consulted generally include, in this order, the following information: a document description; the date, if known; the collection abbreviation; series abbreviation; carton number; and dossier number (see the bibliography for definitions).

Introduction

1. Lambolez and Coeur créole, *Saint-Pierre-Martinique*, 330–31. *Bulletin de la Société astronomique de France*, 304–5.
2. "Last Days of Saint-Pierre," 610–33.
3. André Fagel, "Courrier de Paris: La Catastrophe," *L'Illustration: Journal universel*, tome 119 (1902): 342.
4. Mauch and Pfister, *Natural Disasters, Cultural Responses*.
5. Davis, *Ecology of Fear*.
6. Azoulay, "Citizens of Disaster," 105–37.
7. Étienne, *Les compagnies de colonisation*, 13.
8. Renard, "Labour Relations," 37–57; Sainton, *Les nègres en politique*; Heath, *Sugar, Wine*, 55.
9. Duvergier, *Collection complète des lois*, 64–65.
10. Dubois, *Avengers of the New World*; Hunt, *Inventing Human Rights*.
11. Garrigus, "Vincent Ogé Jeune," 33–62; Fick, *Making of Haiti*; Adélaïde-Merlande, *Les origines du mouvement ouvrier en Martinique*.
12. Dumont, *L'amère patrie*, 4.
13. Dumont, *L'amère patrie*, 4.
14. *Bulletin officiel de la Martinique, Année 1882*, 37.
15. At roughly 83,560 constituents per representative in 1891, Martinique's representation in the French state was on par with many departments within metropolitan France: the departments of Loire (87,961); Indre-et-Loire (84,510); Nord (82,683); Haute-Marne (81,198); and Loire-Inférieure

(80,472) all had comparable representative-to-constituent ratios. While the average for France was 66,204 constituents per representative, Martinique's representation fell within the normal distribution of citizens per deputy, and Guadeloupe's only just below it. Both Antillean colonies had more rights than colonies such as Senegal, which had suffrage limited to certain members of the Four Communes and a population of nearly two hundred thousand people represented by a single deputy.

16. Dubois, *Colony of Citizens*; Nicolas, *L'insurrection du sud à la Martinique*.
17. Lara and Hennique, *Contribution de la Guadeloupe à la pensée française*, 192.
18. Knight and Palmer, *Modern Caribbean*, 91–92.
19. Burton, *La famille colonial*; Burton and Réno, *French and West Indian*; Périna, *Citoyenneté et sujetion aux Antilles francophones*; Sainton, *Les nègres en politique*; Mam Lam Fouck, *L'histoire de l'assimilation*.
20. Boittin, *Colonial Metropolis*; Wilder, *French Imperial Nation-State*; Edwards, *Practice of Diaspora*; Peabody and Stovall, *Color of Liberty*; Chapman and Frader, *Race in France*; Keaton, Sharpley-Whiting, and Stovall, *Black France/France Noire*.
21. Cottias, "Le silence de la nation," 21–45.
22. Heath, *Wine, Sugar, and the Making of Modern France*.
23. Richardson, *Economy and Environment in the Caribbean*.
24. Weber, *Peasants into Frenchmen*, 492.

1. French Race, Tropical Space

1. Cohen, *Rulers of Empire*, 44–45.
2. Dislère, *Notes*, 5.
3. Dislère, *Notes*, 13.
4. Nellis, *Shaping the New World*, 31.
5. See Williams, *Capitalism and Slavery*.
6. While Dislère and other contemporaries, particularly members of the Parti Colonial, argued that the new colonies were financially beneficial to the French state, historians doubt they significantly contributed to the French economy. Most likely the colonies never absorbed more than 10–15 percent of French exports, and trade with the colonies never made up more than 10 percent of French commerce. See Caron, *Economic History*, 109; Spruyt, *Ending Empire*, 68.
7. A popular weekly periodical similar to *National Geographic* with a focus on the French empire. The French Ministry of Education had a subscription to the journal for its use as a pedagogical tool.

8. Nardal, *Guide des colonies françaises*, 5.
9. Garrigus, *Before Haiti*, 1–20; also see Debbasch, *Couleur et liberté*, and the collected volume by Brunet, *Mariage et métissage*.
10. Heuer, "One-Drop Rule," 515–48.
11. Conklin, *Mission to Civilize*, 164–72.
12. See the incorporation of mixed-race orphans in West Africa in White, *Children of the French Empire*, 1–9, 111; as well as what Emmanuelle Saada calls "inclusive racism" in Indochina in *Empire's Children*, 180–81.
13. Jennings, *Curing the Colonizers*, 1–9.
14. Betts, *Assimilation and Association*, 106–32; Prochaska, *Making Algeria French*, 1–28.
15. While the term "mulatto" is considered offensive in anglophone countries today, the French usage of the word is preserved here, as it was used by historical contemporaries and is still used by French Antilleans today.
16. Daniel, "Mars 1900," 76.
17. Irénée Blanc, "Notre programme," *La Liberté colonial*, 26 June 1888.
18. G.F., "La Guadeloupe en 1899," 524–25.
19. Dreyfus and Berthelot, "Guadeloupe," *La Grande encyclopédie*, vol. 19, 485–86.
20. Rey, *Étude sur la colonie de la Guadeloupe*, 7.
21. FM SG GUA 267, d.1628, ANOM.
22. Malte-Brun, *La France illustrée*, 23–36.
23. The emancipation of 1848 has a contentious history in Martinique, as French politicians today stress the humanitarianism of the mother country while underplaying the role of Antillean maroons and slave rebellions in securing emancipation. See Reinhardt, *Claims to Memory*; Nicolas, *La Révolution antiesclavagiste de mai 1848 à la Martinique*; Schloss, *Sweet Liberty*.
24. Blackburn, *Overthrow of Colonial Slavery*, 477, 493–506; Johnson, *Fear of French Negroes*, 133–56; Schmidt, *Abolitionnistes de l'esclavage et réformateurs des colonies*, 340–48.
25. Nicolas, *Histoire de la Martinique*, 36; Lara, *La liberté assassinée*.
26. Renard, "Labour Relations in Martinique and Guadeloupe," 37–57.
27. Renard, "Labour Relations in Martinique and Guadeloupe," 52.
28. Heath, *Wine, Sugar*, 55.
29. Martinique and Guadeloupe each received one deputy in the chamber following the ratification of the Constitution of 1875. The law of 28 July 1881 increased that number to two deputies each.

30. Reisch, "French Experience with Representative Government in the West Indies," 480.

31. FM SG GUA 21, d.228, ANOM; quoted in Sainton, *Nègres*, 152.

32. Mam Lam Fouck, *L'histoire de l'assimilation*, 9–26.

33. Isaac, *Question coloniales*, 151.

34. Bouinais, *Guadeloupe*, 71.

35. Schnakenbourg, "La création des usines en Guadeloupe," note 45.

36. Schnakenbourg, "La création des usines en Guadeloupe," 21–115.

37. Burac and Calmont, *La question de la terre*, 123.

38. Buffon, "La crise sucrière de 1882–1886 à la Guadeloupe," 311–31.

39. Schnakenbourg, "La création des usines en Guadeloupe," 23l; Fallope, *Esclaves et citoyens*, 529.

40. Adélaïde-Merlande, *Origines*, 21–30; Burac and Calmont, *La question de la terre*, 126.

41. Fallope, *Esclaves et citoyens*, 529.

42. Burac and Calmont, *La question de la terre*, 126.

43. Schnakenbourg, "La disparition des 'habitation-sucreries' en Guadeloupe," 257–309.

44. Nicolas, *Histoire de la Martinique*, 151.

45. Schnakenbourg, "La création des usines en Guadeloupe," 21–115; Schnakenbourg, "From Sugar Estate to Central Factory," 83–91.

46. Adélaïde-Merlande, *Origines*, 21–30.

47. Pluchon and Abénon, *Histoire des Antilles et de la Guyane*, 419.

48. Northrup, "Indentured Indians in the French Antilles," 246–71.

49. Adélaïde-Merlande, *Origines*, 37.

50. Quoted in Schnakenbourg, *Histoire de l'industrie sucrière*, 75.

51. Pichevin, "Bulletin de l'Union coloniale française," 151–52.

52. Peck, *Report of the Commissioner-General*, 394; Heath, *Wine, Sugar*; Tomich, *Slavery in the Circuit of Sugar*; Schnakenbourg, *Histoire de l'industrie sucrière*.

53. Quoted in Louisiana Sugar Planters' Association et al., "The French Colonies at the Paris Exhibition," *The Louisiana Planter and Sugar Manufacturer*, 8.

54. Peck, *Report*, 394; Tisserand, *Statistique agricole*, 118.

55. Blancan, *La crise de la Guadeloupe*.

56. Heath, *Wine, Sugar*, 257–58.

57. Reisch, "French Experience," 485.

58. "Miscellaneous," *Beet Sugar Gazette*, 109; *Exposition Universelle Internationale de 1900*, 330; Hélot, *Le sucre de betterave en France*, 214.

59. "Miscellaneous," 109; *Exposition Universelle Internationale de 1900*, 330; Hélot, *Le sucre de betterave en France*, 214.

60. France, *Bulletin: 1889*, 183; Hélot, *Le sucre de betterave en France*, 214.

61. Sonthonnax, *Deux mois*, 4–5.

62. "Séance du 17 Novembre 1910," *Annales du Sénat* 78 (1911): 77–89.

63. "Le Coin des Rieurs," *L'Aurore*, 27 February 1910.

64. "Les journaux du matin," *L'Aurore*, 7 March 1910.

65. Heath, *Wine, Sugar*, 257–65.

66. Mote, *Industrial Arbitration*, 102.

67. Saint-Real, "L'Anniversaire de la commune," *Le Gaulois*, 28 May 1900.

68. Picard, *Exposition universelle*, 181; Maurice Normand, "Coup d'oeil sur l'exposition," *L'Illustration* 2981 (14 April 1900), 222.

69. Boyd, *Paris Exposition of 1900*, 457–60.

70. Peck, *Report*, 394.

71. Louisiana Sugar Planters' Association et al., *Louisiana Planter* 4, 1890: 8.

72. Terrier, "Le Journal des voyages," 332.

73. Alexandre, "Les femmes de l'exposition," 232–33.

74. Terrier, "Le Journal des voyages," 333; "Exposition Universelle de 1900: Martinique," *Journal Officiel de la République Française*, 29 October 1900.

75. Alexandre, "Les femmes de l'exposition," *L'Illustration*, 20 October 1900, 242–43.

76. Alexandre, "Les femmes de l'exposition," *L'Illustration*, 13 October 1900, 232–33.

77. Chotard, *Quelle peut être la garantie*, 9-10.

78. *La Martinique républicaine à la France républicaine*, 1–12.

79. "Conseil du contentiuex—Elections municipales de Fort-de-France," 271.

80. Dislère, *Notes*, 39.

81. Pluchon, *Toussaint Louverture*, 449–50; quoted in Laurent Dubois, *Avengers*, 259.

82. *Exposition universelle international de 1900 a Paris: Rapports*, 639.

83. Picard, *Exposition universelle: Rapport général administratif et technique*, 108.

84. Bouinais, *Guadeloupe*, 162.

85. Harris, *West Indies as an Export Field*, 310.

86. Nardal, *Guide des colonies françaises*, 1.

87. Nardal, *Guide des colonies françaises*, 2.

88. Nardal, *Guide des colonies françaises*, 2.

89. Lucrèce, *Histoire de la Martinique*, vii.

90. Fouret quoted in Lucrèce, *Histoire de la Martinique*, v–vi.

91. Lucrèce, *Histoire de la Martinique*, ix.

92. Lucrèce, *Histoire de la Martinique*, 151.

93. Lucrèce, *Histoire de la Martinique*, 156.

94. Bouinais, *Guadeloupe*, 89.

95. Bouinais, *Guadeloupe*, 92.

96. Garaud, *Trois ans*, 86.

97. Garaud, *Trois ans*, 227.

98. Périna, *Citoyenneté et sujétion*, 98–99.

99. Mam Lam Fouck, *Histoire de l'assimilation*, 100–101.

100. Corre, *Nos Créoles*, 1.

101. Corre, *Nos Créoles*, 222.

102. Corre, *Nos Créoles*, 229.

103. Corre, *Nos Créoles*, 1.

104. Claude Blanckaert argues that the discussion of racial mixing in France followed its own scientific progression separate from political aims. Though he does not deny that this discourse followed a colonial logic and that it was appropriated for imperialist aims, he argues that it should also be situated within a scientific problematic and not seen as strictly the transposition of colonial events. For more about the scientific discussion of racial mixing during the eighteenth and nineteenth centuries, see Claude Blankaert, "Of Monstrous Métis?," 42–70.

105. The idea that the Antilles were the younger children of France characterized the relationship of the colonies to the metropole, and it also largely shaped the movement for assimilation. With respect to the old colonies, France's role as the motherland was to raise these children to maturity. This familial rhetoric was commonplace and is the topic of Richard Burton's analysis of colonial relations in Burton, *La famille coloniale*.

106. Deniker, "Race," 26.

107. Delavaud, "Martinique," 345.

108. Garaud, *Trois ans*, 242.

109. Garaud, *Trois ans*, vii–viii.

110. Garaud, *Trois ans*, 216.

111. "Base de données des députés français depuis 1789," online.

112. Mismer, *Souvenirs*, 11.

113. Mismer, *Souvenirs*, 7–8.

114. Mismer, *Souvenirs*, 104.

115. Both educational underachievement and birth out of wedlock were prevalent in Martinique during the Third Republic. In 1894 only 47,600 people of a population of 187,692 could read and write. That same year it was estimated that three-fourths of children were born out of wedlock. By 1910 the number who could read and write had grown to 69,170 out of a population of 180,428. See *Annuaire de la Martinique*, 630; Reisch, "French Experience with Representative Government," 310.

116. Garaud, *Trois ans*, 221.

117. Verschuur, *Voyage*, 13.

118. Bouinais, *Guadeloupe*, 95–103.

119. Monet, *La Martinique*, 11–12.

120. Rossignol, "Séance du lundi 23 mai 1898," 306.

121. Godefroy et al., "Assessment of Seismic Hazard," 455–60.

122. "Tropical Cyclone Climatology," online.

123. Romer, *Les Cyclones de la Martinique*, 3.

124. Schwartz, "Hurricanes," 381–409; Schwartz, *Sea of Storms*.

125. Schwartz, "Hurricanes," 386.

126. Richardson, *Igniting*, xi.

127. "Renseignements complémentaires sur les effets du cyclone du 9 7bre — tremblement du terre à la Martinique," 29 September 1875, FM SG MAR 72, d.581, ANOM; Godefroy et al., "Assessment of Seismic Hazard," 455–60.

128. Godefroy et al., "Assessment of Seismic Hazard," 455–60.

129. Verschuur, *Voyage*, 14.

130. Cuzent, *Epidémie*, 3–4.

131. Bouinais, *Guadeloupe*, 44–45.

132. Cuzent, "Ouragan," 261–62.

133. Cuzent, *Eau thermo-minérale*, 107–9.

134. Breton, *Relations*, 31.

135. Bouinais, *Guadeloupe*, 17, 41.

136. Osborne, *Nature*, xii–xvi.

137. For an account of how the French colonial policy of "association" informed the development of urban colonial architecture in the early twentieth century, see Wright, *Politics of Design*. For the British context of how European imperial ideals were replicated in colonial architecture in India, see Metcalfe, *An Imperial Vision*.

138. Bouinais, *Guadeloupe*, 11–12.

139. Dreyfus and Berthelot, "Guadeloupe,"
 La grande encyclopédie, 19: 487.

140. Bouinais, *Guadeloupe*, 90–91.

141. Bouinais, *Guadeloupe*, 69.

142. Bérenger-Féraud, *Traité clinique*, 473.

143. Hélénon, *French Caribbeans*, 77–96.

144. Bérenger-Féraud, *Traité clinique*, 473.

145. Garaud, *Trois ans*, 270.

2. The Language of Citizenship

1. Germain Casse, "Le Gouverneur de la Martinique a adressé au Sous-secrétaire d'Etat des Colonies les renseignements suivants sur sujet de l'incendie de Fort-de-France," 2400COL 92, ANOM; "La Martinique," *Le Temps*, 30 June 1890; "La Martinique: L'Incendie de Fort-de-France," *Le Temps*, 25 June 1890.

2. E. Peyron, "Comité de secours aux Incendiés de Fort-de-France (Martinique) et de Port-Louis (Guadeloupe), 2400COL 92, ANOM; "Choses de l'incendie," *Les Antilles*, 28 June 1890; Pelet, *Nouvel Atlas*, xxiv; Janin, "Nos gravures: L'incendie de Fort-de-France," *L'Illustration*, 26 July 1890.

3. "Souscription en faveur des victimes de l'incendie de Fort-de-France," *Le Journal officiel de la Guadeloupe*, 23 June 1890.

4. "Gouvernement de la Guadeloupe," *Le Journal officiel de la Guadeloupe*, 30 June 1890; M. Carnot, "Nouvelles générales," *Le Journal officiel de la Guadeloupe*, 1 July 1890; "Projet de loi allouant, sur l'exercice 1890, une nouvelle subvention de 300.000 francs à la colonie de la Martinique et une subvention de 100.000 francs à la colonie de la Guadeloupe pour venir en aide aux incendiés de Fort-de-France et de Port-Louis," 8 July 1890, 2400COL 92, ANOM.

5. Weber, *Peasants into Frenchmen*, 130.

6. Schafer, *Children*, 37.

7. Chamoiseau, *Texaco*, 178.

8. Report on the earthquake of 1897, FM SG GUA 61, d.430, ANOM.

9. "La Martinique: L'Incendie de Fort-de-France," *Le Temps*, 25 June 1890.

10. Bureau de Recherches Géologiques, *Sismicité historique*, online data set.

11. Report, FM SG GUA 61, d.430, ANOM.

12. Report of the municipal council of Pointe-à-Pitre on a rebuilding project, 18 October 1871, FM SG GUA 38, d.326, ANOM; correspondence, 1879, FM SG GUA 11, d.105, ANOM.

13. Richardson, *Igniting*, 64.

14. "Une catastrophe à Fort-de-France," *Le Petit Journal*, 25 June 1890.

15. Letter from the governor of Guadeloupe to the undersecretary of state, 10 July 1890, FM SG GUA 65, d.470, ANOM; "Au Port-Louis," *Le Progrès de la Guadeloupe*, 2 July 1890.

16. Janin, "Nos gravures: L'incendie de Fort-de-France," *L'Illustration*, 26 July 1890.

17. "La catastrophe du chef-lieu," *Les Antilles*, 25 June 1890.

18. Germain Casse, "Le Gouverneur de la Martinique à M. le Sous-Secrétaire d'Etat," 27 June 1890, printed in "Incendie de Fort-de-France," *La Journal officiel de la Guadeloupe*, 4 July 1890.

19. "La catastrophe du chef-lieu," *Les Antilles*, 25 June 1890.

20. "Choses de Fort-de-France," *Les Antilles*, 8 July 1890.

21. "La catastrophe du chef-lieu," *Les Antilles*, 25 June 1890.

22. Germain Casse, "Le Gouverneur de la Martinique à M. le Sous-Secrétaire d'Etat," 27 June 1890, printed in "Incendie de Fort-de-France," *La Journal officiel de la Guadeloupe*, 4 July 1890. The fire destroyed the boulevard Dourzelot, rue Blondel, rue Isambert, rue du Bord-de-la-Mer, rue Saint-Laurent, rue Victor-Hugo, rue Blenac, rue Saint-Louis, rue Sainte-Catherine, and rue des Fossés. The fire also consumed three-quarters of the rue du Gouvernement and rue Perrinon.

23. "L'Incendie de Fort-de-France," *L'Univers illustré*, 5 July 1890; "L'Incendie de Fort-de-France," *Le Temps*, 27 June 1890.

24. "La Martinique: L'Incendie de Fort-de-France," *Le Temps*, 25 June 1890.

25. "Une catastrophe à Fort-de-France," *Le Petit Journal*, 25 June 1890.

26. "La Guadeloupe," *Le Temps*, 2 July 1890.

27. Investigating judge to the attorney general, 3 July 1890, FM SG GUA 65, d.470, ANOM.

28. *Revue francaise de l'etranger*, 185.

29. "Ce qui se passe: Echoes politiques," *Le Gaulois*, 2 July 1890; "L'incendie de la Guadeloupe," *Le Matin*, 2 July 1890.

30. Letter from A. Le Boucher, 18 September 1890, FM SG GUA 65, ANOM.

31. Janin, "Nos gravures: L'Incendie de Fort-de-France," *L'Illustration*, 26 July 1890.

32. "Appel à la France," *Les Tablettes Coloniales*, 6 July 1890.

33. "Catastrophe du chef-lieu," *Les Antilles*, 25 June 1890.

34. "Les choses de l'incendie," *Les Antilles*, 28 June 1890.

35. "Gouvernement de la Guadeloupe," *Le Journal officiel de la Guadeloupe*, 27 June 1890; "Tombola du 14 Juillet," *Le Journal officiel de la Guadeloupe*, 1 July 1890.

36. Governor of Guadeloupe to the undersecretary of state, 10 July 1890, FM SG GUA 65, d.470, ANOM.

37. L. Blanchard, "Extrait d'un rapport au sujet des secours et des vivres distribués à Fort-de-France après l'incendie du 22 juin 1890," 4 February 1892, FM SG MAR 72, d.581, ANOM.

38. Donations made to fire victims of Point-à-Pitre, FM SG GUA 52, d.383, ANOM.

39. "Extraits du Moniteur du mercredi," *Les Antilles*, 28 June 1890.

40. "Collectes paroissiales," *Les Antilles*, 12 July 1890.

41. "Seance du 29 Décembre 1891," *Annales de la Chambre des Deputés: 1892*, 1269–70.

42. "Derniers renseignments," *Les Antilles*, 25 June 1890.

43. "Nouvelles generals," *La Journal officiel de la Guadeloupe*, 4 July 1890.

44. "Les choses de l'incendie," *Les Antilles*, 28 June 1890; Blanchard, "Extrait d'un rapport."

45. Blanchard, "Extrait d'un rapport."

46. Germain Casse, "Le Gouverneur de la Martinique a adressé au Sous-secrétaire d'Etat des Colonies les renseignements suivants sur sujet de l'incendie de Fort-de-France," FM 2400COL 92, ANOM.

47. "Dernier heure," *Les Antilles*, 19 July 1890.

48. "La Martinique," *Le Temps*, 26 June 1890; "Le Sinistre de Fort-de-France," *Le petit journal*, 26 June 1890. Also, "Le Sinistre de Fort-de-France," *Le petit journal*, 27 June 1890.

49. "Peyron, Alexandre," *Dictionnaire des parlementaires*, vol. 4, 612; "Etienne, Eugène," *Dictionnaire des parlementaires*, vol. 2, 576.

50. E. Étienne, "Le S.S d'Etat à Monsieur le Vice Amiral Peyron," FM 2400COL 92, ANOM.

51. Donation sheets, FM 2400COL 92, ANOM.

52. Letters between the director of the General Transport Company and the undersecretary of state, 22 November 1890, FM 2400COL 92, ANOM.

53. Amiral Peyron, "Rapport fait au Comité sur les opérations de son Bureau et les résultats obtenues," FM 2400COL 92, ANOM.

54. *Salaires et durée du travail*, vol. 4, 16–17.

55. "Loi qui accorde, sur l'exercice 1890, une subvention à la colonie de la Martinique pour secours aux victims de l'incendie de Fort-de-France du 23 juin," in Duvergier, *Collection complète des lois*, 446.

56. M. Carnot, "Projet de loi allouant, sur l'exercice 1890, une nouvelle subvention de 300.000 francs," 8 July 1890, FM 2400COL 92, ANOM.

57. "Séance du vendredi, 11 Juillet 1890," Chambre des députés, 5ᵉ legislature, session de 1900, C/I/448, ANPS.

58. Senator Peyron to the undersecretary of state for the colonies, 25 July 1890, FM 2400COL 92, ANOM.

59. Blanchard, "Extrait d'un rapport."

60. Blanchard, "Extrait d'un rapport."

61. Blanchard, "Extrait d'un rapport."

62. *Commercial Relations of the United States*, 562.

63. "Affaires coloniales: la Martinique," *Le Temps*, 17 August 1890.

64. Blanchard, "Extrait d'un rapport," FM SG MAR 72, d.581, ANOM.

65. "Commune du Port-Louis," *Le Journal officiel de la Guadeloupe*, 29 July 1890.

66. Desnier, "Martinique," 135.

67. Daughton, *An Empire Divided*, 6.

68. *General Catalog: Archival Collection Description*, 26J1, ADM; Hélénon, *French Caribbeans in Africa*, 4.

69. Inspector of the Colonies E. Chaudié to the undersecretary of state for the colonies, 15 January 1892, FM SG MAR 72, d.581, ANOM.

70. Andrieu, *Bibliographie générale*, 145; Bangou, *Le Parti socialiste français*, 39; Corre, *Nos créoles*, 222.

71. Lara and Hennique, *Contribution de la Guadeloupe*, 190–95.

72. Lara and Hennique, *Contribution de la Guadeloupe*, 190.

73. "Nouvelles de la semaine: Une nouvelle épuration en persepective," *La Gazette agricole*, 31 August 1890; Pierre Véron, "Courrier de Paris," *Le Monde illustré*, 9 April 1887.

74. "Antilles," *Le Temps*, 6 July 1890.

75. E. Peyron, "Comité de secours aux incendiés de Fort-de-France (Martinique) et de Port-Louis (Guadeloupe)," FM 2400COL 92, ANOM.

76. "L'incendie de Fort-de-France," *Les Tablettes Coloniales*, 29 June 1890.

77. "L'incendie de Fort-de-France."

78. "À la cité bordelaise," *Les Antilles*, 26 July 1890.

79. F. M., "L'Incendie de Fort-de-France," *L'Illustration*, 5 July 1890.

80. "L'incendie de Fort-de-France," *Les Tablettes Coloniales*, 29 June 1890.

81. F. M., "L'Incendie de Fort-de-France," *L'Illustration*, 5 July 1890.

82. F. M., "Les sinistres du monde: L'Incendie de Fort-de-France," *Journal des voyages et des aventures de terre et de mer*, no. 684 (17 August 1890).

83. Chambre de Commerce de Marseille, *Compte rendu de la situation commerciale*, 208.

84. *Mines and Quarries*, 395.

85. "Nouvelles Scientifiques," *La Nature: Revue des sciences et de leurs applications aux arts et à l'industrie*, no. 1254, 5.

86. "Social, Demographic, and Educational Data for France, 1801–1897," ICPSR00048-VI, Interuniversity Consortium for Political and Social Research (distributor), accessed 20 February 2009.

87. Harp, *Learning to Be Loyal*, 3–18.

88. "Dernier heure," *Les Antilles*, 19 July 1890.

89. E. Étienne, "S.S. d'Etat à M. Le Préfet de Meurthe-et-Moselle à Nancy," FM 2400COL 92, ANOM. "Le Feu," *Les Colonies*, 11 April 1891.

90. "Nouvelles du mardi," *Les Antilles*, 25 June 1890.

91. "Derniers renseignements," *Les Antilles*, 25 June 1890.

92. "Nouvelles du mardi," *Les Antilles*, 25 June 1890; "Choses de l'incendie," *Les Antilles*, 28 June 1890.

93. Cole et al., "Making Sense of a Hurricane"; Tierney, Bevc, and Kuligowski, "Metaphors Matter."

94. Anderson and Dynes, "Civil Disturbances and Social Change."

95. Miles, "Levees, Looters, and Lawlessness"; Potter, "Reframing Crime in a Disaster"; Anderson and Dynes, "Civil Disturbances and Social Change."

96. Drabek, *Human System Responses to Disaster*, 133.

97. Singer, "An Introduction to Disaster," 137.

98. Quarantelli, "Panic Behavior," 336–50; Quarantelli and Dynes, "Response to Social Crisis and Disaster."

99. Tierney, Bevc, and Kuligowski, "Metaphors Matter."

100. "Extraits du Moniteur de mercredi," *Les Antilles*, 28 June 1890; Germain Casse, "Le Gouverneur de la Martinique à M. le Sous-Secrétaire d'Etat," 27 June 1890, printed in "Incendie de Fort-de-France," *Journal officiel de la Guadeloupe*, 4 July 1890.

101. "Le feu," *Les Colonies*, 15 April 1891.

102. "Echos du jour," *Les Colonies*, 2 July 1890.

103. "Dernier renseignements," *Les Antilles*, 25 June 1890.

104. "Choses de l'incendie," *Les Antilles*, 28 June 1890; "Aux électeurs de Fort-de-France," FM 2400COL 92, ANOM.

105. "Le Feu," *Les Colonies*, 11 April 1891.

106. "Echos du jour," *Les Colonies*, 2 July 1890.

107. "Dernier renseignements," *Les Antilles*, 25 June 1890.

108. "Dernier renseignements," *Les Antilles*, 25 June 1890.

109. In 1885 the Republican Party split when Marius Hurard reached out to the wealthy *békés* who sought autonomy for Martinique, and Ernest Deproge continued to advocate for full assimilation into France. Cleaving the Republican Party in twain, Hurard created the Progressive Republican Party, and Deproge the Radical Socialist Party. See Nicolas, *Histoire de la Martinique de 1848 à 1939*, 141–46.

110. Klein, *Shock Doctrine*, 3–26.

111. "Souscription en faveur des incendiés de Fort-de-France et de Port-Louis," FM 2400COL92, ANOM.

112. "Dernier renseignements," *Les Antilles*, 25 June 1890.

113. "L'Enquête," *Les Antilles*, 20 August 1890.

114. "L'Enquête," *Les Antilles*, 20 August 1890.

115. "Affaires colonials," *Le Temps*, 25 August 1890.

116. "Le rapport de la commission d'enquete," *La Petite France*, 6 December 1890, FM SG MAR 72, d.581, ANOM.

117. "Another Mining Disaster, Loss of 200 Lives," *Press*, 6 July 1889, 5.

118. "Explosion de grisou: 200 victimes," *Le Figaro*, 4 July 1889.

119. "Note sur l'explosion de grisou du puits Verpilleux," *Annales des mines*, 397–408.

120. "Le explosion de grisou," *Le Figaro*, 6 July 1889.

121. "Note sur l'explosion," *Annales des mines*, 401–3.

122. "Dernière heure," *Le Patriote savoisien*, 31 juillet 1890.

123. "1890: Le puits Pélissier de la Compagnie de Villeboeuf," retrieved from Mémoire et actualité en Rhône-Alpes on 16 April 2012 at http://www.memoireetactualite.org/dossiers/catastrophes-minieres/1890-le-puits-pelissier-de-la-compagnie-de-villeboeuf/.

124. "La Catastrophe de Saint-Étienne," *L'Univers*, 31 July 1890. Depending on the source, estimates on the dead ran between 113 and 120, while estimates on the wounded ran from thirty-five to forty.

125. "The Late Mining Disaster: The Explosion at Saint Etienne—Terrible Loss of Life," *New York Times*, 22 February 1876.

126. "Catastrophe à Saint-Étienne," *Le Temps*, 31 July 1890; *L'Illustration: Journal universel*, 13 July 1889.

127. "Nos gravures," *L'Illustration*, 11 July 1889.

128. Massing, "From Greek Proverb to Soap Advert."

129. Hale, *Races on Display*, 24–28.

130. Neville, "The Courrières Colliery Disaster, 1906," 33–52.

131. Wright, *Twelfth Special Report*, 183.

132. Letters from the Society of Harmony of the Familistère of Guise, December 1890, FM 2400COL, d.92, ANOM.

133. Simon et al., *Faisons la chaine*, preface; FM 2400COL, d.92.

134. Simon et al., *Faisons la chaine*, preface.

135. Port-Louis, lists of subscriptions, FM SG GUA 57, d.404, ANOM.

136. Letters from donors, 26 November 1890 to 4 May 1891, ANOM FM 2400COL, d.92.

137. "Un juste tribute," *La Verité de la Guadeloupe*, 6 July 1890.

3. The Calculus of Disaster

1. Cole, *Power of Large Numbers*, 1–20.

2. Rappaport and Fernandez-Partagas, "Deadliest Atlantic Tropical Cyclones," online.

3. Rappaport and Fernandez-Partagas, "Deadliest Atlantic Tropical Cyclones," online; Romer, *Les Cyclones de la Martinique*, 7, 13–14.

4. Report to the Chamber of Deputies on damages of the hurricane of 18 August 1891, November 1891, FM SG MAR 72, d.581, ANOM.

5. Report to the Chamber of Deputies on damages of the hurricane.

6. *Annales de la Chambre des Députés*, 38, 76–77.

7. Report to the Chamber of Deputies on damages of the hurricane.

8. "Gouverneur Martinique à Colonies, Paris. Télégramme no. 11," 20 August 1891, FM SG MAR 76, d.620, ANOM.

9. "Proces verbal constatant les pertes occasionnées par le cyclone du 18 août 1891," 20 September 1891, FM SG MAR 72, d.581, ANOM.

10. Eugene Étienne, "Du Moniteur du 21 août," *Les Antilles*, 25 August 1891.

11. "Gouverneur Martinique à Colonies, Paris. Télégramme no. 18," 28 August 1891, FM SG MAR 76, d.620, ANOM; L. Blanchard, "Extrait d'un rapport au sujet des secours et des vivres distribués à Fort-de-France après l'incendie du 22 juin 1890," 4 February 1892, FM SG MAR 72, d.581, ANOM.

12. Undersecretary of the colonies to president of the colonial section of the council of state, 1891, FM SG MAR 72, d.581, ANOM.

13. Undersecretary of the colonies to governor of Martinique, telegram, 23 August 1891, FM SG MAR 72, d.583, ANOM.

14. "État des ordres de recettes emis au compte sources en faveur des victimes du Cyclone du 18 aout 1890," FM SG MAR 72, d.582, ANOM.

15. Americus, "Le Travail à la Martinique."

16. Schoelcher, *La vérité aux ouvriers*, 294.

17. "Echoes du jour," *Les Colonies*, 29 August 1891.

18. There are conflicting copies of the telegram: one that says "populations annihilated" and another "plantations annihilated." While it is likely that the real telegram said plantations, the slippage is interesting, because it suggests the tension between attention to the economy and to human suffering.

19. Governor to undersecretary of the colonies, 23 August 1891, FM SG MAR 72, d.582, ANOM; "Parvenir au département par les soins de M. le Gouverneur," August 1891, FM SG MAR 72, d.582, ANOM.

20. Louisiana Geographic Information Center, "Saffir-Simpson Hurricane Scale," accessed 5 April 2017, http://lagic.lsu.edu/hurricanes/saffir-simpson.htm.

21. Pielke et al., "Normalized Hurricane Damage," 29–42; Elsner and Kara, *Hurricanes of the North Atlantic*, 23.

22. Report to the Chamber of Deputies on the damages of the hurricane of 18 August 1891.

23. National Hurricane Center (NOAA), "Saffir-Simpson Hurricane Wind Scale," accessed 5 April 2017, http://www.nhc.noaa.gov/aboutsshws.php.

24. Report to the Chamber of Deputies on the damages of the hurricane.

25. Chaudié to undersecretary of the colonies, 15 January 1892, FM SG MAR 72, d.581, ANOM.

26. Chaudié to undersecretary of the colonies.

27. Chaudié to undersecretary of the colonies.

28. Chaudié to undersecretary of the colonies.

29. "Commission coloniale Martinique à Colonies, Paris. Télégramme no. 19," 28 August 1891, FM SG MAR 76, d.620, ANOM.

30. Report to the Chamber of Deputies on the damages of the hurricane of 18 August 1891.

31. Jules Roche and Maurice Rouvier, "Project de loi portant ouverture, au Ministre du Commerce, de l'Industrie et des Colonies (3e section—Service coloniale), sur l'exercice 1892, d'un credit extraordinaire de 3.000.000 francs à titre d'avance à la colonies de la Martinique," FM SG MAR 72, d.582, ANOM.

32. Minister of finance to undersecretary of the colonies, 26 August 1891, FM SG MAR 72, d.583, ANOM.

33. Deliberations of the Colonial Commission, 26 August 1891, FM SG MAR 72, d.582, ANOM.

34. *Salaires et durée*, 16–17.

35. "Seance du 26 mars 1900," *Annales de la Chambre des Députés* 60, 1232; *Annales Des Mines: Mémoires*, 473.

36. Circular to the mayors from the directorate of the interior, 5 September 1891, FM SG MAR 72, d.581, ANOM.

37. "Extrait d'une lettre du Contre-Amiral Gouverneur de la Martinique," 5 October 1875, FM SG MAR 103, d.931, ANOM; Governor Moracchini to undersecretary of the colonies, 29 October 1891, FM SG MAR 72, d.581, ANOM.

38. Chaudié to undersecretary of the colonies, 15 January 1892, FM SG MAR 72, d.581, ANOM.

39. Communal reports, 1891, FM SG MAR 72, d.581, ANOM.

40. "La Martinique," *Le Peuple*, 3 September 1891.

41. Minutes of the Central Commission for the Relief of Victims of the Cyclone of 18 August 1891, 27 August 1891, FM SG MAR 72, d.582, ANOM.

42. Deliberations of the Colonial Commission, 26 August 1891, FM SG MAR 72, d.582, ANOM.

43. Governor of Martinique to undersecretary of the colonies, 28 September 1891, FM SG MAR 72, d.582, ANOM.

44. "La Martinique," *Le Peuple*, 3 September 1891.

45. "Le Cyclone du 18 Aout 1891 à la Martinique," *Les Antilles*, 25 August 1891.

46. B. Guliet, "Le Cyclone de la Martinique," *Journal des Voyages et des aventures de terre et de mer*, no. 750, 22 November 1890.

47. David Northrup, "Indentured Indians," 245–71.

48. J. M., "La Question du travail aux colonies: Immigration," *Bulletins de la Société Bretonne de Géographie*, no. 24–25 (May–August 1886), 125.

49. "Correspondances," *Les Colonies*, 29 August 1891.

50. Chaudié to undersecretary of the colonies, 15 January 1892, FM SG MAR 72, d.581, ANOM.

51. Minutes of the Central Commission for the Relief of Victims of the Cyclone of 18 August 1891, Third Meeting, 26 September 1891, FM SG MAR 72, d.582, ANOM.

52. E. Chaudié, Report on distribution of food in the Gros-Morne commune, 20 January 1892, FM SG MAR 72, d.582, ANOM.

53. Minutes of the Central Commission for the Relief of Victims of the Cyclone of 18 August 1891, Third Meeting, 26 September 1891; E. Chaudié, Report on distribution of food in the Sainte-Marie commune.

54. Chaudié's letters, FM SG MAR 72, d.582, ANOM.

55. Chaudié to undersecretary of the colonies, 15 January 1892, FM SG MAR 72, d.581, ANOM.

56. Chaudié to undersecretary of the colonies, 14 January 1892, FM SG MAR 72, d.582, ANOM.

57. Chaudié to undersecretary of the colonies, 15 January 1892, FM SG MAR 72, d.581, ANOM.

58. Chaudié to undersecretary of the colonies, 22 December 1891, FM SG MAR 72, d.581, ANOM.

59. L. Blanchard, Extract of a report on the subject of foodstuffs distributed in Fort-de-France after the fire of 22 June 1890, 4 February 1892, FM SG MAR 72, d.581, ANOM.

60. Governor Moracchini to undersecretary of the colonies, 30 January 1892, FM SG MAR 72, d.581, ANOM.

61. Chaudié to undersecretary of the colonies, 15 January 1892, FM SG MAR 72, d.581, ANOM.

62. Messina, "Assessment of Hurricane Charley's Impact of Cuba," 1–8; Food and Agriculture Organization of the United Nations, *Roots, Tubers, Plantains, and Bananas in Human Nutrition*, 7; Otero and Marti, *Impacts of Natural Disasters on Developing Economies*, 11–15.

63. Bayliss-Smith et al., *Islands, Islanders, and the World*, 85; United Nations Environment Programme, *Environmental Guidelines for Settlements Planning and Management*, 6.

64. "Seance du 29 Décembre 1891," *Annales de la Chambre des Députés*, 1269–70.

65. "Annexe No 2125. Séance du 31 Mai 1892," *Annales de la Chambre des Députés* 38, 76–77.

66. "Annexe No 2125. Séance du 31 Mai 1892," *Annales de la Chambre des Députés* 38, 76–77.

67. "Renseignements complémentaires sur les effets du cyclone du 9 7bre—tremblement du terre à la Martinique," FM SG MAR 103, d.931, ANOM.

68. Zébus, "Paysannerie et économie de plantation," 2–20.

69. Vibert, *La colonisation pratique et comparée*, 281.

70. Vibert, *La colonisation pratique et comparée*, 281.

71. Denise, "Une histoire évolutive de l'habitat Martiniquais," 1–11.

72. Garaud, *Trois ans*, 167–216.

73. August Terrier, "Le Journal des voyages à l'exposition universelle," *Journal des voyages et des aventures de terre et de mer*, 21 October 1900; Bouinais, *Guadeloupe*, 71.

74. Heath, *Wine, Sugar*, 168–85.

75. Report to the Chamber of Deputies on the damages of the hurricane of 18 August 1891, November 1891, FM SG MAR 72, d.581, ANOM.

76. Allègre to Undersecretary Étienne, 9 November 1891, FM SG MAR 72, d.581, ANOM.

77. Allègre to Undersecretary Étienne.

78. Fort-de-France to undersecretary of the colonies, telegram, 18 November 1891, FM SG MAR 72, d.583, ANOM.

79. Martinique's director of the interior to undersecretary of state, 19 November 1891, FM SG MAR 72, d.581, ANOM.

80. "Annexe No 2125. Séance du 31 Mai 1892," *Annales de la Chambre des Députés* 38, 76–77; M. Chautemps, "Rapport fait au nom de la commission du budget chargée d'examiner le project de loi portant ouverture, au Ministre de la Marine et des Colonies (2e section.—service colonial), sur l'exercise 1892 d'un crédit de 3,000,000 de francs à titre d'avances à la colonie de la Martinique," Chambre des députés, 5ᵉ législature, session de 1892, FM SG MAR 72, d.582, ANOM.

81. Report to the Chamber of Deputies on the damages of the hurricane of 18 August 1891.

82. "Annexe No 2125. Séance du 31 Mai 1892."

83. "Annexe No 2125. Séance du 31 Mai 1892."

84. Notes from the General Council regarding the earthquake in Alpes-Maritime, 22 July 1887, FM SG MAR 72, d.581, ANOM.

85. Undersecretary of the Colonies to Senator Allègre, 21 November 1891, FM SG MAR 72, d.581, ANOM.

86. Crédit Foncier de France to undersecretary of state, 25 November 1891, FM SG MAR 72, d.581, ANOM.

87. Crédit Foncier de France to undersecretary of state.

88. Director general of the Caisses d'Amortissements to undersecretary of state, 16 January 1892, FM SG MAR 72, d.581, ANOM.

89. Undersecretary of state to Caisses des Dépôts, 27 January 1892, FM SG MAR 72, d.581, ANOM.

90. Director general of the Caisses d'Amortissements to undersecretary of state," 29 February 1892, FM SG MAR 72, d.581, ANOM.

91. Head of the Third Bureau to Chamber of Commerce of Bordeaux, 29 September 1891, FM SG MAR 72, d.581, ANOM.

92. President of Chamber of Commerce of Marseille to undersecretary of the colonies, 7 November 1891, FM SG MAR 72, d.581, ANOM.

93. Saint-Félix, *Rapport de la Commission spéciale du Conseil Général sur le cyclone du 18 aout 1891*, FM SG MAR 72, d.581, ANOM.

94. Austin, *World's Sugar Production*, 2607. Rutter, *International Sugar Situation*, 58.

95. Governor Moracchini to undersecretary of state, transmittal of a letter from representatives of the sugar industry, 4 March 1892, FM SG MAR 72, d.581, ANOM.

96. Governor Moracchini to undersecretary of state.

97. Chaudié to undersecretary of the colonies, 15 January 1892, FM SG MAR 72, d.581, ANOM.

98. Minutes of the Central Commission for Relief of Victims of the Cyclone of 18 August 1891, fourth session, 13 Novembre 1891, FM SG MAR 72, d.582, ANOM.

99. "Annexe No 2125. Séance du 31 Mai 1892," *Annales de la Chambre des Députés* 38, 76–77.

100. "Annexe No 2125. Séance du 31 Mai 1892," *Annales de la Chambre des Députés* 38, 76–77.

101. "Loi portant ouverture au ministre de la marine et des colonies (2e section—Service colonial), sur l'exercice 1892, d'un crédit de 3 millions à titre d'avance à la colonie de la Martinique," *Journal officiel de la République Française*, no. 196 (21 July 1892).

102. Hobsbawm, *Age of Capital*, 16.

103. See Smith, *Tariff Reform in France*.

104. Duigan and Gann, "Introduction," 9

105. Schnakenbourg, *Histoire de l'industrie sucrière*, 23.

106. Schnakenbourg, *Histoire de l'industrie sucrière*, 23.

107. Governor of Guadeloupe to minister of the colonies, 29 April 1899, ADG, 1 Mi 677.
108. Légier, *La Martinique et la Guadeloupe*, 178.
109. Levasseur, *La France et ses colonies*, 322–24.
110. Levasseur, *La France et ses colonies*, 322–24.
111. Chaudié to undersecretary of the colonies, 15 January 1892, FM SG MAR 72, d.581, ANOM.
112. See Cole, *Power of Large Numbers*.
113. Hunt, *French Revolution and Human Rights*, 101–18.

4. The Political Summation

1. Sainton, *Nègres en politique*, 190–249.
2. Nicolas, *Histoire de la Martinique*, 124.
3. Letter from Senator Gerville-Reache, 1897, FM SG GUA 61, d.430, ANOM.
4. Letter from A. Isaac, 1897, FM SG GUA 61, d.430, ANOM.
5. See Thiébaut. *Guadeloupe 1899*.
6. *Bulletin officiel du ministère des colonies*, 1899, 1251.
7. Governor of Guadeloupe to minister of the colonies, 29 April 1899, 1 Mi 677, ADG.
8. Governor of Guadeloupe to minister of the colonies, 29 April 1899.
9. "Séance du 29 Mai 1899," *Annales du Sénat* 54–55, 797.
10. Jacques Prolo, "Haine de Races," *Le Peuple*, 7 October 1899.
11. Prolo, "Haine de Races."
12. Bouinais, *Guadeloupe*, 79–80.
13. "M. Isaac Sur-Directeur de l'Intérieur à la Guadeloupe du 20 Mars 1879 au 24 Aout 1882," 1 Mi 677, ADG.
14. List of condemnations, 1879–82, 1 Mi 677, ADG.
15. Bouinais, *Guadeloupe*, 80.
16. *Le Courrier de la Guadeloupe*, 30 May 1899, quoted in Thiébaut, *Guadeloupe 1899*, 18.
17. "L. Girard, Procureur général, au Gouverneur de la Guadeloupe: Au sujet des incendies 11 et 15 Juin 1898 à Pointe-à-Pitre," 1 Mi 677, ADG.
18. Governor of Guadeloupe to minister of the colonies, 22 June 1898, 1 Mi 677, ADG; report of attorney general on fires in Port-Louis, 29 June 1898, 1 Mi 677, ADG.
19. *La Sucrerie Indigène et Coloniale*, 64:622.
20. Northrup, "Indentured Indians," 246.

21. Heath, *Wine, Sugar,* 251.

22. Report of attorney general, March 1899, 1 Mi 677, ADG.

23. Republicans of Baie-Mahault to president of the republic, 26 January 1900, 1 Mi 678–1, ADG.

24. Thiébaut, *Guadeloupe 1899,* 194.

25. Report of attorney general, 19 December 1898, 1 Mi 677, ADG.

26. Banque de Consignations to minister of the colonies, 10 April 1899, 1 Mi 677, ADG.

27. Governor to minister of the colonies, 29 April 1899, 1 Mi 677, ADG.

28. Attorney general to governor of Guadeloupe, 14 March 1899, 1 Mi 677, ADG.

29. Republicans of Baie-Mahault to president of the republic, 26 January 1900, 1 Mi 678–1, ADG.

30. Attorney general to governor of Guadeloupe, 11 March 1899, 1 Mi 677, ADG.

31. *Séisme du 29 avril 1897 à la Guadeloupe,* 1–4.

32. Schnakenbourg, "La Banque de la Guadeloupe et la crise de change," 31–95.

33. Bangou, *La Guadeloupe,* 34; Légier, *La Martinique et la Guadeloupe,* 33.

34. Schnakenbourg, "La Banque," 89–95.

35. Qtd. in Légier, "La Martinique et la Guadeloupe: Notes de voyage," 680.

36. Légier, *La Martinique et la Guadeloupe,* 33.

37. Governor of Guadeloupe to attorney general, 15 March 1899, 1 Mi 677, ADG.

38. Governor of Guadeloupe to attorney general, 15 March 1899.

39. Légier, *La Martinique et la Guadeloupe,* 21.

40. Schnakenbourg, "La Banque," 76–77.

41. Governor of Guadeloupe to attorney general, 15 March 1899, 1 Mi 677, ADG.

42. France, *Annuaire statistique* 15, 734; Rolph, *Something about Sugar,* 242.

43. France, *Annuaire statistique* 15, 734; Rolph, *Something about sugar,* 242.

44. "Séance du 30 Mars 1898," *Débats parlementaires. Comte Rendu in Extenso,* 459.

45. Governor of Guadeloupe to attorney general, 15 March 1899, in 1 Mi 677, ADG.

46. Report of attorney general on fires in Grande-Terre, 1 Mi 677, ADG.

47. "Séance du 29 Mai 1899," *Annales du Sénat,* 793; "Séance du 8 Février 1898," *Annales: Débats parlementaires* 54: 623.

48. "Immigration: Circulaire," *Le Moniteur de la Martinique*, 27 April 1880.

49. Governor of Guadeloupe to minister of the colonies, 30 March 1899, 1 Mi 677, ADG.

50. Governor of Guadeloupe to minister of the colonies, 29 April 1899, 1 Mi 677, ADG.

51. Republicans of Baie-Mahault to president of the republic, 26 January 1900, 1 Mi 678–1, ADG.

52. Republicans of Baie-Mahault to president of the republic.

53. Thiébaut, *Guadeloupe 1899*, 43–49.

54. Prolo, "Haine de Races."

55. Attorney general to governor of Guadeloupe, 14 March 1899, 1 Mi 677, ADG.

56. Attorney general to governor of Guadeloupe, 14 March 1899.

57. Prosecutor of the Republic to attorney general, 25 March 1899, 1 Mi 677, ADG.

58. Report of attorney general, 31 March 1899, 1 Mi 677, ADG.

59. Republicans of Baie-Mahault to president of the republic, 26 January 1900, 1 Mi 678–1, ADG.

60. "Terrible Incendie à la Guadeloupe," *L'Illustration* 113 (1899), 340.

61. "Terrible Incendie à la Guadeloupe," 340.

62. "Séance du 29 Mai 1899," *Annales du Sénat* 54–55, 789.

63. "Séance du 29 Mai 1899," 789.

64. "Séance du 29 Mai 1899," 789.

65. Havre Colonial Society to minister of the colonies, 11 August 1899, SG GUA 424, ANOM.

66. Thompson, "Moral Economy of the English Crowd," 76–136.

67. Banque de Consignations to minister of the colonies, 1 Mi 677, ADG.

68. "Troubles in Guadeloupe," *New York Times*, 24 August 1899.

69. "La Guadeloupe: Incendie," *Le Temps*, 20 April 1899.

70. "Séance du 29 Mai 1899," *Annales du Sénat*, 789.

71. Note from minister of the colonies, 1 Mi 677, ADG.

72. "Condamnations prononcées contres des incendiaires," governor to minister of the colonies, 29 April 1899, 1 Mi 677, ADG.

73. "Séance du 29 Mai 1899," *Annales du Sénat*, 789.

74. "Séance du 29 Mai 1899," 789.

75. "Causes des incendies à la Guadeloupe," 29 April 1899, 1 Mi 677, ADG.

76. "Causes des incendies à la Guadeloupe."

77. Heath, *Wine, Sugar*, 151.

78. Republicans of Baie-Mahault to president of the republic, 26 January 1900, 1 Mi 678–1, ADG.

79. Shorter and Tilly, *Strikes in France*, 116–27, 142–48.

80. "Causes des incendies à la Guadeloupe," 29 April 1899, 1 Mi 677, ADG.

81. Republicans of Baie-Mahault to president of the republic, 26 January 1900.

82. Ramnath, *Decolonizing Anarchism*, 149.

83. Merriman, *Dynamite Club*, 1–6

84. See Charle, *Social History of France*, particularly 218–61; "Causes des incendies à la Guadeloupe," 29 April 1899, 1 Mi 677, ADG.

85. Banque de Consignations to minister of the colonies, 1 Mi 677, ADG.

86. "Declaration," *La Cravache*, 17 October 1899.

87. "The West India Hurricane: Much Damage in Guadeloupe," *New York Times*, 9 August 1899.

88. Pointe-à-Pitre to Paris, Colonial Ministry, telegram, 15 August 1899, 1 Mi 678–1, ADG.

89. Pointe-à-Pitre to Paris, telegram.

90. Port-au-Prince to Paris, Colonial Ministry, telegram, 11 August 1899, 1 Mi 678–1, ADG.

91. Governor of Guadeloupe to minister of the colonies, 1 September 1899, SG GUA 424, ANOM.

92. "Guadeloupe, cyclone du 7 août: Délégation de crédit," 23 September 1899, Mi 678–1, ADG.

93. "Approvisionnements, etc.," 20 September 1899, Mi 678–1, ADG.

94. "Approvisionnements, etc.," 20 September 1899, Mi 678–1, ADG.

95. "Approvisionnements, etc.," 20 September 1899.

96. A. N., "Secours de la Métropole," *Le Peuple*, 7 October 1899.

97. Havre Colonial Society to minister of the colonies, 11 August 1899 SG GUA 424, ANOM.

98. Transmission of claims made by various agents of Guadeloupe, 6 February 1900, 1 Mi 678–1, ADG.

99. For more on this, see Tierney, "Social Inequality, Hazards, and Disasters"; Jones and Murphy, *Political Economy of Hazards and Disasters*; Républicains de la Baie-Mahault au président de la République, 26 January 1900, 1 Mi 678–1, ADG.

100. Emprunt de 3,000,000 francs, 20 November 1899, 1 Mi 678–1, ADG.

101. Gerville-Réache to minister of the colonies, 26 February 1900, 1 Mi 678–1, ADG.

102. Minister of the colonies to Deputy Gerville-Réache, 15 January 1900, 1 Mi 678–1, ADG.

103. U.S. Department of State, *Commercial Relations,* 551.

104. Havre Colonial Society to minister of the colonies, 11 August 1899 SG GUA 424, ANOM.

105. Fallope, *Esclaves et citoyens,* 543; Heath, *Wine, Sugar,* 191.

106. Heath, *Wine, Sugar,* 213.

107. Cherdieu, "L'échec d'un socialisme colonial," 308–33.

108. Sainton, *Nègres en politique,* 605. Also see Adélaïde-Merlande, *Troubles sociaux en Guadeloupe.*

109. Adélaïde-Merlande, *Origines,* 143–71.

110. Reisch, "Labor Relations," 490.

111. "Incendiarism in Martinique: Rioters Set Fire to Plantations—France Sends a Warship," *New York Times,* 15 February 1900; "Martinique Troubles Continue," *New York Times,* 26 February 1900; "More Fires in Martinique: French Cruiser Returns to St. Pierre to Quell Trouble," *New York Times,* 21 February 1900.

112. "Bulletin social: les greves," *L'Aurore,* 18 February 1900; "Un 'Fourmies' colonial," *L'Aurore,* 16 February 1900; "Un 'Fourmies' colonial," *L'Aurore,* 15 February 1900.

113. Schnakenbourg, *Histoire de l'industrie sucrière,* 73–81.

114. Ministère du Commerce, *Statistiques des grèves,* 610.

115. Ministère du Commerce, *Statistiques des grèves,* 348.

116. Mote, *Industrial Arbitration,* 102.

117. "More Rioting in Martinique," *New York Times,* 14 February 1900.

118. "Incendiarism in Martinique," *New York Times,* 23 February 1900.

119. "The Martinique Situation," *New York Times,* 2 March 1900.

120. "Un Fourmies Colonial," *L'Aurore,* 11 February 1900.

121. Reisch, "Labor Relations," 488.

122. P. Deschanel, "Chambre: Séance du 26 mars," *Journal des débats,* 28 March 1900.

123. "Séance du 11 décembre 1900," *Annales de la Chambre des Députés,* 7me législature, 978.

124. Adélaïde-Merlande, *Origines,* 141; "Les Colonies: La grève à la Martinique," *Le Figaro,* 12 February 1900.

125. "Séance du 12 février 1900," *Annales de la Chambre des Députés,* 7me législature, 497.

126. "Bombs in Paris Markets," *Chicago Daily*, 14 February 1900.

127. "Les Colonies: La grève à la Martinique," *Le Figaro*, 12 February 1900.

128. E. Terrée-Potino, "Le temps des grèves," 381–82.

129. *Délibérations du Conseil général*, 79.

130. P. Bluysen, "Un Débat Sterile," *Journal des débats*, 28 March 1900.

131. Waldeck-Rousseau, *Politique Française et étrangère*, 276–77.

132. *Deuxième congrès général des organisations socialistes*, 77–78.

133. Nestor, "La grève générale des travailleurs agricoles," 566.

134. P. Bluysen, "Un Débat Sterile," *Journal des débats*, 28 March 1900.

135. Saint-Réal, "L'Anniversaire de la commune," *Le Gaulois*, 28 May 1900.

136. "French Labor Troubles," *New York Times*, 24 December 1900; "Strike Riots at Chalon-sur-Saone," *New York Times*, 4 June 1900.

137. *Deuxième congrès général des organisations socialistes*, 96–98.

138. "Aux travailleurs de la Martinique," *Troisième congres général des organisations socialistes françaises*, 497–98.

139. Nestor, "La grève générale des travailleurs agricoles," 568.

140. *Le Courrier de la Guadeloupe*, 9 May 1899, cited in Université Antilles-Guyane, *La Caraïbe au tournant de deux siècles*, 88–92.

141. "Renseignements Politiques," *Questions diplomatiques et coloniales: Revue de politique extérieure*, 1 March 1900, 312.

142. "History of the Trouble," *Chicago Daily Tribune*, 16 February 1900.

143. P., "Les Troubles de la Martinique," *L'Illustration*, 17 February 1900, 101.

144. M. Landry, "Les colonies," *Le Figaro*, 14 February 1900.

145. E. Terrée-Potino, "Le temps des greves," 382.

146. In 1894 the French military falsely convicted, discharged, and imprisoned a Jewish military captain, Alfred Dreyfus, for selling military secrets to the German government. By 1896 an internal investigation led by George Picquart had uncovered evidence of Dreyfus's innocence. This scandal split French society into two camps, the *dreyfusards* championing Dreyfus's innocence, and by proxy the ability of Jews to be committed to French ideals, and the *anti-dreyfusards* who argued for his guilt, and by extension the inability of Jews to incorporate fully into the French nation. This scandal, only nominally resolved with Dreyfus's reinstatement in 1906, became so politically charged that it bled into all avenues of social life.

147. "Nouvelles militaires," *Le Gaulois*, 7 July 1900.

148. "Labor Disorders in Martinique," *Washington Post*, 10 February 1900.

149. "The Troubles in Martinique," *New York Times*, 15 February 1900.

150. "The Situation in France's Colonies: Many Believe a Rebellion Is in Progress in Martinique," *New York Times*, 18 February 1900.

151. J. Corenely, "Les Troubles de la Martinique," *Le Figaro*, 23 February 1900; "Renseignements Politiques," 313.

152. Bluysen, "Un Débat Sterile," *Journal des débats*, 28 March 1900.

153. Adélaïde-Merlande, *Origines*, 158.

154. See Díaz, *The Virgin, the King, and the Royal Slaves of El Cobre*, 1–28.

155. Klooster, "Slave Revolts, Royal Justice, and a Ubiquitous Rumor in the Age of Revolutions," 401–24; Dubois, *Colony of Citizens*, 85–123.

156. "Martinique Is Jubilant," *Chicago Daily Tribune*, 6 May 1900.

157. "La Séance Hier," *Journal des débats*, 28 March 1900.

158. "La Séance Hier," *Journal des débats*.

159. "French Deputies in a Fight: Interpellation on Martinique Riots Leads to Fisticuffs in the Chamber," *Washington Post*, 27 March 1900.

160. P. Deschanel, "Chambre: Séance du 26 mars," *Journal des débats*, 28 March 1900.

161. "La Séance Hier," *Journal des débats*, 28 March 1900.

162. Waldeck-Rousseau, *Politique Française et étrangère*, 277.

163. L. Resse, "Les Allumettiers et l'Etat," *La Presse*, 24 October 1900.

164. Letter from Guadeloupean Republicans, 1900, 1 Mi 678–1, ADG.

165. "Faits Divers," *Journal des débats*, 26 July 1900.

166. Auguste Terrier, "Le Journal des voyages à l'exposition universelle," *Journal des voyages et des aventures de terre et de mer* (21 October 1900): 332.

167. "Une vengeance ministérielle: Renvoi et disgrace de M. Picanon," *La Presse*, 11 October 1900; "Séance du 11 décembre 1900," 977.

168. "Le retour de M. Picanon," *Journal des débats*, 29 August 1901.

169. "Senat: Séance du 19 juin," *Journal des débats*, 21 June 1900; "Lieutenant to Blame: Fired Too Hastily on Strikers in the Island of Martinique," *San Francisco Call*, 20 June 1900.

170. P. R., "Une affaire à éclaircir," *Le Gaulois*, 9 September 1900.

171. "Le Grand Banquet pour les travailleurs de l'Exposition," *La Presse*, 15 October 1900.

172. "Les interpellations a la Chambre," *La Presse*, 15 December 1900.

173. "Séance du 21 décembre 1900," *Annales de la Chambre des Députés, 7me législature*, 1190.

174. "Séance du 11 décembre 1900," 982.

175. Séance du 21 décembre 1900," 1194.

176. Ministère du Commerce, *Statistiques des grèves*, 298–300.

177. *Délibérations du Conseil général: Session ordinaire, Novembre 1900*, 79.

178. Adélaïde-Merlande, *Origines*, 171.

179. Sainton, *Les nègres en politique*, 189; Russo, "Grèves et socialism à la Guadeloupe," 486–500.

180. "Protestation," *Le Temps*, 12 May 1902.

5. Marianne Decapitated

1. Boyer de Peyreleau, *Les Antilles françaises*, 173.

2. "The Last Days of Saint-Pierre," *Century Magazine*, 615.

3. Zebrowski, *Last Days of St. Pierre*, 82.

4. Scarth, *La Catastrophe*, 190.

5. Scarth, *La Catastrophe*, 77.

6. "Télégrammes du cable français," *Journal officiel de la Martinique*, 6 May 1902.

7. Quoted in Scarth, *La Catastrophe*, 87.

8. Zebrowski, *Last Days of St. Pierre*, 79–80.

9. Scarth, *Vulcan's Fury*, 169.

10. "Which Eruptions Were the Deadliest?," *Cascades Volcano Observatory*, U.S. Geological Survey, retrieved 30 August 2013 from http://vulcan.wr.usgs.gov/LivingWith/VolcanicFacts/deadly_eruptions.html.

11. Eyewitness accounts conflict about the number of survivors, and it was never entirely clear whether the story of the lone survivor, Louis-Auguste Cyparis, was actually true. It is true, however, that several eyewitnesses from the environs of Saint-Pierre, as well as from the harbor, survived. See Scarth, *La Catastrophe*. For more about Cyparis see Flaugh, *Operation Freak Narrative*.

12. "Mont Pelée, West Indies," *Cascades Volcano Observatory*, U.S. Geological Survey, retrieved 30 August 2013 from http://vulcan.wr.usgs.gov/Volcanoes/WestIndies/Pelee/description_mont_pelee.html.

13. Telegraph service, Commandant Arrondissement and Commandant Brigade, August to September 1902, 4M11459/ C, ADM.

14. "Projet de loi tendant à ouvrir au Ministre des Colonies un crédit extraordinaire de sept millions de francs," FM SG MAR 58, d.486, ANOM.

15. Remy Saint-Maurice, "Les désastres de la Martinique," *L'Illustration: Journal universel* 119 (1902), 466–69. In 1906, two thousand pounds sterling

would be equivalent to about fifty thousand francs, with a conversion rate of 24.9:1 francs to pounds. The average yearly salary was approximately 1,080 francs for a metropolitan French worker. See *Diplomatic and Consular Reports*, 17.

16. Scarth, *La Catastrophe*, 212.

17. "Observations suite à l'éruption," 4M11459, ADM.

18. "Divers projets de la loi relatifs à l'ouverture de crédits extraordinaire," FM SG MAR 58, d.486, ANOM.

19. "Souscription nationale au profit des sinistrés de la Martinique: Appel du Comité official d'assistance et de secours," 1902, FR CAOM 9Fi30, ANOM.

20. Letters from diplomats and colonial governors, FM SG MAR 58, d.476, ANOM.

21. G. d'Oussouville au Ministre des Colonies, 17 June 1902, FM SG MAR 58, d.476, ANOM.

22. Jules Cambon, French ambassador in Washington, to M. Delcassé, minister of foreign affairs, 14 May 1902, FM SG MAR 58, d.477, ANOM.

23. Cambon to Delcassé.

24. Cambon to Delcassé.

25. Remy Saint-Maurice, "Les désastres de la Martinique," *L'Illustration: Journal universel* 119 (1902): 466–69. Reports vary as to whether she was asked to pay 280, 320, or 350 francs. There was also quite a bit of confusion as to the nationality of the child and her governess. In any case, however, it sparked substantial criticism in the press.

26. "Commission des secours aux sinistrés: Séance du 26 juin 1902," *Journal officiel de la Martinique*, 12 August 1902.

27. "Remerciements et nouvel appel du comité officiel d'assistance et de secours aux sinistrés de la Martinique," October 1902, FR CAOM 9Fi91, ANOM.

28. "Listes de souscriptions pour les sinistrés de la Martinique (suite): 123e liste," FM SG MAR 58, d.476, ANOM.

29. "Comité d'assistance aux sinistrés, Paris, Rapport," FM SG MAR 58, d.479, ANOM.

30. "Note," September 1902, FM SG MAR 58, d.479 ANOM.

31. "Martinique Fund in United States," 1 November 1902, FM SG MAR 58, d.477, ANOM.

32. French Ambassador to M. Delcassé, Minister of Foreign Affairs, 2 November 1904, FM SG MAR 58, d.477, ANOM.

33. "Nos gravures: La France vient au secours de la Martinique," *Le Petit journal: Supplément du dimanche*, 1 June 1902.

34. "Comité d'assistance aux sinistrés, Paris, Rapport," FM SG MAR 58, d.479, ANOM.

35. Aid tables: FM 1AFFPOL 1091, ANOM; 1AFFPOL 1092, ANOM; FM SG MAR 19, ANOM; 1AFFPOL 1100, ANOM.

36. "Comptabilité de secours accordés, demande de fonds, 1903," FM 1AFFPOL 1092, ANOM.

37. Aid tables and explicatory notes, FM 1AFFPOL 1092, ANOM.

38. "Commission des secours aux sinistrés: Séance du 10 juin 1902," *Journal officiel de la Martinique*, 12 August 1902; "Décision fixant la ration à allouer à tous sinistrés," *Journal officiel de la Martinique*, 29 August 1902.

39. Tables: aid to widows, orphans, and the infirm, FM 1AFFPOL 1092, ANOM.

40. Martinique relief proposals, general summary table no 10, FM 1AFFPOL 1092, ANOM.

41. Lists of aid, FM 1AFFPOL 1100, ANOM.

42. Légier, *La Martinique et la Guadeloupe*, 20.

43. "Séance du 29 Décembre 1891," *Annales de la Chambre des Deputés*, pub. 1892, 1269–70.

44. Lists of aid, orphans, FM 1AFFPOL 1100; proposals for permanent relief for orphans, 1AFFPOL 1092, ANOM.

45. Lists of aid, orphans, FM 1AFFPOL 1100, ANOM.

46. Appended tables: proposals for relief of Martinique, FM 1AFFPOL 1092, ANOM.

47. Proposals for relief of Martinique: general summary table, FM 1AFFPOL 1100, ANOM; proposal of law, no. 63, FM SG MAR 58, d.488, ANOM.

48. Lists of aid, widows, FM 1AFFPOL 1100, ANOM.

49. "Déclaration des pertes," FM SG MAR 58, d.475, ANOM.

50. "Comité official d'assistance et de secours aux sinistrés de la Martinique," FR CAOM 9Fi29, ANOM.

51. "Comité d'assistance aux sinistrés, Paris, Rapport," FM SG MAR 58, d.479, ANOM.

52. "Comité d'assistance aux sinistrés, Paris, Rapport."

53. Letters from the University of France, French Academy, and Committee of Assistance and Aid for Victims of the Catastrophe of Martinique, FM SG MAR 58, d.478, ANOM.

54. "Sinistrés de la Martinique dont la famille habitait la Martinique, en dehors de St. Pierre, au moment de la catastrophe," FM SG MAR 58, d.478, ANOM.

55. "Séance du 13 Mai: Comité officiel d'assistance et de secours aux victimes de la catastrophe de la Martinique," FM SG MAR 58, d.479, ANOM.

56. Passenger documents and ships' manifests, F/5B/138 2/2 & 139 1/2, ANPS.

57. Miller, *Martinique Horror and St. Vincent Calamity*, 348.

58. "Commission des secours aux sinistrés: Séance du 10 juin 1902," *Journal officiel de la Martinique*, 12 August 1902.

59. "Société anonyme par actions de bateaux à vapeur de la Martinique," *Journal officiel de la Martinique*, 21 July 1903. "Société anonyme par actions de de l'usine du Lamentin," *Journal officiel de la Martinique*, 14 July 1903.

60. Quoted in Alwyn Scarth, *La Catastrophe*, 209.

61. "Commission des secours aux sinistrés," *Journal officiel de la Martinique*, 21 July 1902.

62. "Note," September 1902, FM SG MAR 58, d.479, ANOM.

63. Governor Lhueure to the Ministry of the Colonies, telegram, 16 May 1902, FM SG MAR 58, d.483, ANOM.

64. Quoted in Royce, *Burning of St. Pierre and the Eruption of Mont Pelée*, 97–98.

65. "Histoire de la semaine: France," *L'Illustration: Journal universel* 119 (1902), 374.

66. Desnier, "Martinique: Before and After," 137.

67. Shorter and Tilly, *Strikes in France*, 43, 81–82.

68. Shorter and Tilly, *Strikes in France*, 43.

69. Loomis, "Mine Explosions in France," 339–43.

70. Jannesson, *Monographie et histoire de la ville de Saint-Etienne*, 128–35.

71. Branciard and Gonin, *Le Mouvement ouvrier, 1815–1976*, 71.

72. Senator Knight to the Ministry of the Colonies, telegram, 18 May 1902, FM SG MAR 58, d.483, ANOM.

73. Telegram from Governor Lemaire, 5 June 1903, FM SG MAR 58, d.483, ANOM.

74. Alexander, "Study of Natural Disasters."

75. Alexander, "Study of Natural Disasters."

76. "La Catastrophe de la Martinique," *Le Temps*, 5 May 1902.

77. "Note," 8 July 1902, FM SG MAR 58, d.477, ANOM.

78. "Envoi du 3e proces-verbal de réunion de la Commission des pertes," 3 July 1902, FM SG MAR 58, d.488, ANOM.

79. Letters to and from the governor with included committee notes, June-July 1902, FM SG MAR 58, d.488, ANOM.

80. "Note," 8 July 1902, FM SG MAR 58, d.477, ANOM.

81. Desnier, "Martinique: Before and After," 135.

82. Hess, *La catastrophe de la Martinique*, i.

83. Knight and Palmer, *Modern Caribbean*, 91.

84. Lambolez and Coeur créole, *Saint-Pierre-Martinique, 1635–1902*, 301.

85. "La Catastrophe de la Martinique," *Le Temps*, 15 May 1902.

86. "Nos gravures: La France vient au secours de la Martinique," *Le Petit journal: Supplément du dimanche*, 1 June 1902.

87. André Fagel, "Courrier de Paris: La Catastrophe," *L'Illustration: Journal universel* 119 (1902), 342. Italics added for emphasis.

88. G. Cerbelaud, "L'Éruption de la Martinique: Volcans et tremblements de terre; Les zones dangereuses," *L'Illustration: Journal universel* 119 (1902): 423–27.

89. Scarth, *La Catastrophe*, 19.

90. "Eruption volcanique: Recherche d'emplacement pour la construction d'abris et proces verbaux de la commission coloniale," 1M11454, ADM.

91. "La Catastrophe de la Martinique," *Le Temps*, 10 May 1902.

92. President of the Chambre des Négociants Commissionnaires to minister of the colonies, 19 July 1902, FM SG MAR 58, d.475, ANOM.

93. German consul to governor, 12 May 1902, FM SG MAR 58, d.476, ANOM.

94. "Les Congrès," *L'Aurore*, 12 May 1902.

95. Ernest Vaughan, "Fêtes de charité," *L'Aurore*, 13 May 1902.

96. Letter from Charles Depince, 17 February 1903, FM SG MAR 58, d.475, ANOM.

97. "Aux Antilles: La Martinique," *Journal des voyages et des aventures de terre et de mer*, no. 287 (1 June 1902): 5–6.

98. "Aux Antilles: La Martinique."

99. Heilprin, *Mont Pelée*, 6–8.

100. For more on the image of women of color within France, see Mitchell, "*Les ombres noires de saint domingue*," 246.

101. "Une Martiniquaise," *L'Illustration: Journal universel* 119 (1902), 356.

102. "Gde Fête de Bienfaissance au benefice des incendiés de la Martinique et de la Guadeloupe," *Le Courrier Français*, 3 August 1890.

103. Heath, *Wine, Sugar*.

104. R. Pichevin, "Bulletin de l'Union coloniale française," *Quinzaine colonial*, 10 March 1906, 151–52.

105. "Projet de loi, No. 4454," FM 1AFFPOL 770, ANOM.

106. Royce, *Burning of St. Pierre*, 78.

107. Quoted in H. N. Dickson, "The Eruptions in Martinique and St. Vincent," 50–60.

108. Lambolez, *Saint-Pierre-Martinique, 1635–1902*, 300–301.

109. Summary of disaster relief in France, FM 1AFFPOL 1092, ANOM.

110. Summary of disaster relief in France for the elderly, FM 1AFFPOL 1092, ANOM.

111. Final list of relief, extracted from *Journal Officiel* of 19 January and 9 August 1904, FM 1AFFPOL 1100, ANOM.

112. Newspaper clipping included in letters, "Une autre catastrophe peut menacer Saint-Pierre," 15 February 1922, FM 1AFFPOL 770, ANOM.

113. Notes for the minister's office, FM 1AFFPOL 772/1 and FM 1AFFPOL 773, ANOM; "Mont Pelee Erupts; Sixth time in 2 weeks," *New York Times*, 1 November 1929.

114. Telegraphic dispatches, January and February 1930; note for the director of political affairs, 25 February 1930, FM 1AFFPOL 782/2, ANOM.

115. Newspaper clipping included in letter, "Une autre catastrophe peut menacer Saint-Pierre," 15 February 1922, FM 1AFFPOL 770, ANOM.

116. Head of the Third Office to the Chamber of Commerce of Bordeaux, 29 September 1891, FM SG MAR 72, d.581, ANOM.

117. *Le Progrès de la Guadeloupe*, 25 July 1890.

Epilogue

1. Gainot, *Les officiers de couleur dans les armées de la République et de l'Empire*, 5–19.

2. Weber, *Peasants into Frenchmen*, 292–302.

3. Georges Poulet, "Habitants de la Martinique: La guerre est déclarée," *Journal officiel de la Martinique*, 4 August 1914.

4. Dumont, "La figure de l'ennemi," 135–51; Dumont, "Conscription antillaise," 101–16; Fallope, *Esclaves et citoyens*, 53.

5. Fallope, *Esclaves et citoyens*, 53.

6. Galmot, *La Guyane française et la guerre*, 21–22.

7. Cited in Douaire, "Traces et absences de la Grande Guerre aux Antilles," 135.

8. Galmot, *La Guyane française et la guerre*, 1–32; Dumont, "Santé et conscription creole," 223.

9. Chotard, *Quelle peut être la garantie*, 3–15.
10. Gallaher, *General Alexandre Dumas*, 97.
11. Pichevin, *Rapport sur la création d'un gouvernement général des Antilles et de la Guyane*, 1–53.
12. Banchelin, "La Guadeloupe," 131.
13. Fogarty. *Race and War in France*, 100–103.
14. Andrivon-Milton, *Lettres de poilus martiniquais*, 121–22.
15. Andrivon-Milton, *Lettres de poilus martiniquais*, 12.
16. Andrivon-Milton, *Lettres de poilus martiniquais*, 12.
17. Andrivon-Milton, *Lettres de poilus martiniquais*, 12.
18. Andrivon-Milton, *Lettres de poilus martiniquais*, 109–12.
19. Andrivon-Milton, *Lettres de poilus martiniquais*, 131.
20. *La Démocratie coloniale*, 20 March 1918, cited in Dumont, "Conscription antillaise et citoyenneté," 101–16.
21. "La Defense du Drapeau," *Le monde colonial illustré*, January 1936, cited in Bangou, *La Guadeloupe*, 148.
22. "Voyages aux Antilles," *Le Monde illustré*, 18 January 1936.
23. "Ministère des pensions—1919," 3R1, ADG.
24. Jules Monnerot, *Revue Martinique*, 1935, n. 14; Dumont, *L'amère patrie*, 55–88.
25. Monnerot, *Revue Martinique*, 1935, n. 14; Dumont, *L'amère patrie*, 55–88.
26. Hélénon, *French Caribbeans in Africa*, 63.
27. Dumont, *L'amère patrie*, 29.

BIBLIOGRAPHY

Archival Sources

Archives départementales de la Guadeloupe, Basse-Terre (ADG)
  Archives publiques—Époque moderne (1816–1947)
    Affaires militaires série (R): 1 R18–23; 3R1
    Microfilms série (Mi): 1 Mi 677; 1 Mi 678-1; 4 Mi 150; 4 Mi 160;
      4 Mi 162; 1 Mi 191
    Périodiques série (PER): PER 199-1
Archives départementales de la Martinique, Fort-de-France (ADM)
  Archives anciennes, moderne et contemporaines
    Administration générale et économie série (M): 1M11454;
      M11459; 1M9891/A
    Fonds de l'association diocésaine de la Martinique (J) : 26J1
  Archives postérieures à 1790
    Affaires militaires série (H): H410779.
    Microfilms série (MI): 1M11470
Archives nationales d'outre-mer, Aix-en-Provence (ANOM)
  Fonds ministériels (FM)
    Affaires politiques (AFFPOL): FM 1AFFPOL 770; FM 1AFFPOL 772/1; FM
      1AFFPOL 773; FM 1AFFPOL 782/1; FM 1AFFPOL 782/2; FM 1AFFPOL
      783; FM 1AFFPOL 1091; FM 1AFFPOL 1092; FM 1AFFPOL 1100; FM
      1AFFPOL 1138
    Ministère des Colonies. Série géographique Amérique (2400COL): FM
      2400COL 92
    Séries géographiques, Guadeloupe (SG GUA): FM SG GUA 11; FM SG
      GUA 38; FM SG GUA 52; FM SG GUA 57; FM SG GUA 61; FM SG GUA 65;
      FM SG GUA 69; FM SG GUA 222; FM SG GUA 267

Séries géographiques, Martinique (SG MAR): FM SG MAR 19; FM SG MAR 58; FM SG MAR 72; FM SG MAR 76; FM SG MAR 103

Bibliothèque (BIB)

Ministère des Colonies (section Outre-mer) (SOM): BIB SOM d/res/664

Press d'outre-mer (POM): BIB POM/e/558; BIB POM/e/653

Documents iconographiques (Fi)

Centre des archives d'outre-mer, France (FR CAOM): FR CAOM 9Fi29; FR CAOM 9Fi30; FR CAOM 9Fi474; FR CAOM 9Fi91

Archives nationales de la France, Pierrefitte-sur-Seine (ANPS)

Archives postérieurs 1789

Assemblées nationales, Secondes minutes des procès-verbaux des séances des assemblées (C/I): C/I/448

Versements des ministères et des administrations qui en dépendent, Ministère de l'Intérieur—Comptabilité départementale (F/5): F/5B/138 2/2; F/5B/139 1/2

Published Works

"Acclimatization or Acquisition of Immunity from Yellow Fever." *Annual Report of the National Board of Health, 1880.* Washington DC: Government Printing Office, 1881.

Adélaïde-Merlande, Jacques. *Les origines du mouvement ouvrier en Martinique: 1870–1900.* Paris: Karthala, 2000.

———. *L'Historial antillais.* Vol. 4. Fort-de-France: Société Dajani, 1980.

———. *Troubles sociaux en Guadeloupe à la fin du XIXe siècle et au début du XXe siècle (1895–1910).* Pointe-à-Pitre: Groupe universitaire de recherches inter-Caraïbes, 1971.

Alexander, David. "The Study of Natural Disasters, 1977–97: Some Reflections on a Changing Field of Knowledge." *Disasters* 21 (1997): 284–304.

Alexandre, Arsène. "Les femmes de l'exposition." *L'Illustration,* 13 October 1900.

Americus. "Le Travail à la Martinique." *Revue géographique internationale,* 1894, 146–47.

Anderson, William A., and Russel R. Dynes. "Civil Disturbances and Social Change: A Comparative Analysis of the United States and Curaçao." *Urban Affairs Review* 12, no. 37 (1976): 37–56.

Andrieu, Jules. *Bibliographie générale de L'Agenais, et des parties du Condomois et du Bazadais incorporées dans le département de Lot-Et-Garonne, etc.* Paris: Agen, 1886.

Andrivon-Milton, Sabine. *Lettres de poilus martiniquais*. Lamentin: SAM Éditions, 2008.

Annales de la Chambre des députés. Paris: Imprimerie des journaux officiels, 1892.

Annales de la Chambre des députés: Documents parlementaires. Vol. 38. Paris: Imprimerie des journaux officiels, 1893.

Annales de la Chambre des députés, 7me législature: Débats parlementaires; Session extraordinaire de 1900. Paris: Imprimerie des journaux officiels, 1901.

Annales des mines, ou Recueil de mémoires sur l'exploitation des mines et sur les sciences et les arts qui s'y rapportent. 8e série, vol. 20. Edited by Ch. Dunod. Paris: Corps nationaux des ponts et chaussées, des mines, et des télégraphes, 1891.

Annales du Sénat: Débats parlementaires. Vols. 54 and 55. Paris: Imprimerie des journaux officiels, 1900.

Annales du Sénat: Débats parlementaires. Vol. 78. Paris: Imprimerie des journaux officiels, 1911.

Annuaire de la Guadeloupe et dépendances: Année 1901. Basse-Terre: Imprimerie du gouvernement, 1901.

Annuaire de la Martinique. Fort-de-France: Imprimerie du gouvernement, 1900.

Annuaire de la Martinique. Fort-de-France: Imprimerie du gouvernement, 1901.

Austin, O. P. *The World's Sugar Production and Consumption Showing the Statistical Position of Sugar at the Close of the Nineteenth Century*. Washington DC: U.S. Department of the Treasury, 1902.

"Aux travailleurs de la Martinique." *Troisième congres général des organisations socialistes françaises: Tenu à Lyon du 26 au 28 Mai 1901; Compte rendu sténographique officiel*. 497–98. Paris: Georges Bellais, 1901.

Azoulay, Ariella. "Citizens of Disaster." *Qui Parle* 15, no. 2 (2005): 105–37.

Banchelin, Saint-Luce. "La Guadeloupe." *L'Exposition nationale colonial de Marseille décrite par ses Auteurs*. Marseille: Commissariat General de L'Exposition, 1922.

Bangou, Henri. *La Guadeloupe, les aspects de la colonisation, 1848–1939*. Vol. 2. Paris: l'Harmattan, 1987.

———. *Le Parti socialiste français face à la décolonisation: De Jules Guesde à François Mitterrand; Le cas de la Guadeloupe*. Paris: L'Harmattan, 1985.

Barton, Allen H. *Communities in Disaster: A Sociological Analysis of Collective Stress Situations*. Garden City NY: Doubleday, 1969.

"Base de données des députés français depuis 1789." *Assemblée nationale*. Accessed 17 September 2010. http://www.assemblee-nationale.fr/sycomore/index.asp.

Bayliss-Smith, Tim, Richard Bedford, Harold Brookfield, and Marc Latham. *Islands, Islanders, and the World: The Colonial and Post-Colonial Experience of Eastern Fiji*. Cambridge, UK: Cambridge University Press, 1988.

Bérenger-Féraud, L. J. B. *Traité clinique des maladies des européens aux Antilles (Martinique)*. Vol 2. Paris: Octave Doin, 1881.

Betts, Raymond. *Assimilation and Association in French Colonial Theory, 1890–1914*. New York: Columbia University Press, 2005.

Blackburn, Robin. *The Overthrow of Colonial Slavery, 1776–1848*. London: Verso, 1988.

Blancan, André. *La crise de la Guadeloupe: Libres réflexions à nos compatriotes; Comment attirer les capitaux à la Guadeloupe? Un programme, autonomie ou assimilation, un referendum indispensable, les réformes*. Paris: A. Rousseau, 1906.

Blankaert, Claude. "Of Monstrous Métis? Hybridity, Fear of Miscegenation, and Patriotism from Buffon to Paul Broca." In Peabody and Stovall, *Color of Liberty*, 42–70.

Block, Maurice. *Statistique de la France comparée avec les divers pays de l'Europe*. Vol. 2. Paris: Guillaumin, 1875.

Boittin, Jennifer Anne. *Colonial Metropolis: The Urban Grounds of Anti-Imperialism and Feminism in Interwar Paris*. Lincoln: University of Nebraska Press, 2010.

Bouinais, A. *Guadeloupe: Physique, politique, économique; Avec une notice historique*. Paris: Challamel, 1881.

Boyd, James P. *The Paris Exposition of 1900: The Century's Last and Grandest All-World Exposition; A Vivid Descriptive View and Elaborate Scenic Presentation of the Site, Plan, and Exhibits*. Philadelphia: P. W. Ziegler, 1900.

Boyer de Peyreleau, Eugène Edouard. *Les Antilles françaises, particulièrement la Guadeloupe, depuis leur découverte jusqu'au 1er janvier 1823*. Vol. 1. Paris: Brissot-Thivars, 1823.

Branciard, Michel, and Marcel Gonin. *Le Mouvement ouvrier, 1815–1976*. Paris: Montholon-Services, 1977.

Breton, Raymond. *Relations de l'île de la Guadeloupe*. Basse-Terre: Société d'histoire de la Guadeloupe, 1978.

Budget des recettes et des dépenses départementale. Fort-de-France: Imprimerie du gouvernement, 1901–18.

Buffon, Alain. "La crise sucrière de 1882–1886 à la Guadeloupe." *Revue française d'histoire d'outre-Mer*, 1987, 311–31.

Bulletin de la Société astronomique de France. Vol. 16. Paris: Sociétés Savantes, 1902.

Bulletin officiel de la Martinique. Vol. 15, *Année 1882.* Fort-de-France: Imprimerie du gouvernement, 1887.

Bulletin officiel du ministère des colonies: 13ᵉ année 1899. Paris: Imprimerie nationale, 1900.

Burac, Maurice, and André Calmont. *La question de la terre dans les colonies et départements français d'Amérique, 1848–1998.* Paris: Karthala and Géode, 2000.

Bureau de recherches géologiques et Minières (BRGM)/SisFrance-Antilles. *Sismicité historique de la France: Antilles-Guyane-Mer des Caraibes.* 2016. Data set distributed by BRGM. http://www.sisfrance.net/Antilles/.

Burton, Richard D. E. *La famille coloniale: La Martinique et la mère patrie, 1789–1992.* Paris: L'Harmattan, 1994.

Burton, Richard D. E., and Fred Réno. *French and West Indian: Martinique, Guadeloupe, and French Guiana Today.* Charlottesville: University Press of Virginia, 1995.

Brunet, Guy. *Mariage et métissage dans les sociétés coloniales: Amériques, Afrique, et iles de l'Océan Indien (XVIᵉ–XXᵉ siècles)—Marriage and Misgeneration in Colonial Societies: Americas, Africa, and Islands of the Indian Ocean, XVIth–XXth Centuries.* Bern: Peter Lang, 2015.

Byas, Vincent W. "Whither Martinique?" *Phylon* 3, no. 3 (1942): 277–83.

Caron, François. *An Economic History of Modern France.* New York: Columbia University Press, 1979.

Chambre de commerce de Marseille. *Compte rendu de la situation commerciale et industrielle de la circonscription de Marseille pendant l'année 1892.* Marseille: Barlatier et Barthelet, 1893.

Chamoiseau, Patrick. *Chronicle of the Seven Sorrows.* Translated by Linda Coverdale. Chapel Hill: University of North Carolina Press, 1986.

———. *Texaco.* Translated by Rose-Myriam Réjouis and Val Vinoku. New York: Pantheon, 1997.

Chapman, Herrick, and Laura Levine Frader. *Race in France: Interdisciplinary Perspectives on the Politics of Difference.* New York: Berghahn Books, 2004.

Charle, Christophe. *Social History of France in the Nineteenth Century.* Oxford: Berg, 1994.

Charles-Roux, Jean. *Exposition universelle de 1900: L'organisation et le fonctionnement de l'exposition des colonies et pays de protectorat; Rapport général.* Paris: Imprimerie nationale, 1902.

Chemin-Dupontes, P. *Les Petites Antilles: Étude sur leur évolution économique (1820–1908).* Paris: Désormeaux, 1979.

Cherdieu, Philippe. "L'échec d'un socialisme colonial: La Guadeloupe (1891–1914)." *Revue d'histoire moderne et contemporaine* 31, no. 2 (1984): 308–33.

Chotard. *Quelle peut être la garantie de la République française dans ses colonies des Antilles.* Paris: Courcier, 18—.

Cohen, William. *Rulers of Empire: The French Colonial Service in Africa.* Palo Alto CA: Stanford, 1971.

Cole, Angela P., Terri Adams-Fuller, O. Jackson Cole, Olge Kruglanski, and Angela Glymph. "Making Sense of a Hurricane: Social Identity and Attribution Explanations of Race-Related Differences in Katrina Disaster Response." In Potter, *Racing the Storm,* 3–32.

Cole, Joshua. *The Power of Large Numbers: Population, Politics, and Gender in Nineteenth-Century France.* Ithaca NY: Cornell University Press, 2000.

Collection complete des lois, décrets, ordonnances, règlements, et avis du Conseil d'Etat. Vol. 90. Edited by J. B. Duvergier. Paris: L. Larose et Forcel, 1890.

Commercial Relations of the United States with Foreign Countries. Vol. 1. Washington DC: Bureau of Foreign Commerce U.S. Department of State, 1903.

Conklin, Alice. "Boundaries Unbound: Teaching French History as Colonial History and Colonial History as French History." *French Historical Studies* 23, no.2 (2000): 215–38.

———. *A Mission to Civilize: The Republican Idea of Empire in France and West Africa.* Stanford CA: Stanford University Press, 1997.

"Conseil du contentiuex: Elections municipales de Fort-de-France." *Bulletin officiel de la Martinique.* No. 387. Fort-de-France: Imprimerie du gouvernement, 1908.

Cooke, James J. *New French Imperialism, 1880–1910: The Third Republic and Colonial Expansion.* Newton Abbot, UK: David and Charles, 1973.

Cooper, Frederick. *Colonialism in Question: Theory, Knowledge, History.* Berkeley: University of California Press, 2005.

Corre, Armand. *Nos créoles.* Paris: Tresse et Stock, 1902.

Cottias, Myriam. "Le silence de la nation: 'Les vieilles colonies' comme lieu de définition des dogmes républicains (1848–1905)." *Outre-Mers,* 2003, 21–45.

Cotton, Allison M. "Stipulations: A Typology of Citizenship in the United States after Katrina." In Potter, *Racing the Storm,* 157–70.

Cuzent, Gilbert. *Eau thermo-minérale de la Ravine-Chaude du Lamentin (Guadeloupe).* Pointe-à-Pitre: Imprimerie du Commercial, 1864.

———. "Ouragan de la Guadeloupe du 6 September 1865." *L'Illustration: Journal universel,* vol. 46. Paris: [L'Illustration], 1865), 261–62.

Cuzent, Gilbert Henri. *Epidémie de la Guadeloupe, 1863–1866*. Paris: Masson, 1867.

Da Cunha, A. *Les Travaux de L'Exposition de 1900*. Paris: Masson, 1900.

Daniel, André. "Mars 1900." *L'Année politique* 27 (1901): 76.

Daughton, J. P. *An Empire Divided: Religion, Republicanism, and the Making of French Colonialism, 1880–1914*. New York: Oxford University Press, 2006.

Davis, Mike. *Ecology of Fear: Los Angeles and the Imagination of Disaster*. New York: Metropolitan Books, 1998.

Débats parlementaires: Comte rendu in extenso. Paris: Imprimerie des journaux officiels, 1899.

Debbasch, Yvan. *Couleur et liberté: Le jeu de critère ethnique dans un ordre juridique esclavagiste*. Paris: Dalloz, 1967.

Délibérations du Conseil général: Session ordinaire, novembre 1900. Fort-de-France: Imprimerie du gouvernement, 1900.

Denise, Christophe. "Une histoire évolutive de l'habitat Martiniquais." *In Situ: Revue des patrimoines*, no. 5 (2004). http://insitu.revues.org/2381.

Desnier, J. M. "Martinique: Before and after the Disaster of May 8, 1902—Personal Impressions." *Messenger: Monthly Magazine* 39 (1903), 121–40.

Deuxième congrès général des organisations socialistes françaises tenu à paris du 28 au 30 Septembre 1900. Paris: Georges Bellais, 1901.

Díaz, María Elena. *The Virgin, the King, and the Royal Slaves of El Cobre: Negotiating Freedom in Colonial Cuba, 1670–1780*. Stanford CA: Stanford University Press, 2000.

Dickson, H. N. "The Eruptions in Martinique and St. Vincent." *Geographical Journal* 20 (1902): 50–60.

Dictionnaire des parlementaires français depuis le 1er mai 1789 jusqu'au 1er mai 1889. Vols. 2 and 4. Edited by M. M. Adolphe Robert, Edgar Bourloton, and Gaston Cougny. Paris: Bourloton, 1891.

Diplomatic and Consular Reports. Annual Series, no. 4056, part 83. London: Harrison and Sons, 1908.

Dislère, Paul. *Notes sur l'organization des colonies*. Paris: Société d'imprimerie et librairie administratives, 1888.

Domergue, J. "Garaud, Louis." *Dictionnaire de biographie française*. Vol. 15. Paris: Letouzey et Ané, 1933.

Douaire, Anne. "Traces et absences de la Grande Guerre aux Antilles." *Mémoires et antimémoires littéraires au XXᵉ siècle: La Première Guerre mondiale; Colloque de Cerisy-la-Salle*, edited by Annamaria Laserra, Nicole Leclercq, and Marc Quaghebeur. 129–46. 2005. Brussels: PIE Peter Lang, 2008.

Drabek, Thomas E. *Human System Responses to Disaster: An Inventory of Sociological Findings*. New York: Springer-Verlag, 1986.

Dreyfus, Camille, and André Berthelot, eds. *La Grande Encyclopédie, inventaire raisonné des sciences, des lettres et des arts, par une société de savants et de gens de lettres*. 31 vols. Paris: H. Lamirault et cie., 1886.

Dubois, Laurent. *Avengers of the New World: The Story of the Haitian Revolution*. Cambridge MA: Belknap Press, 2004.

———. *A Colony of Citizens: Revolution and Slave Emancipation in the French Caribbean, 1787–1804*. Chapel Hill: University of North Carolina Press, 2004.

Duchateau-Roger, Edith. *Une "histoire vécue" des cataclysmes de la Martinique, 1891–1902*. Lille Desclée, de Brouwer et cie., 1904.

Duigan, Peter J., and Lewis Henry Gann. "Introduction." In *Colonialism in Africa, 1870–1960: The Economics of Colonialism*, vol. 4, edited by Peter J. Duigan and Lewis Henry Gann. 1–32. Cambridge: Cambridge University Press, 1975.

Dumont, Jacques. *L'amère patrie: Histoire des Antilles françaises au XXᵉ siècle*. Paris: Fayard, 2010.

———. "Conscription antillaise et citoyenneté revendiquée au tournant de la première guerre mondiale." *Vingtième siècle: Revue d'histoire*, no. 92 (2006): 101–16.

———. "La figure de l'ennemi: Les Antilles et la première guerre mondiale." *Bulletin de la Société d'Histoire de la Guadeloupe*, no. 168 (2014): 135–51.

———. "Santé et conscription créole: Le tournant de la Première Guerre mondiale." *Outre-Mers: Revue d'histoire* 94, no. 354 (2007): 223–41.

Duvergier, J. B., ed. *Collection complète des lois, décrets, ordonnances, règlements, et avis du conseil d'état*. Vol. 77. Paris: Charles Noblet, 1877.

Dynes, Russell R. *Organized Behavior in Disaster*. Lexington MA: Heath Lexington, 1970.

Edwards, Brent Hayes. *The Practice of Diaspora Literature, Translation, and the Rise of Black Internationalism*. Cambridge MA: Harvard University Press, 2003.

Elsner, James B., and A. Birol Kara. *Hurricanes of the North Atlantic: Climate and Society*. New York: Oxford University Press, 1999.

Étienne, Eugène. *Les compagnies de colonisation: Accompagné de notes explicatives et annexes*. Paris : A. Challamel, 1897.

Exposition universelle de 1900: Les plaisirs et les curiosités de l'Exposition. Paris: Guide Chaix, 1900.

Exposition universelle international de 1900 à Paris: Rapports du jury international. Groupe 1. Paris: Imprimerie nationale, 1902.

Fallope, Josette. *Esclaves et citoyens: Les noirs à la Guadeloupe au XIXe siècle dans les processus de résistance et d'intégration; 1802–1910.* Basse-Terre: Société d'histoire de la Guadeloupe, 1992.

Fick, Carolyn E. *The Making of Haiti: The Saint Domingue Revolution from Below.* Knoxville: University of Tennessee Press, 1990.

Flaugh, Christian. *Operation Freak Narrative, Identity, and the Spectrum of Bodily Abilities.* Montreal: McGill-Queen's University Press, 2012.

Fogarty, Richard. *Race and War in France: Colonial Subjects in the French Army, 1914–1918.* Baltimore: Johns Hopkins University Press, 2008.

Food and Agriculture Organization of the United Nations. *Roots, Tubers, Plantains, and Bananas in Human Nutrition.* Rome: Food and Agriculture Organization of the United Nations, 1990.

France. *Annuaire statistique de la France.* Vol. 15. Paris: Imprimerie nationale, 1894.

———. *Bulletin: Documents officiels, statistique, rapports.* Paris: Imprimerie nationale, 1888.

———. *Bulletin: Documents officiels, statistique, rapports.* Paris: Imprimerie nationale, 1889.

Froidevaux, H. "L'Œuvre scolaire de la France aux Colonies." In *Exposition universelle de 1900: Publications de la commission chargée de préparer la participation du ministère des colonies,* edited by Augustin Challamel. 9–205. Paris: Libraire maritime et coloniale, 1900.

GADM Database of Global Administrative Areas, Version 2, January 2012. Retrieved 12 December 2012 at http://www.gadm.org/.

Gainot, Bernard. *Les officiers de couleur dans les armées de la République et de l'Empire (1792–1815): De l'esclavage à la condition militaire dans les Antilles françaises.* Paris: Karthala, 2007.

Gallaher, John G. *General Alexandre Dumas: Soldier of the French Revolution.* Carbondale: Southern Illinois University Press, 1997.

Galmot, Jean. *La Guyane française et la guerre: Pour la France et pour la petite patrie; L'enthousiasme patriotique à la déclaration de guerre.* Fort-de-France: L. A. Bassières, 1919.

Garaud, Louis. *Rapport sur la situation de l'instruction publique à la Martinique: Année scolaire, 1887–1888.* Fort-de-France: Imprimerie du gouvernement, 1888.

————. *Trois ans à la Martinique*. Paris: Alcide Picard and Kaan, 1892.

Garrigus, John D. *Before Haiti: Race and Citizenship in French Saint-Domingue*. New York: Palgrave Macmillan, 2006.

————. "Vincent Ogé Jeune (1757–91): Social Class and Free Colored Mobilization on the Eve of the Haitian Revolution." *Americas* 68, no. 1 (2011): 33–62.

GEODE, Caraïbe. *Les Antilles, terres à risques*. Paris: Karthala, 1999.

G. F. "La Guadeloupe en 1899," vol. 80 (3 September 1899). In *Le Travail National: Organe de l'Association de l'industrie et de l'agriculture francaises*, 524–25. Paris: Administration et rédaction, 1899.

Gill, André. *Les Hommes d'aujourdhui* 3, no. 133 (1881).

Godefroy, P., E. Leroi, P. Mouroux, B. Sauret, Ch. Paulin, and Ph. Rancon. "Assessment of Seismic Hazard in the Islands of Guadeloupe and Martinique (Antilles)." In *Earthquake Engineering Tenth World Conference*. 455–60. Rotterdam: Balkema, 1992.

Guadeloupe et dépendances: Budget des recettes et des dépenses; Décisions modificatives. Basse-Terre: Imprimerie officiel, 1885–1918.

Guliet, B. "Le Cyclone de la Martinique." *Journal des Voyages et des aventures de terre et de mer*, no. 750 (22 November 1890), 335.

Hale, Dana. *Races on Display: French Representations of Colonized Peoples, 1886–1940*. Bloomington: Indiana University Press, 2008.

Harp, Stephen L. *Learning to Be Loyal: Primary Schooling as Nation Building in Alsace and Lorraine, 1850–1940*. DeKalb: Northern Illinois University Press, 1998.

Harris, Garrad. *The West Indies as an Export Field*. Washington DC: Government Printing Office, 1910.

Heath, Elizabeth. *Wine, Sugar, and the Making of Modern France: Global Economic Crisis and the Racialization of French Citizenship, 1870–1910*. Cambridge, UK: Cambridge University Press, 2014.

Heilprin, Angelo. *Mont Pelée and the Tragedy of Martinique: A Study of the Great Catastrophes of 1902, with Observations and Experiences in the Field*. Philadelphia: J. B. Lippincott, 1903.

Hélénon, Véronique. *French Caribbeans in Africa: Diasporic Connections and Colonial Administration, 1880–1939*. New York: Palgrave Macmillan, 2011.

Hélot, Jules. *Le sucre de betterave en France de 1800 à 1900: Culture de la betterave—législation—technologie*. Cambrai, France: F. et P. Deligne, 1900.

Hess, Jean. *La catastrophe de la Martinique: Notes d'un reporter*. Paris: Charpentier et Fasquelle, 1902.

Heuer, Jennifer. "The One-Drop Rule in Reverse? Interracial Marriages in Napoleonic and Restoration France." *Law and History Review* 27, no. 3 (2009): 515–48.

Hitier, Henri. *Plantes industrielles.* Paris: J.-B. Baillière, 1905.

Hobsbawm, Eric. *The Age of Capital: 1848–1875.* London: Abacus, 1995.

Hunt, Lynn. *The French Revolution and Human Rights: A Brief Documentary History.* Boston: Bedford Books, 1996.

Hunt, Lynn. *Inventing Human Rights: A History.* New York: W. W. Norton, 2008.

Isaac, Alexandre. *Question coloniales: Constitution et Sénatus-consultes.* Paris: Librarie Guillaumin, 1887.

Jackson, Jeffrey H. *Paris under Water: How the City of Light Survived the Great Flood of 1910.* New York: Palgrave Macmillan, 2010.

Jannesson, Victor. *Monographie et histoire de la ville de Saint-Etienne depuis ses origines jusqu'à nos jours.* Saint-Étienne: J. Le Hénaff, 1891.

Jennings, Eric. *Curing the Colonizers: Hydrotherapy, Climatology, and French Colonial Spas.* Durham NC: Duke University Press, 2006.

J. M. "La Question du travail aux colonies: Immigration." *Bulletins de la Société Bretonne de Géographie,* no. 24–25 (May–August 1886): 111–65.

Johnson, Sara. *The Fear of French Negroes: Transcolonial Collaboration in the Revolutionary Americas.* Berkeley: University of California Press, 2012.

Johnson, Sherry. *Climate and Catastrophe in Cuba and the Atlantic World in the Age of Revolution.* Chapel Hill: University of North Carolina Press, 2011.

Jones, Eric C., and Arthur D. Murphy. *The Political Economy of Hazards and Disasters.* Lanham MD: AltaMira Press, 2009.

Keaton, Trica Danielle, T. Denean Sharpley-Whiting, and Tyler Edward Stovall, eds. *Black France/France Noire: The History and Politics of Blackness.* Durham: Duke University Press, 2012.

Klein, Naomi. *The Shock Doctrine: The Rise of Disaster Capitalism.* New York: Metropolitan Books, 2007.

Klooster, Wim. "Slave Revolts, Royal Justice, and a Ubiquitous Rumor in the Age of Revolutions." *William and Mary Quarterly* 71, no. 3 (2014): 401–24.

Knight, Franklin W., and Colin A. Palmer. *The Modern Caribbean.* Chapel Hill: University of North Carolina Press, 1989.

Lambolez, Charles L. [Coeur créole, pseud.]. *Saint-Pierre-Martinique, 1635–1902: Annales des Antilles françaises-journal et album de la Martinique naissance; Vie et mort de la cité créole; Livre d'or de la charité.* Paris: Berger-Levrault et cie., 1905.

Lanessan, J. L. de. *L'expansion colonial de la France: Étude economique, politique, et geographique sur les etablissements français d'outre-mer*, edited by Félix Alcan. Paris: Germier Baillière et cie., 1886.

Lara, Henri Adolphe, and Leon Hennique. *Contribution de la Guadeloupe à la pensée française: 1635–1935*. Paris: J. Crès, 1936.

Lara, Oruno D. *La liberté assassinée: Guadeloupe, Guyane, Martinique, et la Réunion en 1848–1856*. Paris: Harmattan, 2005.

Laserra, Annamaria, Nicole Leclercq, and Marc Quaghebeur. *Mémoires et antimémoires littéraires au XXᵉ siècle la Première Guerre mondiale: Colloque de Cerisy-la-Salle, 2005*. Brussels: PIE Peter Lang, 2008.

"The Last Days of Saint-Pierre." *The Century Magazine*, vol. 64. Edited by Aline Gorren. 610–33. London: Macmillan, 1902.

Légier, Emile. *La Martinique et la Guadeloupe: Considérations économiques sur l'avenir et la culture de la canne*. Paris: Bureaux de la sucrerie indigène et coloniale, 1905.

————. "La Martinique et la Guadeloupe: Notes de voyage." *La sucrerie indigène et coloniale: Revue bedomadaire organes des intérets de la sucrerie et la distillerie*. Paris: Bureaux de la Sucrerie indigène et coloniale, 1904.

Levasseur, Émile. *La France et ses colonies (géographie et statistique)*. Vol. 3. Paris: Librairie Ch. Delagrave, 1893.

Lucrèce, Jules. *Histoire de la Martinique: A l'usage des cours supérieur et complémentaire des écoles primaires*. Paris: Imprimerie des presses universitaires de France, 1933.

Loomis, Francis B., "Mine Explosions in France." In *The Miscellaneous Documents of the House of Representatives for the Second Session of the Fifty-First Congress*. 339–43. Washington DC: Government Printing Office, 1891.

Louisiana Sugar Planters' Association, Louisiana Sugar Chemists' Association, and American Cane Growers' Association. *The Louisiana Planter and Sugar Manufacturer*. Vol. 4. New Orleans: Louisiana Planter and Sugar Manufacturer Company, 1890.

Malte-Brun, Victor Adolfe. *La France illustrée: Géographie, histoire, administration, statistique*. Vol. 5. Paris: J. Rouff, 1884.

Martin, Frederick, John Scott Keltie, Isaac Parker Anderson Renwick, Mortimer Epstein, S. H. Steinberg, John Paxton, and Barry Turner. *The Statesman's Year-Book: Statistical and Historical Annual of the States of the World*. New York: St. Martin's Press, 1880–1920.

Mam Lam Fouck, Serge. *L'histoire de l'assimilation des "vieilles colonies" française aux départements d'outre-mer: La culture politique de l'assimilation en Guyane et aux Antilles françaises (XIXe et XXe siècles)*. Matoury, French Guiana: Ibis Rouge, 2006.

"Martinique." *La grande encyclopédie*. Vol. 23. Paris: Société Anonyme de la Grande Encyclopédie, 1885–1902.

La Martinique républicaine à la France républicaine. Fort-de-France: Imprimerie de la France Colonial, 1908.

Massing, Jean Michel. "From Greek Proverb to Soap Advert: Washing the Ethiopian." *Journal of the Warburg and Courtauld Institutes* 58 (1995): 180–201.

Mauch, Christof, and Christian Pfister. *Natural Disasters, Cultural Responses: Case Studies toward a Global Environmental History*. Lanham MD: Lexington Books, 2009.

McNeill, John Robert. *Mosquito Empires: Ecology and War in the Greater Caribbean, 1620–1914*. New York: Cambridge University Press, 2010.

McWilliam, Neil. *Monumental Intolerance: Jean Baffier, a Nationalist Sculptor in fin-de-siècle France*. University Park: Pennsylvania State University Press, 2000.

Nellis, Eric. *Shaping the New World: African Slavery in the Americas, 1500–1888*. Toronto: University of Toronto Press, 2013.

Merriman, John. *The Dynamite Club: How a Bombing in Fin-de-Siècle Paris Ignited the Age of Modern Terror*. Boston: Houghton Mifflin Harcourt, 2009.

Messina, William A., Jr. "An Assessment of Hurricane Charley's Impact of Cuba." FE494. Gainesville: University of Florida, IFAS Extension, 2004.

Metcalfe, Thomas. *An Imperial Vision: Indian Architecture and Britain's Raj*. Berkeley: University of California Press, 1989.

Michel, Jean-Baptiste, et al. "Quantitative Analysis of Culture Using Millions of Digitized Books." *Science* 331, no. 6014 (14 December 2011): 176–82. doi: 10.1126/science.1199644.

Miles, Michelle. "Levees, Looters, and Lawlessness: Race, Rumor, and the Framing of Hurricane Katrina." PhD diss., University of Colorado at Boulder, 2008.

Miller, James Martin. *The Martinique Horror and St. Vincent Calamity*. Philadelphia: National Publishing, 1902.

Mines and Quarries: General Report and Statistics for 1902. Part 4. *Colonial and Foreign Statistics*. Edited by Clement Le Neve Foster. London: His Majesty's Stationary Office, 1902.

Ministère du Commerce. *Statistiques des grèves et des recours à la conciliation et à l'arbitrage survenus pendant l'année 1900*. Paris: Imprimerie nationale, 1901.

"Miscellaneous." *Beet Sugar Gazette* 4, no. 4. (June 1902): 109.

Mismer, Charles. *Souvenirs de la Martinique et du Mexique pendant l'intervention française*. Paris: Librarie Hachette, 1890.

Mitchell, Robin. "*Les ombres noires de saint domingue*: The Impact of Black Women on Gender and Racial Boundaries in Eighteenth- and Nineteenth-Century France." PhD diss., University of California, Berkeley, 2010.

Monet, Henri. *La Martinique*. Paris: A. Savinne, 1892.

Mote, Carl H. *Industrial Arbitration: A World-Wide Survey of Natural and Political Agencies for Social Justice and Industrial Peace*. Indianapolis: Bobbs-Merrill, 1916.

Mulcahy, Matthew. *Hurricanes and Society in the British Greater Caribbean, 1624–1783*. Baltimore: Johns Hopkins University Press, 2008.

Murphy, Arthur D. *The Political Economy of Hazards and Disasters*. Lanham MD: AltaMira Press, 2009.

Nardal, Paulette. *Guide des colonies françaises: Martinique, Guadeloupe, Guyane, St. Pierre-Miquelon*. Paris: Société d'éditions géographiques, maritimes, et coloniales, 1931.

La Nature: Revue des sciences et de leurs applications aux arts et à l'industrie. No. 1254. Edited by Henri de Parville. Paris: Masson et cie., 1897.

Nestor, P. "La grève générale des travailleurs agricoles." *Le mouvement socialiste: Revue bi-mensuelle internationale*. No. 150. Paris: Edouard Cornély, 1905, 563–67.

Neville, R. G. "The Courrières Colliery Disaster, 1906." *Journal of Contemporary History* 13 (1978): 33–52.

Nicolas, Armand. *Histoire de la Martinique de 1848 à 1939*. Vol. 2. Paris: L'Harmattan, 1996.

———. *L'insurrection du sud à la Martinique (septembre 1870)*. Fort-de-France: Imprimerie populaire, 1971.

———. *La Révolution antiesclavagiste de mai 1848 à la Martinique*. Fort-de-France: Imprimerie populaire, 1967.

Northrup, David. "Indentured Indians in the French Antilles. Les immigrants Indiens engagés aux Antilles françaises." *Revue française d'histoire d'outre-mer* 87, no. 326 (2000): 245–71. http://www.persee.fr/doc/outre_0300-9513 _2000_num_87_326_3777.

Osborne, Michael A. *Nature, the Exotic, and the Science of French Colonialism*. Bloomington: Indiana University Press, 1994.

Otero, Romulo Caballeros, and Ricardo Zapata Marti. *The Impacts of Natural Disasters on Developing Economies: Implications for the International Develop-*

ment and Disaster Community. Yokohama, Japan: World Conference on Natural Disaster Reduction, 1994.

Peabody, Sue, and Tyler Edward Stovall. *The Color of Liberty: Histories of Race in France.* Durham NC: Duke University Press, 2003.

Peck, Ferdinand Wythe. *Report of the Commissioner-General for the United States to the International Universal Exposition, Paris, 1900.* Vol. 5. Washington DC: Government Printing Office, 1901.

Pelet, Paul. *Nouvel Atlas des colonies françaises, dressé par ordre de l'administration des colonies.* Paris: A. Challamel, 1891.

Perina, Mickaella. *Citoyenneté et sujétion aux Antilles francophones: Post-esclavage et aspiration démocratique.* Paris: l'Harmattan, 1997.

Peyreleau, Eugène Edouard Boyer de. *Les Antilles françaises, particulièrement la Guadeloupe, depuis leur découverte jusqu'au 1er janvier 1823.* Vol. 1. Paris: Brissot-Thivars, 1823.

Picard, Alfred. *Exposition universelle internationale de 1900 à Paris: Le bilan d'un siècle (1801–1900).* Vol. 6. Paris: Imprimerie nationale, 1906.

———. *Exposition universelle internationale de 1900 à Paris: Rapport général administratif et technique.* Vol. 6. Paris: Imprimerie nationale, 1903.

Pichevin, Roland. "Bulletin de l'Union coloniale française." *Quinzaine colonial,* 10 March 1906, 151–52.

———. *Rapport sur la création d'un gouvernement général des Antilles et de la Guyane, présentée à la section des Anciennes Colonies de l'Union Coloniale.* Paris: Imprimerie de P. Dupon, 1906.

Pielke, Roger A., Joel Gratz, Christopher W. Landsea, Douglas Collins, Mark A. Saunders, and Rade Musulin. "Normalized Hurricane Damage in the United States: 1900–2005." *Natural Hazards Review,* February 2008, 29–42.

Piketty, Thomas. *Les hauts revenus en France au XXe siècle: Inégalités et redistributions, 1901–1998.* Paris: Bernard Grasset, 2001.

Pluchon, Pierre. *Toussaint Louverture: Un révolutionnaire noir d'ancien régime.* Paris: Fayard, 1989.

Pluchon, Pierre, and Lucien-René Abénon. *Histoire des Antilles et de la Guyane.* Toulouse: Privat, 1982.

Potter, Hillary. "Reframing Crime in a Disaster: Perception, Reality, and Criminalization of Survival Tactics among African Americans in the Aftermath of Katrina." In Potter, *Racing the Storm,* 51–67.

———, ed. *Racing the Storm: Racial Implications and Lessons Learned from Hurricane Katrina.* Lanham MD: Lexington, 2007.

Prochaska, David. *Making Algeria French: Colonialism in Bône, 1870–1920.* Cambridge, UK: Cambridge University Press, 1990.

Projet de budget (Département de la Martinique). Fort-de-France: Imprimerie du gouvernement, 1913.

Projet de budget (Département de la Martinique). Fort-de-France: Imprimerie du gouvernement, 1914.

Quarantelli, E. L. "Panic Behavior: Some Empirical Observations." In *Human Response to Tall Buildings,* edited by D. J. Conway. 336–50. Stroudsburg PA: Dowden, Hutchinson, and Ross, 1977.

Quarantelli, E. L., and Russel R. Dynes. "Response to Social Crisis and Disaster." *Annual Review of Sociology* 3 (1977): 23–49.

Ramnath, Maia. *Decolonizing Anarchism: An Anti-Authoritarian History of India's Liberation Struggle.* Edinburgh: AK Press, 2012.

Rappaport, Edward, and José Fernandez-Partagas. "The Deadliest Atlantic Tropical Cyclones, 1492–1996." National Hurricane Center, National Oceanic and Atmospheric Administration, 1997. http://www.nhc.noaa.gov/pastdeadly.shtml.

Reinhardt, Catherine A. *Claims to Memory: Beyond Slavery and Emancipation in the French Caribbean.* New York: Berghahn Books, 2006.

Reisch, R. S. "French Experience with Representative Government in the West Indies." *American Historical Review* 6, no. 3 (1901): 475–97.

Renard, Rosamunde. "Labour Relations in Martinique and Guadeloupe, 1848–1870." *Journal of Caribbean History* 26, no. 1 (1992): 37–57.

Rey, Henri. *Étude sur la colonie de la Guadeloupe, topographie médicale, climatologie, démographie.* Paris: Berger-Levrault et cie., 1878.

Richardson, Bonham C. *Economy and Environment in the Caribbean: Barbados and the Windwards in the Late 1800s.* Kingston, Jamaica: University of the West Indies Press, 1997.

———. *Igniting the Caribbean's Past: Fire in British West Indian History.* Chapel Hill: University of North Carolina Press, 2004.

Rolph, George Morrison. *Something about Sugar: Its History, Growth, Manufacture and Distribution.* San Francisco: John J. Newbegin, 1917.

Romer, A. *Les Cyclones de la Martinique.* Fort-de-France: Imprimerie du gouvernement, 1932.

Rossignol, G. "Séance du lundi 23 mai 1898 de la conférence de M. Samuel Verneuil sur les Antilles françaises." In *Revue de géographie commerciale de Bordeaux,* edited by J. Gebelin. 305–7. Bordeaux: Feret et Fils, 1898.

Royce, Frederick. *The Burning of St. Pierre and the Eruption of Mont Pelée: A Graphic Account of the Greatest Volcanic Disaster in the History of the World.* Chicago: Continental Publishing, 1902.

Russo, L. "Grèves et socialism à la Guadeloupe." *La Vie Ouvrière: Revue syndicaliste bi-mensuelle,* no. 26 (1910): 486–500.

Rutter, Frank Roy. *International Sugar Situation: Origin of the Sugar Problem and Its Present Aspects under the Brussels Convention.* Washington DC: Government Printing Office, 1904.

Saada, Emmanuelle. *Les enfants de la colonie: Les métis de l'Empire français entre sujétion et citoyenneté.* Paris: La Découverte, 2007.

Saffache, Pascal, Jean-Valéry Marc, and Olivier Cospar. *Les cyclones en Martinique: Quatre siècles cataclysmiques; Éléments pour une prise de conscience de la vulnérabilité de l'ile de la Martinique.* Fort-de-France: Ibis Rough, 2002.

Saffache, Pascal, Jean-Valéry Marc, and Vincent Huyghes-Belrose. *Les cyclones en Guadeloupe: Quatre siècles cataclysmiques.* Fort-de-France: Ibis Rough, 2003.

Sainton, J. P. *Les nègres en politique: Couleur, identités, et stratégies de pouvoir en Guadeloupe au tournant du siècle.* Lille, France: Presses universitaires du Septentrion, 2000.

Salaires et durée du travail dans l'industrie française: Résultats généraux. Vol. 4, *Ministère du commerce, de l'industrie, des postes, et des télégraphes.* Paris: Imprimerie nationale, 1897.

Scarth, Alywn. *La Catastrophe: The Eruption of Mount Pelée, the Worst Volcanic Eruption of the Twentieth Century.* Oxford: Oxford University Press, 2002.

———. *Vulcan's Fury: Man against the Volcano.* New Haven CT: Yale University Press, 2001.

Schafer, Sylvia. *Children in Moral Danger and the Problem of Government in Third Republic France.* Princeton NJ: Princeton University Press, 1997.

Schloss, Rebecca Hartkopf. *Sweet Liberty: The Final Days of Slavery in Martinique.* Philadelphia: University of Pennsylvania Press, 2009.

Schmidt, Nelly. *Abolitionnistes de l'esclavage et réformateurs des colonies, 1820–1851: Analyse et documents.* Paris: Karthala, 2001.

Schnakenbourg, Christian. "La Banque de la Guadeloupe et la crise de change, 1895–1904." *Bulletin de la Société d'histoire de la Guadeloupe* 87–90, no. 318 (1991): 31–95.

———. "La création des usines en Guadeloupe (1843–1884)." *Bulletin de la Société d'histoire de la Guadeloupe,* nos. 124–25 (2000): 21–115.

———. "La disparition des 'habitation-sucreries' en Guadeloupe (1848–1906): Recherche sur la désagrégation des structures préindustrielles de la production sucrière antillaise après l'abolition de l'esclavage." *Revue française d'histoire d'outre-mer* 74, no. 276 (1987): 257–309.

———. "From Sugar Estate to Central Factory: The Industrial Revolution in the Caribbean (1840–1905)." In *Crisis and Change in the International Sugar Economy, 1860–1914*, edited by Bill Albert and Adrian Graves. 83–91. Norwich, UK: ISC Press, 1984.

———. *Histoire de l'industrie sucrière en Guadeloupe aux XIXe et XXe siècles.* Vol. 3. Paris: L'Harmattan, 2008.

Schoelcher, Victor. *La vérité aux ouvriers et cultivateurs de la Martinique, suivie des rapports, décrets, arrêtes, projets de lois, et d'arrêtés concernant l'abolition immédiate de l'esclavage.* Paris: Pagnette, 1849.

Schwartz, Stuart B. "Hurricanes and the Shaping of Circum-Caribbean Societies." *Florida Historical Quarterly* 83, no. 4 (2005): 381–409.

———. *Sea of Storms: A History of Hurricanes in the Greater Caribbean from Columbus to Katrina.* Princeton NJ: Princeton University Press, 2015.

Séisme du 29 avril 1897 à la Guadeloupe. Paris: Ministère du l'Écologie, du Développement durable et de l'Énergie, April 2013.

Shorter, Edward, and Charles Tilly. *Strikes in France, 1830–1968.* London: Cambridge University Press, 1974.

Simon, Jules, et al. *Faisons la chaine, contes, nouvelles et récits.* Paris: Levy, 1890.

Singer, Timothy J. "An Introduction to Disaster: Some Considerations of a Psychological Nature." *Aviation, Space, and Environmental Medicine,* March 1982, 245–50.

Smith, Michael. *Tariff Reform in France, 1860–1900: The Politics of Economic Interest.* Ithaca NY: Cornell, 1980.

"Social, Demographic, and Educational Data for France, 1801–1897." Interuniversity Consortium for Political and Social Research. 1984. Accessed April 2, 2017. doi:10.3886/ICPSR00048.VI.

Sonthonnax, L. *Deux mois aux Antilles françaises.* Lyon: Imprimerie de A. Rey, 1898.

Soppelsa, Peter. "Paris's 1900 Universal Exposition and the Politics of Urban Disaster." *French Historical Studies* 36, no. 2 (Spring 2013): 271–98.

Special Commission, Saint-Félix. *Rapport de la Commission spéciale du Conseil Général sur le cyclone du 18 août 1891,* FM SG MAR 72, d.581, ANOM.

Spruyt, Hendrik. *Ending Empire: Contested Sovereignty and Territorial Partition.* Ithaca NY: Cornell University Press, 2005.

Steinberg, Theodore. *Acts of God: The Unnatural History of Natural Disaster in America.* New York: Oxford University Press, 2000.

A Study of the Great Catastrophes of 1902, with Observations and Experiences in the Field. Philadelphia: J. B. Lippincott, 1903.

La Sucrerie Indigène et Coloniale. Vol. 64. Paris: Bureaux de la sucrerie indigène et coloniale, 1904.

Terrier, Auguste. "Le Journal des voyages à l'exposition universelle," *Journal des voyages et des aventures de terre et de mer*, 21 October 1900.

Terrée-Potino, E. "Le temps des grèves." In *L'Historial Antillais*, edited by Tony Djian. 381–82. Fort-de-France: Société Dajani, 1980.

Thiébaut, Claude. *Guadeloupe 1899: Année de tous les dangers*. Paris: Éditions L'Harmattan, 1989.

Thomas, Gordon, and Max Morgan Wits. *The Day the World Ended: Mont Pelée Earthquake 1902*. New York: Stein and Day, 1969.

Thompson, E. P. "The Moral Economy of the English Crowd in the Eighteenth Century." *Past and Present*, no. 50 (1971): 76–136.

Tierney, Kathleen. "Social Inequality, Hazards, and Disasters." In *On Risk and Disaster*, edited by Ronald J. Daniels, Donald F. Ketti, and Howard Kunreuther. 109–28. Philadelphia: University of Pennsylvania Press, 2011.

Tierney, Kathleen, Christine Bevc, and Erica Kuligowski. "Metaphors Matter: Disaster Myths, Media Frames, and Their Consequences in Hurricane Katrina." *Annals of the American Academy of Political and Social Science* 604, no. 1 (March 2006): 57–81.

Tisserand, Eugène. *Statistique agricole de la France (Algérie et colonies) résultats généraux de l'enquête décennale de 1882*. Nancy: Imprimerie administrative Berger-Levrault et cie., 1887.

Tomich, Dale. *Slavery in the Circuit of Sugar: Martinique and the World Economy, 1830–1848*. Baltimore: Johns Hopkins University Press, 1990.

"Tropical Cyclone Climatology." *National Weather Service: National Hurricane Center*. 18 June 2012. Retrieved 20 August 2012 from http://www.nhc.noaa.gov/climo/.

United Nations Environment Programme, and United Nations Centre for Human Settlements. *Environmental Guidelines for Settlements Planning and Management*. Nairobi, Kenya: United Nations Environment Programme, 1987.

Université Antilles-Guyane. *La Caraïbe au tournant de deux siècles: Commémoration du premier centenaire de la guerre hispano-cubano-américaine et de la république de Cuba, 1902*. Paris: Karthala, 2004.

U.S. Department of State. *Commercial Relations of the United States with Foreign Countries during the Year 1901*. Washington DC: Government Printing Office, 1902.

Verschuur, G. *Voyage aux trois Guyanes et aux Antilles.* Paris: Hachette, 1894.

Vibert, Paul. *La colonisation pratique et comparée: Colonies françaises, colonisation pratique; Colonies étrangères, colonisation comparée; Deux années de cours libres à la Sorbonne.* Paris: É. Cornély et cie., 1904.

Waldeck-Rousseau, P. *Politique française et étrangère,* edited by Eugène Fasquelle. Paris: Bibliothèque-Charpentier, 1903.

Weber, Eugen. *Peasants into Frenchmen: The Modernization of Rural France, 1870–1914.* Stanford CA: Stanford University Press, 1976.

White, Owen. *Children of the French Empire: Miscegenation and Colonial Society in French West Africa, 1895–1960.* New York: Oxford University Press, 1999.

Wilder, Gary. *The French Imperial Nation-State: Negritude and Colonial Humanism between the Two World Wars.* Chicago: University of Chicago Press, 2005.

———. "Unthinking French History: Colonial Studies beyond National Identity." In *After the Imperial Turn: Thinking with and through the Nation,* edited by Antoinette Burton. 134–35. Durham NC: Duke University Press, 2003.

Williams, Eric. *Capitalism and Slavery.* New York: Russell and Russell, 1961.

Wright, C. *Twelfth Special Report of the Commissioner of Labor: Coal Mine Labor in Europe.* Washington DC: Government Printing Office, 1905.

Wright, Gwendolyn. *The Politics of Design in French Colonial Urbanism.* Chicago: University of Chicago Press, 1991.

Yacou, Alain. *Les catastrophes naturelles aux Antilles: D'une Soufrière à une autre.* Pointe-à-Pitre, Guadeloupe: CERC, 1999.

Zebrowski, Ernest. *The Last Days of St. Pierre: The Volcanic Disaster That Claimed 30,000 Lives.* New Brunswick NJ: Rutgers University Press, 2002.

Zébus, Marie-Françoise. "Paysannerie et économie de plantation: Le cas de la Guadeloupe, 1848–1980." *Ruralia: Revue de l'Association des ruralistes francais* 5 (1999). https://ruralia.revues.org/110.

INDEX

Page numbers followed by *f* indicate figures.
Page numbers followed by *m* indicate maps.
Page numbers followed by *t* indicate tables.

Monet on, 50–51; Louis Garaud on, 60; and Méline Tariff, 142–44; overview, 15, 109–13, 144–46; political consequences of, 147, 149, 152–56; and racism, 109, 112, 126, 128, 133, 139, 145; on Saffir-Simpson hurricane scale, 114; and slavery, 112–13, 132–33, 144–45

hurricane of 7 August 1899 (Guadeloupe), 148, 156–57, 165–70, 188, 221

hurricanes: in general, 3–5, 11, 22, 52–53, 53f, 54f, 56, 58–60, 63, 65; hurricane of 1780, 110; hurricane of 1813, 110. *See also* hurricane of 18 August 1891 (Martinique); hurricane of 7 August 1899 (Guadeloupe)

Hurricanes and Society (Mulcahy), 9

imperialism, French, key motifs of, 17

incendiarism, 15, 55, 148, 150–65, 170, 185, 187–89. *See also* fires

indentured servants, 3, 28, 123, 151, 159, 178, 202

Isaac, Alexandre, 22, 148–49, 158–59, 162, 165

Jackson, Jeffrey, 9
Jennings, Eric, 20
Johnson, Sherry, 9

Kahn, Lieutenant, 175, 178–79, 181, 185–86
King, Clara, 199, 274n25
Klein, Naomi, 95

Laborieux, Marie-Sophie, 65
Labor Law of 1892, 172–73
labor unrest, 2, 15, 33–35, 95, 148–49,

162–64, 171–73, 178, 181, 184–85, 189–90. *See also* strike activity

La famille coloniale (Burton), 9, 252n105

laicization, 77–78

Law of 5 April 1844, 152

Law of 28 July 1881, 7–8, 249n29

Law of Labor Arbitration of 1892, 33

League of the Rights of Man and the Citizen, 35

Légitimus, Hégésippe Jean, 149–50, 160, 175

Le Savon Dirtoff, 99, 102f

Les nègres en politique (Sainton), 9

L'histoire de l'assimilation (Mam Lam Fouck), 9

liquefaction, earthquake, 55

Lucrèce, Jules, 39–40

malaria, 23, 56

Mam Lam Fouck, Serge, 9

manioc, 71, 131–32, 154–55, 167, 202

Marianne, 44, 225f, 226, 228–29

Martinican pit viper, 50–51, 191

Martinique: citizenship rights in, 6–9; civil strife in, 22–23; civil unrest and legislative catastrophe at turn of century, 147–90; climate in, 50–61; departmental status of, 16–18, 21–23, 26, 109, 134–46, 197, 214, 231, 234, 238, 244, 247n15; early history of, 2–3; and earthquakes, 51–52, 55, 65–66; educational system in, 37–49, 77, 204–6, 211, 242, 253n115; and Law of 28 July 1881, 7–8, 249n29; national identity after World War I, 236–46; as part of old France,

Martinique (*continued*)
38–49; political aspirations and economic reality, 23–38; race and racism in, 17–23; racism and assimilation in, 17–23; representation in French national government, 25, 247n15, 249n29. *See also* great Antillean fires of 1890; hurricane of 18 August 1891 (Martinique); Mount Pelée eruption; strike of 1900 (Martinique)

Matheiu, Louisy, 24

Maximin, Daniel, 109

Méline, Jules, 142

Méline Tariff of 1892, 142–44, 154

métissage, 19–20, 45, 60. *See also* mulattos; race and racism

Millerand, Alexandre, 186

mine collapse. *See* Saint-Étienne Mine Collapse

Ministry of the Colonies, 7, 152, 188, 208

miscegenation, 19–20, 44. *See also* mulattos; race and racism

Mismer, Charles, 48, 61

A Mission to Civilize (Conklin), 20

Monet, Henri, 50–51, 58–59, 230–31

Moracchini, Delphino, 96, 111–12, 119, 123, 149, 152–55, 159, 163–69

Mortenol, Camille, 240

Mount Pelée eruption, 191–231; described, 192–96; economic and cultural consequences of, 212–28, 213f, 217f, 218–19f, 223f, 224f, 225f, 227f; as French national emergency, 196–212, 205t; overview, 1–2, 16, 191–92; and racism, 191–92;

and slavery, legacy of, 219, 222; sole survivor of, 195, 273n11; and sugar economy, 194, 202, 212–14, 213f, 228

mulattos: attitudes toward, 22; demographics, 210; and departmentalization, 21; education of, 87; historical usage of term, 249n15; images of, 223f, 224f, 225f; as political activists, 24–26, 35–36, 42–49, 79; romantic idealization of, 220–26, 228–29, 235; status of, 56–61, 92, 204–7, 221; and turn-of-the-century social and political discord, 151, 166, 169–70

Mulcahy, Matthew, 9

Nardal, Paulette, 19, 39

Nos Creoles (Corre), 42

Notes on the Organization of the Colonies (Dislère), 17

out of wedlock births, 253n115

Parel, Gabriel, 1, 221

Paris Under Water (Jackson), 9

Peck, Ferdinand, 30

Périna, Mickaella, 9, 42, 49

Perrinon, François, 24

Peyron, Alexandre, 73, 80

phylloxera, 10, 135, 144

Picanon, Édouard, 175, 179, 185–87, 189

Picard, Alfred, 37–38

Pichevin, Roland, 239

Picquart, George, 271n146

pit viper, 50–51, 191

Pointe-à-Pitre earthquake of 1843, 65

Pointe-à-Pitre fires, 15, 66, 71, 148, 150–52, 159, 161–65, 178

strike of 1900 (Martinique) (*continued*) 181–85, 183*f*; invoking Labor Law of 1892, 172–73; and Mount Pelée eruption, 214, 221–22; overview, 2, 4, 15, 47, 95, 144, 148–50, 170–72, 187–90; Picanon report on, 185–87; and racism, 178–81; in school books, 40

strike of 1910 (Guadeloupe), 10, 23, 32, 169

subsistence farmers, 116, 120–21, 196. See also *cultivateurs*

sugar economy: and abolition of slavery, 23–27; in the Antilles vs. the Metropole, 106*f*; and civil unrest at turn of the century, 147–63, 156*f*, 157*f*, 158*f*; crisis on Guadeloupe, 22–23; decline of, 147–90, 156*f*, 228; and fires of 1890, 67–68, 82–83, 95, 98, 104, 106*f*; and hurricane of 18 August 1891, 109–46, 116*t*, 117*m*, 122*f*, 125*t*, 126*t*, 129*t*, 130*t*; and hurricane of 7 August 1899, 166–70; industrialization of, 27–32, 29*f*; and labor unrest, 32–33; and Mount Pelée eruption, 194, 202, 212–14, 213*f*, 228; overview, 2–3, 5, 8–11, 14–15, 18, 61, 234–36; and strike of 1900 on Martinique, 170–83, 183*f*; and Universal Exposition of 1900, 33–35; and World War I, 240, 245

tafia, 5, 120, 131, 135, 139, 147
Tahiti, 220
tectonic plates, 3, 51, 65
Terrier, Auguste, 14, 133
Texaco (Chamoiseau), 65
Treaty of Amiens, 24
tropical diseases: cholera, 56, 147, 166; malaria, 23, 56; typhoid, 56; yellow fever, 23, 45, 56, 147
typhoid, 56

Universal Exposition of 1900, 33–35, 37, 185–86, 222

vagabondage laws, 6–7, 25
Vaughan, Ernest, 218
Vesuvius, 191, 215, 228–29

Waldeck-Rousseau, Pierre, 173–77, 182–84, 186–89
Weber, Eugen, 11, 64, 99
Wilder, Gary, 9, 107, 235
World War I, 16, 236–44

yellow fever, 23, 45, 56, 147

To order or obtain more information on these or other
University of Nebraska Press titles, visit nebraskapress.unl.edu.

CPSIA information can be obtained
at www.ICGtesting.com
Printed in the USA
LVOW11*1347121217

559528LV00002B/5/P